Teaching Video Game Design Fundamentals

This comprehensive guide provides educators with everything they need to teach video game design fundamentals. With ready-made lesson plans, practical examples, assignment templates, exercises, video walkthroughs, and learning materials in a modular format that allows for customisation, it makes it easy to tailor lesson plans to meet the unique needs of your students, turning your classroom into an immersive learning environment that inspires creativity and innovation.

This book offers a variety of exercises and learning materials to engage all types of learners, additionally with materials designed for different learning speeds that help them progress at a pace that suits them. With this book, you can ensure that all students have the opportunity to succeed and reach their full potential.

This book will be vital reading to both educators teaching, and students learning, game design.

Andy Sandham has spent over a decade teaching game design at some of Europe's premier game development schools, with a passion for inspiring the next generation of game designers. He is an experienced subject leader and lecturer of Game Design, with an extensive career in academia, teaching across BA and Master's programmes at several esteemed universities. His previous 20 years of experience in the game industry, working in key roles on several high-profile titles, including *Theme Park*, the original *Tomb Raider* series, and *Magic: The Gathering: Duels of the Planeswalkers*, have armed him with invaluable industry insights which he brings to his teaching, creating inspiring and educational lessons, and earning a reputation as an inspirational lecturer and content creator who arms students with the knowledge to succeed in their careers.

Teaching Video Game Design Fundamentals

A Guide for Educating with Practical Examples and Learning Materials

Andy Sandham

CRC Press is an imprint of the
Taylor & Francis Group, an **informa** business

Designed cover image: Lee Stocks and Andrew Thornton

First edition published 2025
by CRC Press
2385 NW Executive Center Drive, Suite 320, Boca Raton FL 33431

and by CRC Press
4 Park Square, Milton Park, Abingdon, Oxon, OX14 4RN

CRC Press is an imprint of Taylor & Francis Group, LLC

© 2025 Andy Sandham

ISBN: 9781032644714 (hbk)
ISBN: 9781032644707 (pbk)
ISBN: 9781032644721 (ebk)
ISBN: 9781032644738 (eBook+)

DOI: 10.1201/9781032644721

Typeset in Times
by codeMantra

Access the Instructor and Student Resources/Support Material: https://www.routledge.com/ 9781032644707

I would like to dedicate this book to Mum and Dad – thanks for buying my first ZX Spectrum – and for never asking why I didn't do any homework on it.

Contents

Foreword

I believe that being a game developer keeps you young, literally. Enjoying what you do is a core part of staying young – and, I would argue, also core to creating great game experiences. Crafting such experiences is a game design art form that's often difficult to teach, which is where Andy comes in. With his extensive experience across a raft of shipped titles and years of fine tuning his teaching material to deliver the book you now hold in your hands, he shares his knowledge to not only help you craft great game experiences but also, maybe, help you stay young.

Andy and I first met in Breda, Netherlands, at the NHTV University of Applied Science, (now Breda University), one of the top programmes in the world, thanks to its strong ex-game industry lecturers, with myself as Programming lead, where Andy joined the nascent Game Design team. So how do you teach game design to enthusiastic students? Is it just playing games all day? At this point, those wanting to move into the area of teaching Game Design may angrily shout "No!". But, as Andy has taught me, playing games *is* an important part of it. Few teachers take the time to properly play and understand the games their students create, or even play at all. Andy was exceptional at this, always playing students' games, no matter how broken, and providing feedback to help them improve, teasing out the good and giving enough direction for budding designers to evolve positively. His ability as a great teacher was linked to his deep understanding of game design – motivating, rewarding, and providing the right amount of challenge for both players and students, while never forgetting to have fun while doing so.

Sometimes an academic course and its students need time to breathe, and Andy recognised this by encouraging students to take a break and join a jam. Whether it was Brains Eden, Global Game Jam, Ludum Dare, Nordic Game Jam, or any of several other exciting options, allowing students to escape the grading process and focus on their craft. Engaging in jams led to an amazing number of cleverly designed outcomes, some resulting in new student companies and games like "FRU," probably the most innovative use of Microsoft's Kinect we have seen.

Having moved out of academia, and back into game development, I've missed Andy's game design teaching savvy (not to mention our lunches arguing over the merits of grappling hook mechanics in games) – so was thrilled to hear about this book, compiling 12 years of innovative teaching. This is a comprehensive toolkit for educators, offering seven turnkey lesson plans based on his extensive experience across both academia and the games industry, with a practical approach that sets it apart, including dynamic presentations, assignment templates, exercises, video walkthroughs, and more. Andy's expertise and passion for game design education shine through every page, and his commitment to excellence and innovation in teaching is evident, providing educators with a blueprint that is as engaging as it is educational. These resources engage students and simplify the teaching process, doing the heavy theoretical game design lifting and allowing educators to focus on mentoring, teasing out game greatness through iteration – and maybe evens providing the extra time to organise those Game Jams! As you delve into this book, you will find yourself equipped with the tools to not only teach game design but ignite a passion for it in your students – a passion vital to keep the spark fired up through all the hard work required to learn the craft.

This book is an invaluable asset for any educator aiming to cultivate the game designers of tomorrow, and I hope you have as much fun with it as I've had working with Andy.

And who knows? When you use it, maybe you'll even end up feeling a few years younger.

Robbie Grigg
Technical Director, NeoBards Entertainment
Former Director of Games, Media & AI, Breda University of Applied Sciences
Brighton, July 2024

Acknowledgements

I've discovered during this process of writing a book that actually making it into a "thing" requires a lot of help. And I've had a lot. So, I'll use this section to say thank you – but don't worry, I'll keep this short. I know that if you're an educator, game developer, or student, you're probably already looking at your watch and glancing nervously at your inbox and/or game engine.

First up, thanks to my artists, Jack Hollick and Andrew Thornton, for their splendid illustrations and design work, decorating what may otherwise had become somewhat of an exercise on the eyes. As an extension of this, thank you to my fellow lecturers at York St. John, Charlene Clempson and Andrew Byrom, for mentoring these excellent students. And a special thank you must go out to Alex (Camilleri) and Thomas (White), two of my exceptionally talented ex-graduates for their invaluable help.

Thanks to Lee Stocks for taking time out from his fungible tokens to provide some striking cover art. And Stu, thank you for not only some of your classic pixel art but also the mental support needed when digging back through my own work from 30 years ago. And while on that subject, thanks to Heather for uncovering some of her work from the very dawn of game design to include in the book. (Apologies Heather, I should point out you're not actually that old).

Thanks to Rich Chalmers for staying up long after the boys have gone to bed to help research relatively oblique elements of game development, despite deadlines on your own triple masters (I forget which one you're on now).

Big thanks to Mata Haggis and Robbie Grigg for being there at the start, supporting me in a new country and a strange new job, both gently coaxing out those first, wobbly baby steps in my teaching career. (No respite in Robbie's case, this mentoring now translated into spending much of his Sunday nights reviving me in our MP sessions). And kudos to Jack Venegas, another former NHTV lecturer and developer, for convincing me that the book you hold in your hands might actually be of use to the educators of the present and future.

Thanks to my editor Will for his level-headed support, for understanding that the grading period is not the best time to finish a book, and for never cocking a snoot at a late-night request for clearance on an odd image of a spaceman in plimsolls.

And, of course, thanks to my endlessly patient and hugely talented wife Tracey for her unending support, and to Sheila for her backing, and occasional lambasting for "crunch" (a newly learnt word to harangue me with).

And finally, from the perspective of this book being written at all, most of all, thank you to my students, many of whom have not only inspired me to continue teaching and improve my craft over the last 12 years but also gone out into the wide and often terrifying world of game development to inspire others with their huge talent.

Game on!

Introduction

I was there at the birth of Game Design. Quite a statement, right? I remember it well. Back in the 90s, while sitting in the back room of a grubby game studio, absent-mindedly dithering some colour isometric tiles into black and white, when a cool-looking guy entered the room and started chatting with the coder. He turned his attention to me. "You're new." "Yes," I mumbled. "Hi, I'm the Designer." Said cool guy. "Uh?" I blurted, somewhat nonplussed – "You're not an artist or a programmer?" "Nope. I'm a Game Designer." "That's... a job?" I stammered. "Yup. That's a job. Every day is a school day, right?" He grinned. "You should try it. It's fun." And with a wink, he was off. Wow, I thought, looking at this departing guru, with his trendy sneakers (definitely *sneakers*, not drab old trainers, no siree!), cool cornrow hairdo, and hip, non-game developer-looking shell suit. And then I looked down at my stained definitely trainers and back at my dismal black and white 8-bit blocks. And I thought "That Cool guy looked like he was having FUN."

I wanted some of that.

I decided then and there I wanted to be a Game Designer too.

It took a while. Those "First Game Designers ever" ™ didn't have it easy – but gradually, it began to sink in. The industry began to recognise that it needed someone on the team to be managing the overarching game design, the feel, the narrative, the level design, even the UX (which we would have assumed was a new type of petrol if you'd used the term back then). To test it, to iterate it, to correct it. Game design gradually became a "thing." One of, indeed the first step, in the holy triumvirate of game development – Art, Code – and now – Game Design. And as more designers joined the fray, sharing concepts, ideas, and theories, and theoretical game design books began to gain traction, the core principles and theories of game design began to take shape. The discipline of Game Design had been born.

And WOW! Being a Game Designer was everything I wanted it to be. Designing levels, puzzles, mechanics, narratives. Being handed the keys to the sweet shop. Cool guy was right. Making games WAS fun.

And that's what this book is about. Game Design. Not art, programming, or producing. Game Design. More specifically, teaching Game Design, hopefully with at least some of the fun included.

But how do you teach Game Design? Practical application of design techniques in relevant game engines and specific software is obviously vital and has always helped our students find roles across the industry. But I'm guessing you wouldn't navigate into a wilderness without a map, or build a house without a plan, right?

In addition to practical knowledge, the importance of teaching students the theory and principles of game design is now recognised. Teaching game design involves determining the order and priority of these principles, and from my 12 years of gradually adapting and iterating these lesson plans, I would suggest the order and delivery of the foundational steps are key.

These are the seven key theoretical lectures you hold in your hand. The first steps for sending your nascent game design students out into the ever-advancing and inspirational discipline of game design. They are not only "road-tested" and ready to be taught, but also ready for your own personalised iterations, adaptations, and tweaks. Customise as you will. I hope you enjoy teaching these lessons, and ultimately your role in shaping the next generation of game designers, who will almost certainly soon be teaching us a thing or two.

Remember – Every day is a school day!
Andy Sandham
York, 2024

HOW TO USE THIS BOOK: EDUCATOR INSTRUCTION MANUAL

Introduction

The content in the lecture/chapter sections of this book should be fairly self-explanatory. Many chapters have specific instructions, and this guide serves as a general overview for implementing this module into your course structure. The materials in this book are designed to be accessible and hands-on, focusing on practical, nuts-and-bolts, tried-and-tested functional game design, as well as including relevant analysis, such as the psychology behind player motivation and the business and societal aspects of game design, highlighting their potential impact on individuals and society.

They utilise examples of current (at the time of writing) and "classic" games, game design techniques, and case studies to help readers understand how each design element can be applied in real-world situations. The provided examples are included to stimulate the "Eureka!" moment for the students and re-enforce learning, but you'll notice limited examples within certain genres – I haven't included a huge amount of platformers because in my career, I haven't designed a huge amount of platformers. I'd suggest adapting lectures to your area of specialisation to maximise learning. The fundamental tenets taught in the book should be relevant across all genres, so if platformers, or any other genre are much more in your wheelhouse, the examples are there to be swapped out.

Either way, I hope this book inspires you in educating your game designers of the future!

PLEASE NOTE: All included instructor resources can all be downloaded from the **Instructor Hub**

MODULE OVERVIEW: GAME DESIGN FUNDAMENTALS

This covers the first 7 weeks of course materials for introducing students to the first steps in learning the core theory and principles, or indeed, fundamentals of practical Game Design. This content is deliberately designed to be software agnostic and primarily theory based. In addition, the course aims to direct students towards beginning to identify their own unique "voice" that will make them stand out in a crowded market.

MODULE OBJECTIVES AND COURSE OUTCOMES

The primary objective of our courses and modules is not to prop up ailing university coffers, it's to *get our students jobs in industry.*

With this in mind, I suggest that, as a future Game Designer, the important learning and/or artefacts our students need to leave university with are:

Essential

- A portfolio that contains a playable game or prototype, with evidence of clear methodology and progression of ideas of mechanics that display ongoing iteration.
- Evidence of teamwork, or a team-based project example.

Desirable

- A unique game concept, idea, or mechanic, ideally reflecting some demonstrable aspect of the student's personality or a subject they are passionate about.

LECTURE/CHAPTER CONTENT

There are seven core chapters/lectures included in this book. Each lecture follows a similar systematic structure, and this section gives an overview of this.

LECTURE/CHAPTER SUMMARY

Lecture Outline and Objectives

An overview of the topics covered in the lesson, with clear learning objectives, gives the educator an understanding of what the students will learn during that session. The instructional design of the lesson incorporates a theoretical lecture at the outset to introduce students to the specific topic, followed by an exercise or "working class".

Each chapter lecture will build knowledge incrementally over the proposed 7-week duration and will end with a recap of the points covered. From week 4 onwards, recaps are introduced at the start of each lecture to re-iterate the previous week's learning.

Duration

Each PowerPoint lecture will normally run for 1 hour out of a 3-hour teaching block (i.e., 10 am–1 pm). This includes video examples and discussions, and in some cases will be replaced with an end of semester quiz. After this I'd suggest an hour for the online exercise/working class, and after a short break (which I use for a quick look through the delivered exercise/working class) an hour for feedback on the exercise on the main screen as a discussion with the students.[1] I'd note some of the included PowerPoint lectures can run to 70 or so slides. This often reflects "Question slides" (one slide question, one slide answer) which can bloat the slide count, but I'd generally cite 1–2 minutes per (content) slide as the average delivery time.

Delivery

From a delivery perspective, images and video examples help to encourage engagement. Putting a video upfront after the first few slides can allow you to catch your breath, gauge your delivery style, and make the class relax a little (i.e., no opportunity for lecturer asking the class questions!) and feel more comfortable.

LECTURE/CHAPTER COMPONENTS OVERVIEW

Intro

A concise summary of the chapter's main concepts, theories, and research findings, which will help instructors to quickly review the material before teaching it.

Lecture Regulars: Recap of Previous Weeks Learning

Examples are included from week 4.

Lecture Regulars: USP Corner

I always try to expose students to current indie games, usually single-mechanic games with strong Unique selling points or USPs that they might be able to make by the end of the course. Obviously replace with your own, current or favoured examples where you feel necessary.

"Working Class" Exercises and Materials

Examples of "Working class" team exercises that are relevant to each chapter/lesson topic are provided and can be downloaded from the instructor hub. These templates contain both instructions and blank templates for the students to fill out, explained in more detail in the following "working class example walkthrough" These templates should be situated on (your own or a university) shared drive for easy student access, or they can be downloaded, providing students with the opportunity to engage in collaborative learning activities as a team. Additionally, other pedagogical tools are included, such as discussion questions, quizzes, assignments, and suggested readings/games to play, to aid learners in comprehending how video game design principles are applied in the context of published games, with links to a diverse range of real-world game/case study videos. Continuous student-facing access to this material should be provided to support self-directed learning and independent study.

Chapter Boxouts

Key terms will be highlighted and defined throughout the text to help educators build the necessary vocabulary and deepen their understanding of the concepts. These are outside of the timing of the lecture content. (Each lecture should come in at around 45 minutes to an hour.)

Replacing Materials

As mentioned, wherever possible, I've included "classic" examples of games to re-enforce the taught theory, and in some cases (such as "USP corner") more specific current or trending examples. In both cases, these are my own preferences, based around my own experience of designing and playing games. I'd suggest replacing it with relevant examples from your own experience wherever possible, as I'm sure you don't need me to tell you, passion for your subject is half the battle!

ACCESSIBLE CONTENT/DIGITAL MATERIALS

Learning Materials Provided

To enhance the accessibility and flexibility of the instructional materials, the lectures and working classes are provided in editable PowerPoint format. Moreover, links to a video recording of an example delivered lecture is available for guidance.

- 7 PowerPoint slides, one for each week: These include discussion questions and links to quizzes and tests, with links to an array of real-world game and case study videos.
- Working class exercise templates to follow each of the seven lectures.
- Assignment example template with grading rubric.
- Online Quiz example

PLEASE NOTE: All included instructor resources can all be downloaded from the **Instructor Hub**.

PROVIDED POWERPOINTS

Use images from the games or replacement game examples you have chosen to populate your slides. Chunk info on your slides – use the "animations/fade" feature to bring in images one at a time on one slide, and then talk about them in steps. Always note the educational use of copyright materials, often under the concept of "fair use" or "fair dealing," allows for limited use of copyrighted content without permission for purposes such as teaching, research, and scholarship. Educators should always attribute the source and use materials in a manner that doesn't infringe on the original creator's rights.

DEDICATED VIDEO CHANNEL

As well as game example videos, my video channel[3] contains several tutorial videos that can be used for various technical classes. There will be clear links to videos within the chapters, and also a link to where the videos are hosted in the relevant section. Please feel free to use them, and if they are helpful, please consider subscribing to allow me to make more!

PROVIDED WORKING CLASSES

As outlined In class exercises (or "Working classes") run directly after the main lecture and are used to re-enforce what has been taught. The exercise should be hosted on a shareable digital content platform, and the link provided at the end of the lecture. In the example, I've used Google Drive, although you will usually have your own online content platform available at your specific university.

The link leads the students to a set of templates (dependent on class size) numbered and set out based around the taught content, and each team finds their own game examples with which to complete the content (as demonstrated in the following example).

They can be run solo, although teams of two to three seem to work well and introduce students to sharing tasks.

WORKING CLASS EXAMPLE WALKTHROUGH

As described, To re-enforce learning, after the main lecture, there will usually be a working class. The students will have access to the online area with slide templates and "Gamecards" as set out in example slides depicted in Figures HT.1–8 and provided as downloads from the **Instructor Hub**.

Upload these slide templates onto your own collaborative workspace (e.g., OneDrive, Google Drive) and extend the teams as per your class size. (i.e., a class of four students will only need templates for two teams, with two students in each team!)

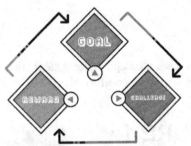

Illustration by Andrew Thornton.

FIGURE HT.1   Working Class Example slide 1.

Slide 1

An introduction to the topic of the exercise.

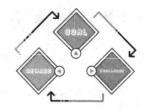

IN TEAMS OF 2-4

FIGURE HT.2   Working Class Example slide 2.

Slide 2

This is primarily a *team* exercise, although make it clear students will be able to take part in a solo capacity if they feel more comfortable participating in that way.

Choose examples from your own favourite games and create your own objective/challenge/reward gamecards! (at least 9!)

FIGURE HT.3   Working Class Example slide 3.

Slide 3

Gives the students their first example of "Gamecards" specific to the exercise (in this case Objective/Challenge/Reward examples).

FIGURE HT.4   Working Class Example slide 4.

Slide 4

Basic instructions for the task.

FIGURE HT.5   Working Class Example slide 5.

Slide 5

Some simple examples help students who are unclear about the task.

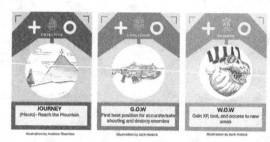

Work on your cards, debate choices with other teams and refine- All finished? We'll look at them on the main screen and discuss as a class.

FIGURE HT.6 Working Class Example slide 6.

Slide 6

Re-enforcing that we will be looking at the exercises on the main screen motivates the students to provide the best possible examples.

TEAM 1:

TEAM NAME:

MEMBERS OF TEAM:

FIGURE HT.7 Working Class Example slide 7.

Slide 7

This is the beginning of the student facing area. You can also denote this with a slide before this area saying something along the lines of "Over to you!"

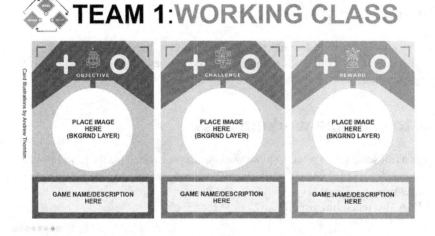

FIGURE HT.8 Working Class Example slide 8.

Slide 8

This is where the students will place their examples. The Gamecards are in layers allowing students to collect relevant images from their game examples from the internet and paste in (or create their own), then describe the specific component example (in this case Objective/Challenge or reward). I usually ask the students to provide at least nine cards per exercise, depending on the taught content that week, but I would note example working class templates are provided for all lectures (1–7).

SETTING UP

At the end of each content lecture, there should be a slide providing a link to the online environment (as per example Figure HT.9). Make sure the slides in the link are set to "Editable!"

LINK HERE:

http://tiny.cc/GDF_WK1_LOOPS

FIGURE HT.9   Working Class Example slide 9.

Before providing the link, I would also suggest walking the students through example slides (Figures HT.1–8), demonstrating the layered nature of the Gamecards, and allowing any questions on the exercise.

Link to example working class

There is a full setup of the week 1 online working class provided via the link. I would note this example is locked to editing, unlike the live version you will provide for your students!
    http://tiny.cc/GDF_WK1_LOOPS
NOTE: A shortened link usually saves time for the class!

Running the Exercise

Move around class during exercise and discuss choices. Once finished, discuss choices on the main screen with the class. Discussion should take 30 minutes to 1 hour (depending on the size of the class)

Final notes

Remember, the more exercises the students complete, the more up-to-date examples from students you will have for future examples and quizzes – it's a never-ending cycle!

FURTHER LEARNING TOOLS: QUIZZES

A competitive online quiz is another excellent way to reinforce taught material, especially if you have a prize to hand, and there is now a wide variety of options available to the educator. In the example provided, I'm using the free version of the teaching tool **Kahoot!**.[2] it's usually an effective method to start the following week's lecture, using it as a recap of the previous material, and a useful tip is to use slides from the previous week's student working class as the basis of the quiz. The provided example utilises repurposed slides from the Components and Loops lecture, and I've provided a **Kahoot!** quiz link and a tutorial on how to translate your quiz into a digital version **(Resource links 1.2, 1.3).**

As a disclaimer, I should note some students feel that Kahoot! is more suited to secondary education than higher education; this ultimately depends on reading the class dynamics, although I usually just find it's a bit of fun to get the class warmed up.

RESOURCE LINK 1.2: KAHOOT QUIZ

http://tiny.cc/GDF1_CompLoop_Quiz

RESOURCE LINK 1.3: CREATING A SIMPLE KAHOOT QUIZ FROM A LECTURE

http://tiny.cc/Lecture2Kahoot

FURTHER LEARNING TOOLS: HOMEWORK

Homework will typically be announced at the end of the lecture and reiterated at the end of the day's classes. A good initial example of a homework assignment would be Assessment point 1, as described in the provided example assignment and rubric document, for delivery in week 2 (see the Instructor Hub/Chapter one resources for the downloadable Assignment example). Students would be tasked with analysing a small segment of a first/third-person game of their choosing, with the goal of later replicating a whitebox of it in a game engine for the second part of the assignment. The purpose of the week 2 presentation is to "set out our stall" and help students become comfortable with presenting as soon as possible, an essential skill in real-world development. Some terminology may be unfamiliar to them at this point, but this method of "front-loading" information is beneficial. Some students may choose to research the terminology online, which is advantageous, while others may remember it due to the challenge of not understanding it initially, leading to greater curiosity when the terms are "officially" taught later in the course. One final note: make it clear that if students are nervous about presenting in front of the class, or have a valid reason not to, private or video presentations can be provided. Most students are comfortable presenting, and I find that those who are not often find that recognising they are in a supportive environment (and that presenting is usually fun!) will lead them to eventually attempt to overcome their concerns and give it a try.

PUTTING YOUR MODULE TOGETHER: ACADEMIC COURSE STRUCTURE NOTES

Module Specs

This module is a theoretical introduction to Game Design fundamentals, intended to run alongside complementary modules. Examples of these might include research-based modules such as "Game Design Analysis," where students learn academic writing and research, and also practical modules involving basic game logic creation such as "paper prototyping." Additionally, students should spend significant time learning and using relevant software.

Learning/Pedagogical Objectives

The learning objectives will fit into the broader course overview to complement all areas of Game Design, i.e., the learning objectives in this module are a small part of the overall 3–4-year structure across several modules to comprehensively teach students Game Design, but I've included an overview of various basic Game Design learning objectives below:

- Game mechanics: The rules, procedures, and systems that govern gameplay.
- Game dynamics: The behaviour of the game system and the player's interaction with it.
- Game aesthetics: The visual and audio elements that create the game's atmosphere and mood.
- Design documentation: The process of creating and documenting the design of a game.
- Prototyping: The process of creating a preliminary version of a game to test and refine its design.
- Playtesting: The process of testing a game with actual players to identify and fix design problems.

Timetabling Your Semester 1 Module

I'd suggest in their first semester, theory – 30%, research – 20%, and learning and utilising game design tools (to re-enforce taught theory) as 50% of this initial learning period.

Suggested Schedule (SEM 1)

12 weeks taught, with the last 2 weeks for support.

DAY 1 EXAMPLE for teaching 1 specific module.
Morning

- 1 hour theory lecture
- 1 hour class exercise (working class)
- 1 hour analysis and discussion of previous exercise on the main screen

Afternoon

- 2 hour tech class – either learning relevant software or re-enforcement of taught materials in these lectures.

Suggested Week Structure

Repeat the formula for other non-research-based modules. Allocate 1.5 days a week for open learning/free studio, with lecturer or technical lecturer support.

A Note on Breaks

I'd suggest breaks every hour for 5–10 minutes when digesting theory after the lecture and after the working class (before moving onto the discussion)

Further Lecture Content: Week 7 Onwards

This book covers the introduction to game fundamentals, spanning weeks 1–7 of a typical UK Higher Education semester (14 weeks total, with 12 taught and 2 for assignment support). Further taught theory suggestions (in an ever-changing and evolving field of study) for the end of semester one include:

- Diversity, equality, and the changing industry
- Accessibility
- Design documentation
- Prototyping
- Playtesting

The Learning Environment

The game design classroom should ideally be a communal space with student work, game posters, and ideally a console "chill out" area for lunchtime gaming sessions. Ideally attempt to replicate industry studio layouts, encouraging working across disciplines (Art, Design, Code) if your university supports that. Include elements that can specifically showcase student games, such as a re-purposed or custom-built arcade cabinet which can be built around a PC. The goal here is for the students to feel that this is their space and become inspired by it.

Getting Them Started

First week activities

- Get them to go out and take photos on their phones for an initial (workshop) "introduction to pipelines" exercise. (e.g., bringing the images into photo editing software or as textures within a game engine.)
- Get them to go to the library and find a section in a game design book that interests them for a short presentation (in groups of two, making sure one in the group is comfortable presenting).
- Mini "random game name generator" game jam, presented in front of class to help them meet classmates and develop initial bonds.
- Establish a habit of doing the same thing at the same time to create a more coherent learning environment.

ASSIGNMENTS

Formative and Summative Assessments

FORMATIVE – Semester One

This is useful for providing feedback in a one-to-one format in their first year without intimidating the student with the threat of grades. Useful at the end of semester one to ensure the student knows how they are progressing. This feedback will highlight any shortfalls, areas that need fixing, and answer any questions the student may have, any help they need, or any areas they want to focus on. In early sessions I'd suggest asking students how they want to receive feedback – written, auditory, or face to face, and adhere to their preferences.

SUMMATIVE – End of Semester Two

A concept document, ideally from a simple provided template (many are available online).

A short playable level replicating some of the level design topics investigated in Assessment 1.

PLEASE NOTE: A full example Assignment can be downloaded from the Instructor Hub/Chapter one resources.

ASSIGNMENT SUBS: CHECKLIST

- **Game Engine Version**

  If you're using game engines, specify the version up front – and emphasise this is the version that will be used for the year (or semester if a semester-based assignment). Students will invariably get "techstruck" and download the latest version of any software at home as soon as it becomes available, usually meaning that any work in the new engine version is redundant when they bring it back to class.

- **Naming conventions**

  Give the students a clear naming convention, i.e., "xxxyournamehere. docx." Note that from experience, first-year students seem to believe the lecturer is "all seeing" and are not convinced that they need to put their name on anything they submit. Do your best to convince them otherwise to avoid spending most of your weekends trying to work out which student submitted what.

- **Backing up work – wake up and back up!**

  Backing up work is crucial in a games course to prevent loss of progress due to technical failures, ensuring that valuable projects, assets, and data are secure. This should become second nature, and allows students to continue their work without significant setbacks, of which, in Game Development, there are many.

- **Video Submissions (YouTube)**

  If your students are going to be using hefty engines or large software packages, video walkthroughs with student narration are the way to go. Most students will have access to a mic, and there are plenty of free video screen capture tools available. The benefits are two-fold: students reflect on and explain their own work, reinforcing learning, and from an educator's perspective, you don't have to spend 3 or 4 hours per submission downloading and unravelling large projects or contacting the student for missing files. I'd also suggest they set up a YouTube account set to "unlisted." Beginner students are often nervous about the general public seeing their work. Ticking "unlisted" (as opposed to "private," which can be problematic at grading time) means only people with the link have access. Good news if they actually provide you with the link!

- **Presenting! (both exercises and assignments)**

  Encourage students to learn how to present, but make it clear they don't HAVE to present if they don't want to – they can present privately, or by video.

SETTING UP YOUR MODULE

Online Digital Learning Environment: Example Layout

- **Splash image**

  Adding a big splash image up front and centre at the top of your online learning environment sets the tone for the course and should capture students' interest from the start, helping to reflect the creative nature of game design.
- **Contact and student absence links**
- **ASSIGNMENT with ASSESSMENT SPECS AND DATE (extensions can be added later)**
- **Link to module guide and grading rubric**

  The grading rubric (example included in example assignment brief) is vital, and one of the first steps I'd suggest walking your students through after introducing your assignment specifications.
- **Week 1: video of lecture, exercise link, further reading**
- **External examiner examples (hidden from students)**

  These will usually be examples from top, middle, and bottom from your student grading. As you proceed with any graded work, drop them in here to prevent end-of-term admin overload.
- **READING LIST**

  Links to your suggested library texts, suggested reading, digital links to online websites such as "Game Developer.com." This is about curation. Direct students towards recognised games outlets for curated design articles and material and encourage them to subscribe to online newsletters. Your first lesson is an opportunity to get your students to sign up to these. I'd try to include as many different type of media sources/resources as possible (as per limited example provided) to not only cater to different learning styles, but also to give the students an overview of the variety of learning resources available.

(SOME EXAMPLES OF) SUGGESTED READING

Salen, K., & Zimmerman, E. (2004). *Rules of Play: Game Design Fundamentals*. Cambridge, MA: The MIT Press.

Fullerton, T. (2008). *Game Design Workshop: A Playcentric Approach to Creating Innovative Games*. Boca Raton, FL: CRC Press.

Schell, J. (2014). *The Art of Game Design: A Book of Lenses*. Boca Raton, FL: CRC Press.

Bogost, I. (2010). *Persuasive games: The expressive power of videogames*. Cambridge, MA: MIT Press.

Game Industry News, Deep Dives, and developer blogs (no date) Game Developer. Available at: https://www.gamedeveloper.com/

Edge: *The Future of Interactive Entertainment*, 1993–ongoing. (Magazine). Future Publishing.

SOME LECTURER TOOLS

Screencasts

There are a number of screencast devices available – this is quite useful if you are running exercises where, for instance, students are using simple editing packages such as the *Portal 2* "perpetual learning initiative" (Valve Corporation, 2011) to build levels, which can then be played by a fellow student on the main screen while other students are able to comment and vocally support (or indeed, question) within the class environment.

Snipping Tool

A useful tool from Microsoft for the students to quickly grab images from game videos for use in exercises.

URL Shorteners

Use URL shorteners to compress your links into readable format – especially useful if you have an onscreen link to an exercise. Again, there are plenty of free versions available.

YouTube (Or Other Video Streaming Service)

YouTube is hugely useful for game playthroughs that can be utilised in exercises (although, as I always stress, there is no real substitute for playing the game yourself). An important element in YouTube is that right clicking on the video will allow you to *copy the video URL at that point*. This obviously saves a lot of scrolling through lengthy playthroughs when discussing on the main screen.

SUCKING EGGS!

And finally, I've included the "sucking eggs" section, named as such because although I'm not attempting to teach anyone to suck eggs, I hope these extra notes detailing some elements that have become apparent during my tenure as an educator may be useful to some; if not, feel free to ignore them!

Find Your Course USP!

Make sure it is clearly "Game Design" first and foremost!

I've included some "Open Day" slide example content, telling prospective students and their parents what is unique about your course:

Example "Open Day" Slide Content

- What we want to help you achieve is an industry-ready portfolio. It is vitally important that we get you something playable in your portfolio, which you can then present to industry professionals. This way, people can play your game, and it can help you secure a job.
- We aim for a small, dedicated cohort of students. A small cohort means students have more time with the lecturers, where they can be guided by industry professionals.
- One day a week "Gamelab" where students from different disciplines (art design, code) replicate an industry environment, working under industry expert supervision to create games
- Collaboration across design departments (i.e. game projects across games, animation, interior design, sound design)
- Specific equipment and resources – Mocap and Mocap actors, VR and VR-specific projects.
- Indie development – a focus on solo or indie team practice.

Finding Out Who Your Students Are

Find which area of design your students are interested in (i.e. narrative, level) and wherever possible, support them in this. Some modules will be more suited than others, and the students' interests may change and evolve over time, but their best work will always come from the design area they are passionate about.

Different Learning Styles

Make sure you accommodate different learning styles, such as visual, auditory, and kinaesthetic within your presentations, class exercises, and feedback. Understanding a particular student's learning styles will help them to produce their best work.

Scaleable Assignments

Make sure the least capable students can still complete the assignment but give the high achievers the opportunity to shine. Offer foundational tasks that everyone can grasp while offering advanced challenges and optional enhancements for more dedicated students. This balance supports an inclusive learning environment where every student can progress and excel at their own pace.

Motivators

Although I'm hesitant to use the terminology "Gamifying the classroom" due to its somewhat negative marketing-based connotations, I would suggest that, in a game design course, competitions and prizes are a relevant part of first-year study. In my own classes, I handed out "Rogue Warrior[4] points" for students who performed best in exercises and gave less vocal students opportunities to add points by supplying new and unique game examples for the "USP CORNER" section of the lecture. This not only kept examples up to date but also taught me about new games to look out for and play. For end-of-semester prizes, I suggest attending any game development conference and stocking up on promotional freebies – I've never had a student complain, even when receiving a small badge from the most obscure game company as a prize.

Diversity! Guest Lectures and Videos

Regardless of who you are as an educator, I'd always suggest introducing the students to as broad a set of voices as possible. If you're unable to get live industry speakers (ask! You'd be surprised how many will say yes), online resources such as the GDC VAULT [5]will allow you to run talks from a huge range of development voices that will help to broaden your students' outlook and understanding of the evolving field of game development.

Taking Notes

Always encourage students to take notes, whether on their phone or otherwise. They often get good ideas when looking back or translating notes into another digital medium. Reviewing notes can inspire new game ideas, making the practice worthwhile.

Game Jams, Trips, and Inter University Competitions

These can be a massive boost for students, and indeed course-level confidence. And indeed in the case of some of the game jams I've attended with my students, direct employment from game companies for the winning students. Job fairs are also frequently available at these events, where industry professionals give their time to give feedback on students' portfolios.

Remember – Teaching is Two Way!

Always offer positive re-enforcement in class – I've always encouraged students to discuss openly, and in doing so have learnt a variety of new design techniques, systems, and new (and frequently baffling) terminology. Every day is a school day!

NOTES

1 A number of lecturers, myself included, used to baulk at the idea of a discussion running for an hour. Dependent on class size (30 upwards) I'd now suggest this is quite common. If this section runs dry, I'd simply move them onto the afternoon technical exercises early.
2 https://kahoot.com/
3. https://bit.ly/UnrealTakeaway
4 Students will always discover the worst games you have ever worked on, usually within the first 10 minutes of the course. Better to embrace this at the outset!
5 https://www.youtube.com/@Gdconf

Getting Started in Game Design

Game Components & Loops

CHAPTER 1
COMPONENTS & LOOPS

LECTURE OVERVIEW

The purpose of this initial chapter is to scaffold Game Design knowledge from its foundational elements, **Game components** and **Gameplay loops**, investigating how the interplay of these elements should combine to produce *Gameplay*.

DOI: 10.1201/9781032644721-1

SECTION 1.1: GAME COMPONENTS – THE BUILDING BLOCKS OF GAMES

Lecture reference: slides 1–4

Games are made up of various components that serve as the building blocks of the experience. I've boiled these down to six key areas: Teaching, Objectives, Mechanics, Challenge, Win Lose, and Social.

GAME COMPONENTS

FIGURE 1.1   Game component types. Illustration by Andrew Thornton.

We'll examine these core components and relevant introductory game development terminology in much greater detail through this initial seven lecture series. But let's use the start of this lecture series to get familiar with these components, starting with an introduction to the **Objectives** component.

Core Component: Objectives

Lecture reference: slide 5

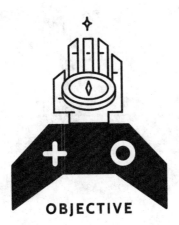

FIGURE 1.2   The objectives game component. Illustration by Andrew Thornton.

In Game Design, it is important for every game to have clear **Objectives** that guide players from beginning to end. These objectives should not only lead to visible *progress* within the game but should also guide the player through *feedback* (see Box 1.1). With the inclusion of challenge and reward systems, this core gameplay loop transforms the experience into a true "game." If a game lacks clear objectives, I question whether it can truly be considered a "game" or if it is more of an "experience."

For a clear, unambiguous example of a game objective, let's look at the classic title *Super Mario Bros.* (Nintendo, 1985): rescuing Princess Peach from the villainous Bowser. Although not explicitly revealed until the end of the original game, this objective evolves throughout the series, sets the goal for players, and is frequently reinforced throughout the later titles via initial cutscenes (where Bowser kidnaps the Princess) or in-game setpieces, which guide and drive the gameplay. This reiteration of the core objective across the series means that when most players sit down to play Mario, even before they select "start game," they know that the primary goal will be to rescue Princess Peach.

FIGURE 1.3 The Princess in the castle. Illustration by Shutterstock/Giuseppe_R.

Even in open-world or sandbox games, which some may feel lack clear objectives, we often find that objectives gradually bubble to the surface. Let's take a look at an example: the sandbox game *Garry's Mod* (Facepunch Studios, 2006). As described on the Steam website, *"Garry's Mod is a physics sandbox. There aren't any predefined aims or goals. We give you the tools and leave you to play. You spawn objects and weld them together to create your own contraptions – whether that's a car, a rocket, a catapult, or something that doesn't have a name yet – that's up to you. You can do it offline or join the thousands of players who play online each day."*[1]

Although this game may not have a specific designer-set end game objective, players will often create their own objectives, wanting to showcase their creations to others in pursuit of positive peer review. From a psychological reward perspective, I like to call this the "Mum factor" – harking back to childhood when we were eager to impress our parents with our latest, possibly slightly underwhelming, drawings or creations, to get the dopamine hit of positive reinforcement from some almost guaranteed praise. This dopamine hit is still relevant regardless of age and can be "designed in" by utilising various systems that we'll look at in later lectures, such as creation mechanics and social game systems that reward with positive feedback from player-peers.

Box 1.1 Progression and Feedback

Progression and feedback are two of the core reward systems in Game Design. They work hand in hand to motivate players to engage with and continue playing the game. Feedback (e.g., sound, visuals, haptics) provides information on player performance, guiding the player and allowing them to correct mistakes and build on successes. This, in turn, drives the game's reward system (e.g., score, levels, narrative), confirming that the feedback has meaning, which in turn encourages further engagement, driving the player further into your game.

Core Component Example: Teaching

Lecture reference: slides 6–7

FIGURE 1.4   The teaching game component. Illustration by Andrew Thornton.

Let's have a brief introduction to another of our core components, **Teaching**, that will be expanded on in subsequent lectures. Teaching is vitally important in guiding the player how to play your game, and is essential, regardless of genre or difficulty level. Players need to learn the mechanics and rules to understand how to engage with your game systems, and there are various techniques to facilitate this learning process. Let's look at some examples of teaching the player, starting with the much-maligned "Game tutorial"

FIGURE 1.5   "Driver." Illustration by Jack Hollick.

The "Gatekeeper" tutorial and its necessary evolution

While an integral element of classic game design, "Gatekeeper" tutorials that are imposed on the player and are necessary for accessing the main game are generally discouraged in modern games due to the expected increase in player *agency* (see Box 1.2) within these titles. Modern players expect to access the game they paid for as soon as they want, and those who are "told" to complete tutorials to reach the main game may instead decide to "tell" the Game (and its designer) where to go. Not so in ye olden times of Game Design. An example of an "old school" tutorial is apparent in the PC/PS1 title *Driver 2* (Reflections Interactive, 2000). In control of a 70s muscle car, the player is enclosed within an underground car park and tasked with a series of increasingly difficult manoeuvres (burnout, slalom, 180, lap, etc.) within a time limit (see video link 1.1). From a game designer's perspective, this "lock-in" is a fantastic way to determine the player's available skills when they leave that garage, enabling level design from that point based around the skills you *know* the player has learned. From a player's perspective, however, perhaps not so great. If you don't complete this incredibly frustrating sequence, you don't get to play the rest of the game that you've just paid for.

VIDEO LINK 1.1: *DRIVER 2* TRAINING TUTORIAL

https://bit.ly/Driver2Tut

"Intuitive" tutorials

As a result, incorporated "intuitive" tutorials have become a prevalent design trend. For example, the initial "bank heist" sequence in *Grand Theft Auto V* (Rockstar North, 2013) effectively teaches players cover mechanics, combat techniques, and driving skills as integral parts of the actual gameplay. I would also note that it clearly delineates itself as a game through the Pac-Man-style pellet cash pickups in the vault, complete with accompanying sound effects, clearly telling us it is *not* trying to be an "interactive movie" (see video link 1.2). Another clear example of intuitive teaching is in the platform game *Super Meat Boy*, (Team Meat, 2010). Players start with easy levels that teach the basics of *traversal* (General movement within the game, e.g., jumping, climbing, ducking, etc.) As the game progresses, new challenges such as saw blades and spikes are gradually introduced, requiring quick thinking and precise timing. Instant respawns encourage repeated attempts, improving skills through trial and error, and replay footage showcases successful player attempts, offering insights into how the player has previously failed, inviting different strategies and creating excitement and anticipation for the next attempt.

VIDEO LINK 1.2: *GRAND THEFT AUTO 5* TUTORIAL SEQUENCE

https://bit.ly/GTAV_TUT

Tutorial videos

Another effective way of teaching players is through tutorial videos that are introduced within the game and can be accessed from the menu whenever necessary. These videos act as useful reminders of specific mechanics, such as combat movesets, or "special moves" such as those featured in the Insomniac games title *Marvel's Spider-Man 2* (Insomniac games, 2023).

Box 1.2   Player Agency

"Player agency" or the "player possibility space"[2] generally refers to the freedom and meaningful choices that the game designer builds into the game systems that allow the player to feel as if they have genuine choice in their actions. Good implementation of agency within your design should allow the player to feel they are fully in control of, and responsible for, their actions, as opposed to the game being unfair or taking the action out of their hands (i.e., the player character being defeated in an unplayable cutscene). Ideally this increases the player "ownership" over their avatar (i.e., the character is an extension of the player), and hence, arguably, increases immersion and engagement.

Let's move onto another brief introduction to a core component, in this case, **Game Mechanics**.

Core Component Example: Mechanics

Lecture reference: slide 8

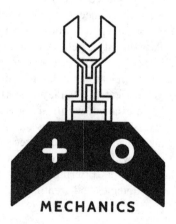

FIGURE 1.6   The mechanic game component. Illustration by Andrew Thornton.

Mechanics encompass a wide range of elements that drive gameplay and player Agency. Mechanics is a catch-all term that includes various specific elements, such as player traversal, combat, puzzles, crafting, and any of the player facing "working parts" of the game. Mechanics are the gears that make the game experience run smoothly. One broken cog, and the engine begins to fail. For example, In the game *Portal* (Valve Corporation, 2007). The core mechanic revolves around using a portal gun to create inter-dimensional portals that enable the player to instantaneously teleport between spaces within the level. This complex core mechanic (adapted from original student designs, see Box 1.3) requires careful scaffolding of game mechanics that often guides the player in stages, culminating in the "Aha!" moment (Bates, 1997), an important climatic dopamine hit for the player when they finally unravel the solution.

Box 1.3 An Inspiration Drop

In 2007, a small team of students from the DigiPen Institute of Technology was hired by the nearby game company Valve to work on a new project. Why were the students hired? Because in 2005, they had come up with a clever teleport mechanic in their student game *Narbacular Drop*. The game's innovative teleport-based mechanics caught the attention of Valve, and impressed by their work, Valve hired them to expand, develop, and refine their concept, ultimately leading to the creation of the critically acclaimed game (you might have guessed this) *Portal*. Many of the team went on to further successes, including the original designer, Kim Swift, who has worked across many high-profile studios and projects to become a hugely influential and inspiring figure in game design and development. Not bad for what started as a simple class assignment!

We'll look at puzzles in more specific detail in the "Challenge" lecture, in the meantime, let's have a quick overview of the **Challenge** component.

Core Component: Challenge

Lecture reference: slide 9

CHALLENGE

FIGURE 1.7 The challenge game component. Illustration by Andrew Thornton.

As previously mentioned, I would suggest a game without a challenge is more an experience than a game. Consider this scenario: Imagine you are in a medium-sized,

FIGURE 1.8   A Samurai swordsman. Illustration by Shutterstock/Rotshild.

featureless room. (Depending on how many rooms you have been in previously, this may not require much imagination.). You are on one side of the room, and on the opposite side, an obvious exit door, your **objective**. If you can effortlessly walk to the door, there is no challenge. However, if there is a peculiarly coloured turtle blocking your path that attacks at speed unless you rapidly jump on its shell, jump off, and *then* reach the door, then you have a challenge – and thus, I would argue, a game. **Challenges** in this respect can be obstacles, puzzles, enemies, or general tasks that test a player's skills. They should add a sense of accomplishment when overcome or reached. Without these challenges, the player is not "earning" their reward, and the objective simply becomes a valueless tickbox.

An example of a game with frequent and difficult challenges is, *Sekiro: Shadows Die Twice* (FromSoftware, 2019). It offers intense "Soulslike" combat encounters where players must learn enemy attack patterns and execute precise timing and movesets to overcome their foes.

This high level of difficulty provides a tremendous sense of achievement when players successfully conquer particularly challenging foes, and this "Risk/Reward" (see Box 1.4) gamble feeds directly into the "Reward" aspect of the core gameplay loop, which we will discuss shortly.

Box 1.4   Risk/Reward

The concept of "Risk/Reward" in game design refers to the method of adding a secondary layer of strategy to gameplay. For example, a player may venture into an area of the map where the enemies are much stronger. The player must then decide whether the potential high-level loot or XP is worth the increased risk of some serious maiming at the hands of some unruly MOB. Similarly, a particularly twinkly pickup placed in a difficult-to-reach location makes the player weigh the risk of retrieval against the value of the possible reward. I say "possible" as in many cases the lure of curiosity may be designed in to drive the player to take that chance. What's in the box?[3]

Core Component: Win/Lose

Lecture reference: slide 10

FIGURE 1.9   The win/lose game component. Illustration by Andrew Thornton.

Let's move onto another core component overview, in this case, **Win/Lose**. The Win/Lose condition is a fundamental component of gameplay. It defines the outcome and can create a sense of achievement, or indeed, disappointment for players.

FIGURE 1.10   "Rocket League." Illustration by Shutterstock/Printon Merchandise.

If we look at the game *Rocket League* (Psyonix, 2015), the "Win/Lose" component is central to the gameplay experience. Basically "football with cars," two teams are assigned a half of the pitch, and play across it, aiming to score more goals than their opponents within a time limit. The team with the most goals at the end of the match wins, the dopamine "hit" from the win encouraging further play. In the case of the losing player or team, various social and psychological reasons can also encourage continued play. These range from the anticipation of re-firing the brain's dopamine pathways with a win, to the desire not to let teammates down, or to resolve the cognitive dissonance between the thoughts "I'm really good at this game!" and the factual "I've lost."

Although we should note, in the case of Games, even a lose can be a win – as games are one of the only mediums where constant failure is utilised as a learning experience.

Core Component: Social

Lecture reference: slide 11

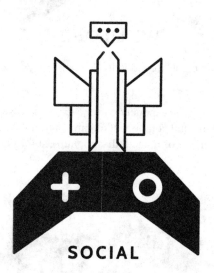

FIGURE 1.11   The social game component. Illustration by Andrew Thornton.

The final component we'll touch on in this initial overview of the core components is **Social**.

In the context of game design, "social" refers to "other players" in either competitive or cooperative multiplayer gameplay scenarios and interactions. Multiplayer can be a distinct and highly specialised area of game design that requires a deep understanding of player psychology and motivation, which can involve utilising player feedback data to iterate and refine game designs, particularly in the field of casual gaming. Social gaming is often seen as crucial within the business side of the gaming industry for player retention and engagement.

Previously, publishers sought to incorporate multiplayer features into many high-budget games, irrespective of suitability, such as the example of *Dead Space 2* (Visceral Games, 2011), (see Box 1.5), However, the trend has shifted towards season-based/subscription models and "games as a service," such as *Call of Duty: Warzone* (Infinity Ward & Raven Software, 2020). This approach ensures a consistent revenue stream through limited updates or downloadable content (DLC), as opposed to developing entirely new games.

Box 1.5   Multiplayer Case Study: *Dead Space 2*

One of the recognised key strengths of the *Dead Space* series is its horror atmosphere, designed primarily around the isolation of a solo experience. The tension and fear generated by the game's single-player campaign were difficult to replicate in what became a 4v4 multiplayer deathmatch experience included in *Dead Space 2* (Visceral Games, 2011). Other issues included the perception (common in many games at the time) that the multiplayer was "tacked on." The limited selection of maps and modes further hindered its support within the core player-base. The game also had to compete with other major titles with established multiplayer modes, such as *Call of Duty: Black Ops* (Activision, 2010). As a result, player numbers dwindled (Chalk, 2023)[4], leading to slow matchmaking and an increasingly worsening experience for those involved. However, it should be noted that the servers for this game continued to operate until December 2023.[5] Some Necromorphs won't go down without a fight.

To finish our overview of Social, let's look at an example featuring common multiplayer tropes in the hit title *Phasmophobia* (Kinetic Games, 2020).

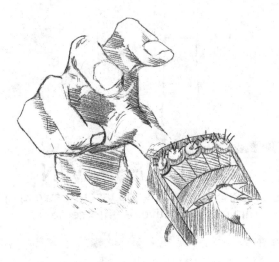

FIGURE 1.12   Ghost hunting. Illustration by Jack Hollick.

In *Phasmophobia*, players explore haunted locations, gather evidence, and attempt to identify supernatural entities. Communication and collaboration are key as players must strategise, share findings, and support each other to identify and survive encounters with ghosts.

Phasmophobia gained popularity due to its unique selling point – immersing players in a paranormal investigation experience, similar to those made popular by television shows such as *Most Haunted*. Designed to be played with friends, with the vibe of a "horror movie night," I'd suggest one of the key design pillars (see Box 1.6) in this case is "being scared together."

Now we've had a brief overview of the six core components of Teaching, Objectives, Mechanics, Challenge, Win Lose, and Social, let's drill down a little deeper with our first **Exercise.**

FIGURE 1.13   An example game card. Illustration by Andrew Thornton.

Lecturer Notes: Game Cards and the "Redaction" Exercise

Before we start, here's a quick overview of this teaching technique, as we'll be using it frequently. Introducing the "Game Cards"[6] (see Figure 1.13). These focus on the taught components that week (e.g., "Objectives") with examples of how the component or techniques is utilised in well-known games, as per the provided example cards. A good way to introduce these example components or techniques is to introduce the card with the details intact, but the title "redacted" (see Figure 1.14). It's a great way of prompting discussion around the design of the featured game, and the students have the anticipation of uncovering the "name" of the described feature, and if correct, with the reward of positive peer and lecturer feedback to re-enforce learning. It should be noted these same cards are also used in the end of the lecture exercise/workshop, which we'll cover in more detail in the appropriate section. In the meantime, let's get on with the exercise!

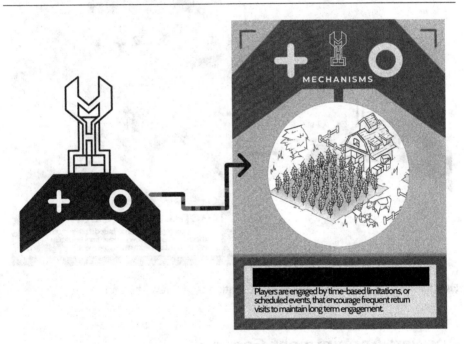

MECHANISMS

Players are engaged by time-based limitations, or scheduled events, that encourage frequent return visits to maintain long term engagement.

FIGURE 1.14 A "Redacted" game mechanic card. Illustration by Andrew Thornton.

IN CLASS EXERCISE 1.1

Lecture reference: slides 12–13
Game Component Discussion: Mechanic
   Let's drill down and examine a specific component, in this example, a game mechanic:

If we look at the featured (Figure 1.14) game mechanic component card, we see a *Farmville*-esque game that has the mechanic description but is missing the mechanic title –

"Players are engaged by time-based limitations, real-time elements, or scheduled events, that encourage frequent return visits to maintaining long term engagement."

Question:

Can you use the description to work out what the title of the game mechanic might be?

Followed by Class Discussion

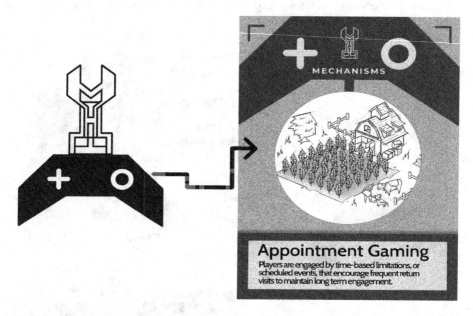

FIGURE 1.15   A game mechanic card. Illustration by Andrew Thornton.

Answer: Appointment Gaming

Games such as *Farmville* (Zynga, 2009) or Sample *Cropout*[7] (Epic Games, 2023) are designed to utilise "Appointment gaming" – a strategy that involves players returning to the game at specific times to obtain rewards, advance their progress, or enjoy special bonuses. This mechanic is particularly common in casual or mobile games, where maintaining and promoting regular re-engagement is crucial to sustain the game's continued income (via advertising revenue or other sources).

Other Example Answers:

Animal Crossing: New Horizons (Nintendo, 2020)
Unless they decide to fiddle with the time settings on their Nintendo Switch, Players are encouraged to play in real-time. They can only perform certain activities, like entering shops or buildings, gathering resources or talking to non-player characters (NPCs), at specific allocated times. This creates a re-engagement cycle which conditions the player to return to the game at specific times, hence "Appointment gaming."

Pokémon GO (Niantic, 2016)
Based around the popular Pokémon series of games, this augmented reality mobile game has real-world locations designated as "Pokéstops" and Gyms. Players can collect items and engage in battles at these real-world locations, which often refresh every few hours, driving scheduled play sessions (appointment gaming). Unfortunately, player "enthusiasm" for capturing some of these rarer Pokémon has resulted in some well-documented accidents (Bogost, 2016)[8].

FIGURE 1.16   Dark city. Illustration by Shutterstock/Little Vignettes Photo.

IN CLASS EXERCISE 1.2: GAME COMPONENTS

In class reference: Lecture slide 15
Game Video Discussion: Game Mechanics
Question:

Try to identify and list as many game mechanic components as you can from the following clip. Watch the video and write them down for discussion afterwards.

EXERCISE 1.2 VIDEO LINK:

Batman: Arkham City (Rocksteady Studios, 2011)
    https://bit.ly/EX1_2_BAT

Notes on the video clip:
In this clip, it appears that Rocksteady, the game developer, aims to capture the essence of Batman by focusing on his use of gadgets. This is crucial for gameplay and likely a priority as one of the core *gameplay pillars* (see Box 1.6). The goal is not only to showcase Batman's tech-based savvy (i.e., his "utility belt" packed with upgradeable gadgets) but also his detective skills, both of which are integral to his character.

Box 1.6   Gameplay Pillars

Gameplay pillars aim to define the essential or signature elements of a game. Typically limited to between three and five (in larger A-AAA titles), they are established early on by the designer or design team to form the game's foundation. These pillars serve as a guiding framework for both player experience and provide structure and direction for the development team. While the pillars may evolve during development, it is often advisable to establish them early on to ensure clear and coherent development objectives. Some developers will print and display them at workstations, or in the case of more specific (not to be named) game studios, pin them up on the inside of the toilet cubicle doors in an effort to force the development team to actually read them. A compelling industry example of the significance of gameplay pillars is the *DOOM* reboot by id Software, released in 2016. Initially announced in 2008, the development team faced challenges that led to criticism from fans who felt that early footage failed to capture the fast-paced action of the original series. Around 2011–2012, the team made the difficult but necessary decision to scrap the project and start anew, focusing on the core pillars of the original *DOOM* – fast traversal, aggressive combat against overwhelming odds, and minimal narrative within a horror setting. After years of refocused efforts based on these pillars, the game was released in 2016 to widespread acclaim. It succeeded in paying homage to the original while also updating it for modern audiences, much to the satisfaction of both new and long-time fans. Finally, DoomGuy had found his new home.

Exercise 1.2 Answers

Lecture reference: slide 16
Now, let's compare the mechanics listed below with your own findings.
How many did you get?

1. **Glide**

   In this case, the glide mechanic is effectively a "controlled fall," enabling a deliberate and gradual descent. It offers designers the opportunity to introduce more verticality to their levels and incorporate gameplay challenges, such as allowing the player to guide Batman's direction towards a target platform, adding some agency to what might otherwise be a fairly vanilla descent.
2. **Detective Mode: (A Subgame)**

   Detective mode is a sub-game in which players use investigative techniques to identify areas within the game environment that can be interacted with. One of the earliest and most widely recognised implementations of this is in the original Batman title from Rocksteady, *Batman: Arkham Asylum* (Rocksteady Studios, 2009). This mode was such an effective piece of design that it quickly influenced numerous other titles from its inception onward. It continues to be utilised in various games, e.g. the spell "Revelio" in *Hogwarts Legacy* (Portkey Games, 2023).
3. **Grapple gun**

   The Grapple Gun introduces us to a gameplay mechanic akin to a set-piece or cutscene. Its functionality involves equipping the gun, locating the relevant highlighted object (in detective mode) and then "firing," initiating an interactive sequence whereby players subsequently "button tap" to complete the action, resulting in a *"Canned animation"* (see Box 1.7) including other elements such as (in this case) dialogue, and particle effects of water and billowing steam as the kiln door is ripped off.

Box 1.7   Canned Animations

"Canned" animations are predefined singular animations that depict specific actions or movements usually performed by a game character, i.e., pulling a rope, opening a door, pushing a lever, reacting to a conversational point. Canned animations allow game developers to re-use common mechanics without the need for resource heavy bespoke animations for each. Sequences or montages of canned animations are sometimes utilised as "Resource light" setpieces or cutscenes.

---

4. **Shimmy**

   Shimmying is an essential component of a *traversal moveset* (see Box 1.8) common in action-adventure titles such as *Tomb Raider* (Core Design, 1996) or it's later stable mate, *Uncharted: Drake's Fortune* (Naughty Dog, 2007). The shimmy mechanic involves finding your way to the next section of the level by carefully manoeuvring along edges or narrow paths. Shimmying can cleverly hide the intended route in plain sight, which forms one of the foundations of effective traversal-based level design. We'll look at level design around traversal mechanics in more detail in later lectures.

Box 1.8   Traversal Mechanics & "Movesets"

Traversal mechanics in video game design describe the general actions and abilities that enable players to navigate and explore the game world, e.g. running and jumping. More complex traversal systems are usually associated with third-person, character-based action-adventure or stealth titles, and these mechanics encompass a range of movements such as climbing, crawling, ducking, rolling, and even, in some cases, when the animator has too much time on their hands, performing hand-stands. These mechanics serve the purpose of surmounting obstacles, accessing new areas, and uncovering hidden secrets throughout the game, and are sometimes also referred to as "movesets."

---

5. **Railing/rope walk**

   More of a traversal design sub-game, and fairly common across action-adventure titles, this requires that the player maintains balance while navigating a narrow and precarious environmental element. In some games, you may need to continuously adjust your controller/keyboard left and right to "balance" and prevent yourself from falling. Again, this is another element of adding challenge and jeopardy to what is effectively moving between points A and B.

6. **Explosive**

   This mechanic involves the utilisation of detective mode, whereby players employ investigative techniques to identify areas within the game environment that can be interacted with. Once such an area is located and interacted with by placing the explosive, a predetermined canned animation sequence is triggered (as per the grapple gun mechanic)

7. **Batarang**

   The Batarang offers three distinct mechanics – the grapple gun for attaching to interactable elements, precision targeting for combat or specific environment-based features, and the explosive attachment. These mechanics add the challenge of skill-based positioning, accuracy, and strategic destruction to the gameplay experience.

GAME COMPONENTS

FIGURE 1.17   Game component types. Illustration by Andrew Thornton.

IN CLASS EXERCISE 1.3: OTHER COMPONENTS

Now let's have a brief look at some of the other components.

Lecture reference: slide 18

Game Video Discussion: Game Components

Question:

Identify the component from the list (see Figure 1.17) in the following video clip:

EXERCISE 1.3 VIDEO LINK:

Super Mario Bros (Nintendo, 1985)**:** World 1-1

https://bit.ly/EX1_3_MAR

Exercise 1.3 Answer

Lecture reference: slide 19

I would suggest the most important component in this sequence is "Teaching".

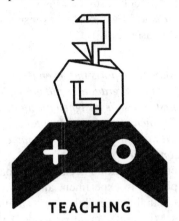

TEACHING

FIGURE 1.18   The teaching game component. Illustration by Andrew Thornton.

Shigeru Miyamoto *on* Super Mario Bros*: World 1-1*

Lecture reference: slide 20

FIGURE 1.19   Shigeru Miyamoto. Illustration by Jack Hollick.

Shigeru Miyamoto, the legendary Japanese game designer, and producer at Nintendo, is often cited as "the Father of modern video gaming[9]" and the creator behind some of the world's best-known game titles, such as *Donkey Kong*, *Super Mario Bros*, and *The Legend of Zelda*. Miyamoto's insights on game design often revolve around the idea of teaching players. Let's have a look at some of his wisdom with specific reference to World 1-1 in *Super Mario Bros* as Miyamoto shares insights on how Nintendo crafted Mario's most iconic level (Robinson, 2015).

Miyamoto:

"We made sure that there were some parts that even if the player felt it would be safe by doing that we wanted the player to gradually and naturally understand what they're doing" he continues – *"the first course Is designed for that purpose – so they can learn what the game is all about but then after that we want them to play more freely – that's the approach we've taken with all the games that we make – once the player realises what they need to do, it becomes their game."*

In game design, this teaching method is called "onboarding" or "on-ramp" and involves a safe space for players to experiment and learn without risks. This area can also be referred to as a "sandbox area," though it should be noted it differs from "sandbox games" (such as Minecraft "creative mode") where players have complete freedom to create and pursue their own objectives. Aarseth (2003) explains that learning in a game involves exploring and experimenting with different techniques.[10] The sandbox area is specifically designed for this purpose, where players are typically required to learn the fundamental aspects of the game system. Just like we used to experiment with toys and play in the physical sandbox as children, Miyamoto believes in giving players the freedom to explore and find their own style in games, and in this first level of *Super Mario Bros*, players feel like they are exploring the game on their own terms – or as Miyamato says *"it becomes their game"* (Robinson, 2015).

Shigeru Miyamoto on User Testing

Lecture reference: slide 21

"There's a lot of testing whilst the game is being built – I don't give any verbal explanation and just watch them play and see how they do it – and most of the time I think they'll play it a certain way or enjoy a certain part and they'll end up not doing that." (Robinson, 2015)

I've included this final section of Miyamoto's interview because it highlights the importance of user testing in game design. Players often surprise us by doing the opposite of what we expect, so it's crucial to keep this in mind throughout the design process. Iteration, the process of making improvements through repetition, lies at the core of practical, hands-on user-centred game design – build, test, iterate, repeat. Designers create prototypes, test them with the *Quality assurance department* (see Box 1.9), gather feedback, make necessary changes, and repeat the cycle until the design meets user needs and expectations. We'll look at user testing in more detail in later lectures.

Box 1.9   Game Testing and Quality Assurance (QA)

In the early days, game testing was typically carried out by a small in-house team, often including the developers themselves. However, with the increasing size and complexity of games, the role of game testers has now transformed into dedicated departments and external quality assurance providers. These teams meticulously test games for bugs and glitches, their data and feedback helping to refine the game before release, aiming to provide players with a playable, friction and error-free experience. It should be noted that game testing is still commonly viewed as an accessible entry point into the industry for game designers.

SECTION 1.2: CORE TECHNIQUES: GAMEPLAY LOOPS

Lecture reference: slide 22

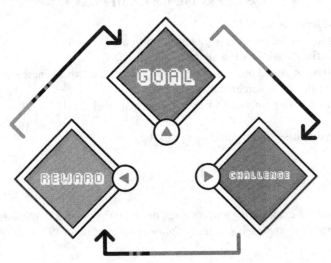

FIGURE 1.20   A gameplay loop. Illustration by Andrew Thornton.

As we've discussed, games consist of various elements or components. Now, let's discuss the next essential technique that emerges from these components: **Gameplay Loops.** These loops revolve around the idea of objectives (or "goals"), challenges, and rewards (see Figure 1.20).

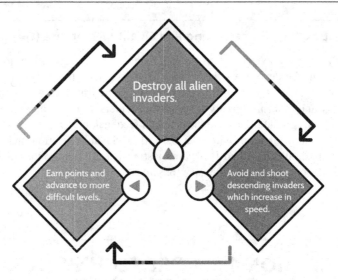

FIGURE 1.21 Example gameplay loop. Illustration by Andrew Thornton.

IN CLASS EXERCISE 1.4: GAMEPLAY LOOPS

Lecture reference: slide 23

Let's look at an example gameplay loop (see Figure 1.19).

Objective/Goal: Destroy all Alien Invaders.

Challenge: Avoid and shoot descending invaders, which increase in speed (the further down the screen they get).

Reward Earn points and advance to more difficult levels.

Question:

Can you guess which game we're talking about?

Exercise 1.4 Answer

If you guessed the exhilarating and complex online universe of *Eve Online* you would, sadly, have been incorrect – It's actually *Space Invaders* (Taito, 1978).

FIGURE 1.22 *"Space Invaders."* Illustration by Jack Hollick.

Lecture reference: slide 24

Despite having some subtler strategies, like the inclusion of bases (protective structures placed at the bottom of the screen), this example showcases a well-defined and uncomplicated gameplay loop.

Now, let's explore a slightly more complex one.

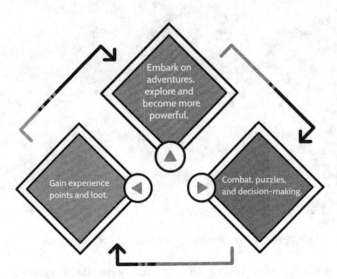

FIGURE 1.23 Example gameplay loop. Illustration by Andrew Thornton.

IN CLASS EXERCISE 1.4: GAMEPLAY LOOPS PART 2

Lecture reference: slide 25
Question:
Which game does the following loop refer to? (see Figure 1.23)
Objective/Goal: Embark on adventures, explore and become more powerful, advance the narrative.
Challenge: Combat, puzzles, and decision-making.
Reward: Gain experience points and loot.

Answer

Lecture reference: slide 26
XP, loot, and exploration – which *type* or *genre* of game could we be talking about here?
   The answer is, of course, a Role-Playing game (or RPG)
This loop encompasses numerous games, and as we'll discover, the core loop is also commonly utilised in non-RPG genre titles. However, before we examine those, let's rewind to patient zero…

The birth of role-playing games

Lecture reference: slides 27–28

FIGURE 1.24   Roleplaying game. Illustration by Shutterstock/paulzhuk.

Back in the early days, when video games were barely past the withering gaze of Nolan Bushnell's bank manager, a game called *Dungeons & Dragons* (TSR Hobbies, 1974) emerged fully formed into the nascent world of tabletop gaming. This game is considered the foundation of all role-playing games (RPGs), and, for the most part involved sitting down with friends, usually a group of four or five, with a nominated *Dungeon Master* (see Box 1.10). The Dungeon master (usually the player group would take turns) would, adhering to a strict set of rules laid out in the "Players' Handbook" (see Figure 1.25) craft that week's adventure. Players would assume a character's role and earn experience points (XP) by completing tasks, rolling against stats controlled by the rules and the dungeon master, and discussing options with the other players (i.e., "Should we try to charm the ogre with a song, or just chuck the bard at it?"). Progression and exploration allow players to enhance specific skills and abilities of their self-created character, fostering a valuable sense of progress and camaraderie.

Box 1.10   "Dungeon Master"

In the early days of RPG gaming, serving as the dungeon master often meant spending evenings meticulously crafting thrilling adventures for your friends and fellow adventurers. You would utilise the game's provided rulebooks, investing time and effort into creating intricate maps, developing characters, constructing narratives, and finalising all necessary details. Once fully prepared, you would bring your hours of carefully prepared plans, documentation, and maps to your friends' homes, eagerly observing as they began playing through the adventure you had designed. And then, much like modern game testing, you would watch with horror as, within the initial 5 minutes, they did exactly the opposite of what you expected and ended up breaking everything.

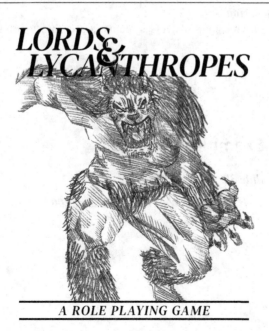

LORDS & LYCANTHROPES

A ROLE PLAYING GAME

FIGURE 1.25   Example "Player's handbook." Illustration by Jack Hollick.

In more detail, some of the key game-changing elements in the RPG systems were.

Personalised character creation
For the first time, RPG's empowered players to craft their own distinctive and personal characters, enabling specialisation in skills such as combat, healing, and magic, altering gameplay and team dynamics while opening a vast array of gameplay possibilities. This approach also fostered a strong sense of "ownership" among players regarding their characters, intensifying the peril of dangerous encounters.

Experience (XP) points
Successful completion of quests and activities earns experience points (XP). When a character accumulates enough XP, they level up, unlocking various benefits and improvements. These can include increasing hit points (HP), gaining new abilities, spells, or skills, and becoming proficient in new weapons or unlocking unique features available in the chosen character class.

Non-linear narrative
As you advance, the narrative unfolds, as managed (and often written by) the "Dungeon Master." This system allows players to perform dice rolls against their character stats to determine outcomes that shape the story, from interactions with other NPC characters and the environment, to combat encounters that ultimately influence the game's final outcome.

EXERCISE 1.5: LOOPS DISCUSSION

Game Loop Discussion – RPG's
 Nowadays, the core loop of RPG systems is a cornerstone of many video game titles.
Question:
 Can you think of any?
In class Discussion

Exercise 1.5 Example Answers

Lecture reference: slide 30

Classic RPG Case study: World of Warcraft (Blizzard, 2004)

FIGURE 1.26 Murloc from *"World of Warcraft."* Illustration by Jack Hollick.

World of Warcraft is a prime example of an exceptionally designed game that illustrates the mechanics of levelling up (XP) and utilising carefully managed reward schedules (which we'll discuss in more detail in a later lecture). The dopamine effect of accumulating XP, which reinforces progress, compels players to continuously enhance their characters and gain access to areas where they might have previously struggled against high-level *mobs* (see Box 1.11) – an underrated design aspect that offers a satisfying sense of "revenge" on foes that previously hammered you at a lower skill level. In addition, you'll instantly recognise the almost Pavlovian rush of euphoria that accompanies the sound of levelling up. *World of Warcraft* has perfected its gameplay loop and reward schedules, and this is not by accident – WoW was one of the first games to tweak, redesign, and update the game based on collected user gameplay data. If you haven't played the game, exploring its exemplary game systems is a useful learning experience for any game designer. However, DISCLAIMER! It's worth noting that participation in *World of Warcraft* may require significant time, financial, and spousal commitment.

Box 1.11 Mobs

"Mob" is a term commonly used to describe hostile NPCs or enemies that players encounter and engage with during gameplay. These mobs are typically designed to exhibit certain behaviours, such as attacking the player, defending specific areas, or following predetermined patrol paths. Mobs play a crucial role in providing obstacles, and combat encounters to enhance the challenge component of the gameplay loop.

Classic RPG Case Study: Assassins Creed 2 (Ubisoft, 2009)

Although not immediately recognisable as an RPG, and not featuring an XP system, *Assassin's Creed 2* introduces a groundbreaking upgrade mechanism by consistently enhancing your initially run-down hometown of "Monteriggioni" – rather than improving your character, you enhance a town. Players can renovate various buildings within the town, unlocking new features, services, and benefits. For instance, restoring the local blacksmith enables players to buy new weapons and armour, while renovating the villa's codex pages reveals hidden knowledge and upgrades. In essence, you are enhancing and upgrading the skillset of the player character, Ezio Auditore, through bricks and mortar.

This concept has been utilised to a lesser extent in subsequent games, ranging from restoring classic Italian villas to the arguably slightly less aesthetically pleasing rebuilding of a series of Viking halls in *Assassin's Creed Valhalla* (Ubisoft, 2020).

Further Examples: Hogwarts Legacy (Portkey Games, 2023)

FIGURE 1.27   Illustration by Shutterstock/Cloudy Design.

In *Hogwarts Legacy* (Portkey Games, 2023), set in the Harry Potter universe, players assume the role of a student at Hogwarts School of Witchcraft and Wizardry. This allows them to customise their character and develop their abilities through RPG elements, progressing from character creation to enhancing magical abilities and acquiring new spells. Players can specialise in different playstyles, such as focusing on dark arts. The branching narrative and decision-making system impact the story and relationships, promoting a sense of "ownership" of the character in true RPG fashion. Furthermore, quests, exploration, interactive dialogue, and magical activities provide a constant reward cycle, encouraging re-engagement and rewarding the player in a classic RPG loop.

Further Examples for Discussion

Borderlands (Gearbox Software, 2009)
The Elder Scrolls V: Skyrim (Bethesda Game Studios, 2011)
Fallout 3 (Bethesda Game Studios, 2008)

Further Examples: Beyond RPG

Lecture reference: slide 31

It's interesting to note that many of the popular, Triple A (AAA) games like *Skyrim* (Bethesda Game Studios, 2011) and *Fallout 3* (Bethesda Game Studios, 2008), share a similar core loop with our RPG games. But now, let's explore how elements of these systems have made their way into different types of games.

Beyond RPG Case Study: Call of Duty: Modern Warfare 2 (Infinity Ward, 2009)

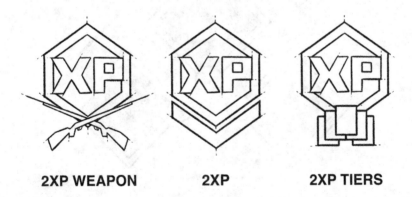

DOUBLE XP WEEKEND

2XP WEAPON   **2XP**   **2XP TIERS**

AVAILABLE APRIL 3- APRIL 6
ON ALL PLATFORMS

FIGURE 1.28   Double XP weekend. Illustration by Andrew Thornton.

As seen in the original *Call of Duty 4: Modern Warfare (Infinity Ward, 2007)*, experience points, or XP, are among the first design elements to transcend their original RPG roots. Nowadays, numerous first-person shooters and multiplayer deathmatches incorporate XP systems into their gameplay. However, as designers, we bear a responsibility to be cautious in our designs. A fundamental aspect of game design is rooted in the fact that humans are naturally driven by rewards. This innate motivation can lead to prolonged play or even addictive behaviour, as reward schedules featuring previously discussed elements like XP, in-game currency (such as loot boxes), or cosmetic items encourage players to keep playing. Game design has faced significant critique regarding the ethics of these systems, and while rewards are widespread in most games, it is crucial to be mindful of their implementation. In subsequent chapters, we will delve further into this subject, exploring the underlying psychology and its impact on the ethics and responsibility of how we design games.

SECTION 1.3: CORE TECHNIQUES: GAMEPLAY LOOPS AND THE OBJECTIVE/GOAL

Lecture reference: slide 32

Now, let's delve into the "objective" or "goal" aspect of the Gameplay loop.

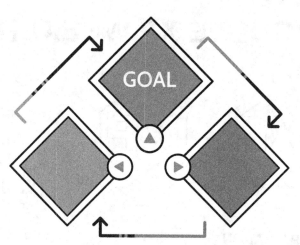

FIGURE 1.29   The Objective/Goal component of the loop. Illustration by Andrew Thornton.

EXERCISE 1.6: GAMEPLAY LOOP EXERCISE

Lecture reference: slide 33
   Game Video Discussion: Objective component
Question:
   Try to identify the objective in the video clip and write it down for discussion afterwards.

Exercise 1.6 Answers

From the video, as we transition into the game's title screen, it becomes clear that the objective is the mountain. This design decision is notable because, unlike in many other games, your objective remains visible for the majority of the game. In most levels in *Journey*, the mountain is visible, serving as a constant reminder of your goal. While you'll encounter challenges such as facing enemies or engaging in cooperative teamwork, the beauty of the design lies in the clarity of this objective.

FIGURE 1.30 "Journey." Illustration by Andrew Thornton.

A similar example can be found in *Half-Life 2* (Valve Corporation, 2004) where the Combine Tower remains visible for most of the game. Both *Journey* and *Half-Life 2* frequently appear on "best games of all time" lists. Does this suggest that maintaining a clear and visible objective throughout a game may be a cornerstone of what makes it great? Answers on a postcard[11] please!

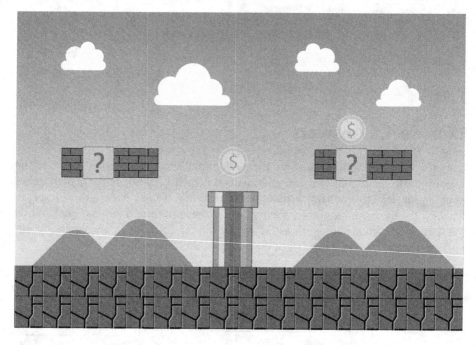

FIGURE 1.31   Classic videogame. Image by Shutterstock/neuralsuperstudio.

IN CLASS EXERCISE 1.7: GAMEPLAY LOOP EXERCISE PART 2

Lecture reference: slides 35–36
Question:
    Let's go back to level 1-1 in *Super Mario Bros*.
    Try to identify the <u>objective</u> in the video clip and write it down for discussion afterwards.

EXERCISE 1.7 VIDEO LINK:

Super Mario Bros (Nintendo, 1985)
    https://bit.ly/EX1_7_MAR

Exercise 1.7 Answers

So, in general, what do you think the core objective is in a platform game?

In *Super Mario Bros* and other early platformers, the main goal is to keep moving forward, with the ultimate objective in many of these games being to progress towards the right side of the screen. As you navigate through the levels in *Super Mario Bros*, you encounter challenges such as enemies like Goombas, and environmental hazards like pits to jump over. Gameplay elements like "Question blocks" are designed to encourage exploration and playfulness. These elements emphasise experimentation, allowing the player to learn, consistent with the previously discussed teaching component.

It's worth noting that over time, the concept of platform game objectives has evolved. In games like *Spelunky* (Yu, 2008), *Hollow Knight* (Team Cherry, 2017), and *Ori and the Blind Forest* (Moon Studios, 2015), the gameplay revolves around the players enjoying the freedom to explore in all directions within the constraints of the 2D environments.

However, if you're finding your feet in 2D platform design, it's probably a good rule of thumb to remember that players often feel a sense of comfort knowing that if they head towards the right, they are on the correct path.

EXERCISE 1.8: GAMEPLAY LOOP EXERCISE PART 3

Lecture reference: slides 37–38
Question:
   Try to identify the objective in the video clip and write it down for discussion afterwards.

EXERCISE 1.8 VIDEO LINK:

Temple Run (Imangi Studios, 2011)
   https://bit.ly/EX1_8_TEMP

Exercise 1.8 Answers

In *Temple Run*, which you may not have played, but will almost certainly have played a variation of, we see a 3D adaptation of the endless runner genre, which was popularised by the game *Canabalt*, created by Adam Saltsman and Semi-Secret Software in 2009. *Temple Run* adopts a third-person, over-the-shoulder perspective. The main objective in *Temple Run* is all about progress and scoring points. As you play, your reward is not only reflected in your score but also in how far you reach in the game. Time becomes a factor in measuring your progress, and the score increases as you continuously collect coins along the way. So, in essence, the *objective* is to keep moving forward, collect as many coins as possible, and achieve the highest score.

It's interesting to note that (after the Flash version) *Temple Run* found its home on smartphone and tablets – which brings up an important point – let's have a look at how gameplay loops vary between devices.

SECTION 1.4: CORE TECHNIQUES: MICRO AND MACRO LOOPS

Lecture reference: slide 39

Micro Loops

Loops vary depending on platform. In mobile games, the gameplay loop is usually much smaller. In *Temple Run*, the challenge is simple – turn left or right or jump – and your reward is your score and progress. It's a "second-by-second" loop. The loops are smaller in mobile games, as mobile games are all about being played in short bursts (usually while on the go), so they require quick and frequent rewards to keep players engaged.

These are *"Micro loops"* (see Box 1.12). They often occur in rapid succession and prioritise immediate gratification and rewards, which in turn should theoretically promote player engagement and retention, vital in mobile and casual games. Why is engagement and retention important in these types of games? Take a few moments to consider/discuss this, as we'll focus on it in more detail in later lectures.

Box 1.12   Micro and Macro (within Game Design)

Micro:

Micro refers to the small elements or mechanics at a granular level. It focuses on individual parts, like a puzzle piece, to understand how they work on their own.

Macro:

Macro refers to the big picture or the entire system as a whole. It looks at how all the puzzle pieces fit together and how they interact to create a complete system.

Macro Loops in the Wild

PC and console games (as opposed to smartphone/tablet) have what we call "Macro Loops" or "Hierarchical loops." These loops are designed for longer gameplay sessions. In these games, there is a main objective, like (for example) assassinating a specific target in *Assassin's Creed 2* (Ubisoft, 2009), but there are also many smaller objectives within that. It's a structure of loops within the game, where you have multiple goals to achieve, one leading to the other.

FIGURE 1.32 "Warrior assassin." Image by Shutterstock/Hoika Mikhail.

For example, during a combat sequence, you might earn experience points and receive rewards that progress the story, leading to new quests. So, while games always have smaller moments of gameplay (micro loops), in bigger games, these micro loops fit together like puzzle pieces to form larger, more time-consuming, Macro objectives.

Box 1.13 "30 Seconds of Fun"

No game design bootcamp is complete without the obligatory mention of the "30 seconds of fun," a concept coined by game designer Jamie Griesemer, who is known for his work on the Halo series. He articulated it as the core gameplay loop that players should encounter consistently every 30 seconds while playing a game. According to Griesemer, this concept underscores the need for games to offer engaging and enjoyable bursts of action, decision-making, or challenge within brief intervals to keep players both entertained and immersed. It highlights the importance of establishing a rhythm and pacing that continuously engages players. However, it's worth noting that there is considerable debate about whether this original quote has been taken out of the context in which Griesemer initially stated it (Kietzmann, 2016).[12] Either way, it's now firmly ingrained in the lexicon of Game Design.

The Strange Case of VR

As of the time of writing, there is no general consensus on an "average" playtime (and hence Micro/Macro Gameplay Loop) for VR games. Playtime typically falls between the point where players feel satisfied after overcoming initial setup challenges – known as "setup friction" – and the point where they start to experience fatigue from wearing the headset for an extended period, often referred to as "headset fatigue." Games in the VR space vary widely, ranging from shorter, casual experiences with repetitive gameplay, e.g. *Beat Saber* (Beat Games, 2018), to longer, intense adventures featuring complex progression systems, such as *Resident Evil: Biohazard* (Capcom, 2017), which engages players for extended periods.

Gameplay Micro Loops Case Study:

Infinity Blade (Chair Entertainment and Epic Games, 2010)

FIGURE 1.33   In the style of *"Infinity Blade."* Illustration by Jack Hollick.

Developed by Chair Entertainment and Epic Games, *Infinity Blade*, released in 2010 on Apple iOS, allowed players to become knights on a quest to defeat the tyrannical "God-King," pitched against huge and intimidating enemies. This game marked a milestone in smartphone gaming, as it was among the first to use Unreal Engine on a handheld device, delivering exceptional graphics and essentially becoming the first AAA game for mobile platforms. Its gameplay loop employed RPG elements that let players improve their abilities by acquiring new weapons and skills. The game's core loop centred on a swipe-based sword and shield combat system, effectively a simple

"Rock/Paper/Scissors" mechanic which, as lead designer Donald Mustard explains, created an engaging micro-loop for players:

> A lot of console games can get away with not having core loops that are good, because there are so many other things they can do. A game that only has your attention for 30 seconds has to be very polished and very tight, and it needs a mechanic that is easy to learn but difficult to master.
>
> *(EDGE Magazine, 2012)*

Let's look at the last part of that quote in more detail.

SECTION 1.5: CORE TECHNIQUES "EASY TO LEARN, BUT DIFFICULT TO MASTER"

Lecture reference: slide 42

FIGURE 1.34 Nolan Bushnell. Illustration by Jack Hollick.

Nolan Bushnell and Early Gameplay Loops

Lecture reference: slide 43

Nolan Bushnell, co-founder of Atari alongside Ted Dabney, is widely regarded as the godfather of video games[13]. Established in 1972, Atari introduced some of the earliest video games, including *Computer* Space, (Nutting Associates, 1971) *Pong*, (Atari Inc., 1972) and *Breakout* (Atari Inc., 1976). Bushnell was a pioneer in developing core gameplay loops focused on a clear objective: keeping players engaged. Crucially, these gameplay loops encouraged players to keep inserting coins into arcade machines, thereby sustaining the fledgling company. His design philosophy of "easy to learn, difficult to master" effectively onboarded players, initially giving them the impression that they could beat the machine. As players continued to engage with the games, however, they soon realised that achieving mastery might require inserting one – or perhaps even a few thousand – more coins.

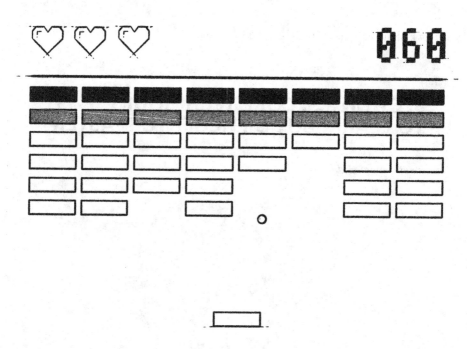

FIGURE 1.35   Early video game. Illustration by Andrew Thornton.

Gameplay Loop Case Study: Breakout (**Atari Inc., 1976**)

Lecture reference: slide 44

One of Nolan Bushnell's early game designs was *Breakout*, released by Atari in 1976. In this game, he took the simple concept of *Pong* and added a layer of complexity by introducing the objective of breaking through a wall. The challenge lies not just in getting the ball to the right place, as in *Pong*, but also in breaking through the wall while employing basic physics principles. This adds a strategic element and opens up a huge range of gameplay possibilities. The ball now bounces between walls and bricks, requiring players to use split-second timing to position their paddles and return the shot, with a complexity similar to the vast strategic variables in a real-world game of squash, but in this case with constant feedback as a reward, as the wall is slowly decimated. The completed wall at the start of the game allows the player the certainty and reward of hitting a brick (easy to learn), but as more and more bricks disappear, the difficulty increases (difficult to master). Time to feed more coins in!

FIGURE 1.36   Image by Shutterstock/NextMarsMedia.

Gameplay Loop Case **Study:** *Flappy Bird* **(Nguyen, 2013)**

Lecture reference: slide 44

Flappy Bird serves as another prime example of a game that is "easy to learn, but difficult to master." The main objective is to tap the screen to keep your bird airborne while guiding it through gaps in pipes. This already requires skill and strategy, but an added layer of challenge emerges as you realise you must also avoid the pipes by not only timing your taps carefully but also adjusting your speed, a highly challenging core loop. This loop onboards players quickly, and almost immediately it becomes apparent just how difficult the game is. This intensifying challenge drives you to chase rewards such as high scores, progression and mastery, urging you to try even harder – or, as in my case, to call it a day and give up.

IN CLASS EXERCISE 1.9: GAMEPLAY LOOP EXERCISE PART 4

Lecture reference: slide 45
Question:
   Try to identify and list the core gameplay loop elements (objective/challenge/reward) from the upcoming clip. Watch the video and write them down for discussion afterwards.

EXERCISE 1.9 VIDEO LINK:

Gears of War (Epic Games, 2006)
   https://bit.ly/EX1_9_GEAR

Exercise 1.9 Answers

Lecture reference: slide 46

So, let's examine the gameplay loop in that specific clip. The objective is to progress to the next level. The challenge lies in avoiding damage, securing advantageous positions, and achieving accurate shots/hits on the enemy. The reward is exploration, which leads to more weapons and more ammo, and narrative progression.

FIGURE 1.37   *"Gears of War"* (Epic Games, 2006). Illustration by Jack Hollick.

We also encounter a design element called "Gating," in this case "Arena gating" which we will explore in more detail in later lectures; in this case enemies burn open a door, granting you access to the next part of the game. This also serves as a progression reward, giving you access to additional ammo, weapons and even narrative, and the tantalising opportunity to further explore the motives and philosophies of the hyper enigmatic polymath Marcus Fenix, within this ultra-macho soap opera.

Conclusion

Lecture reference: slide 47

In this chapter, we've learned that game components and gameplay loops are essential for creating engaging games. These loops, both micro and macro, must work in harmony with clear objectives, challenges, and rewards to offer a compelling player experience. In the next chapter, we'll build on our knowledge by beginning our focus on specific game components, focusing on the vital aspect of "Teaching" and its role within Game Design.

Lecture One Components and Loops: Additional Resources

I have included supplementary materials, some of which are regular weekly exercises (e.g., "Working class") and others designed to give students a "quick boot" into game design. Briefly, they include:

- Working class activity (Examples and week 1-7 Templates)
- Quiz (available in both PowerPoint and Kahoot! formats)
- Assignment example
- Example video of delivered lecture

These included instructor resources can all be downloaded from the **Instructor Hub**.

Lecture One in PowerPoint Format

The lecture is provided in PowerPoint format for this and all seven chapters, cross-referenced with page numbers. Although it's ready to run "out of the box," I suggest replacing some elements (e.g., USP corner, described in Chapter 2) with your own favourites, as the industry moves fast! For further information, please see the chapter "How to Use This Book."

WORKING CLASS

The gamecard-based "working class" will usually take place straight after the lecture to re-iterate the taught material, ideally across the first semester (weeks 1–14)

Simply paste the provided lecture template into a shared drive of your choice (e.g., Google Drive) and make it available to students to complete in class (30 minutes to 1 hour). Follow with discussion on the main lecturer screen afterwards (30 minutes to 1 hour).

Resource link 1.1 will take you to a template exercise example on a shared drive. This example is locked – for your own example, when sharing, make sure it is set "editable" to avoid perplexed students!

Resource LINK 1.1: Example shared working class:
https://bit.ly/TVGDF_Working_Class_1
(For further information, please see the chapter "How to Use This Book.")

Components and Loops: Quiz

A competitive quiz is another excellent way to reinforce taught material, especially if you have a prize to hand. Rather than delivering after the lecture, it's usually an effective method to start the following week's lecture, using it as a recap of the previous material. The provided example utilises repurposed slides from the Components and Loops lecture, although a useful tip is to use slides from the previous week's student working class as the basis of the quiz, as described in the "How to Use This Book" chapter. Additionally, I've provided a Kahoot! quiz link and a tutorial on how to translate your quiz into a digital version (Resource links 1.2, 1.3). As a disclaimer, some students feel that Kahoot! is more suited to secondary education than higher education; this ultimately depends on reading the class dynamics, although I usually just find it's a bit of fun to get the class warmed up. Over to you!

Resource LINK 1.2: Kahoot Quiz
https://bit.ly/TVGDF_KahootQuiz
Resource LINK 1.3: Creating a simple Kahoot Quiz from a lecture
https://bit.ly/TVGDF_How2KAHOOT

Game Design Fundamentals: Example Assignment

This is an example assignment to give an overview of the type of submissions we expect to receive from the student over the 14-week semester. It would usually be introduced at the start of lecture one and added to the top of the online learning environment page for the course, as well as being re-iterated regularly over the 12 weeks with regular opportunities for students to ask questions. At the start of their journey through higher education, students will frequently feel overwhelmed, and the stress of assignments is one of the core friction points in this journey. Make it easier for yourself and the students by re-iterating the specifications, dates and requirements regularly. For further information, please see the chapter "How to Use This Book." Please note that all These included instructor resources can all be downloaded from the **Instructor Hub**.

Game Design Fundamentals: Example Lecture

https://bit.ly/TVGDF_LEC_CLIP

NOTES

1 Available at: https://store.steampowered.com/app/4000/Garrys_Mod/
2 Nutt (2013) *Raph Koster on 'play' - the possibility space for games, Game Developer.* Available at: https://www.gamedeveloper.com/design/raph-koster-on-play---the-possibility-space-for-games
3 From the somewhat unsettling climax of the film "Seven" (New Line Cinema, 1995), aped, fortunately without a similar resolution, in the tagline for Peter Molyneux's game: "Curiosity – What's Inside the Cube?" (22Cans, 2012).
4 Chalk (2023) *Electronic arts is closing the servers for even more old games, including Dead Space 2, crysis 3, and Mirror's Edge Catalyst, pcgamer.* Available at: https://www.pcgamer.com/electronic-arts-is-closing-the-servers-for-even-more-old-games-including-dead-space-2-crysis-3-and-mirrors-edge-catalyst/

5   Electronic Arts (no date) 'Service updates', Electronic Arts. Available at: https://www.
    ea.com/en-gb/legal/service-updates
6   A full set of game cards are provided in the supplementary materials.
7   A handy free RTS Game sample/Game development resource, available from the
    Unreal Marketplace at https://www.unrealengine.com/marketplace/en-US/product/cropout-
    sample-project?sessionInvalidated=true
8   Bogost, I. (2016). The Tragedy of Pokémon Go. The Atlantic, 11 July. Available at: https://
    bogost.com/writing/the-tragedy-of-pokemon-go/
9   *10 questions for Shigeru Miyamoto* (2007) *TIME.com*. Available at: https://web.
    archive.org/web/20120213223257/http:/www.time.com/time/magazine/article/
    0,9171,1645158,00.html
10 Interestingly, the concept of a sandbox environment aligns with the basic learning needs
    of human beings. As Bjorklund and Pellegrini (2002, p. 331) argue in their chapter "Homo
    Ludens," human children have a lot to learn, and they require both time and safe spaces
    to master their future roles as adults, describing, in effect, a physical sandbox or sandpit
    utilised for learning (Sandham, A., 2015).
11 Please replace with relevant, exciting, and up to date tech here.
12 Kietzmann (2016) *Half-minute halo: An interview with Jaime Griesemer, Engadget.
    Available at: https://www.engadget.com/2011–07–14-half-minute-halo-an-interview-with
    -jaime-griesemer.html*
13 Remember, Miyamoto is "the Father of modern video gaming", and Bushnell is the
    "Godfather" Are you keeping up?

REFERENCES

22Cans. (2012). Curiosity – What's Inside the Cube? [mobile game]. Guildford, UK: 22Cans.

Aarseth, E. (2003). Playing research: Methodological approaches to game analysis. In *Proceedings of the Digital Arts and Culture Conference* (pp. 28–29). Melbourne, Australia.

Atari Inc. (1972). *Pong.* [Video game]. Sunnyvale, CA: Atari Inc.

Atari Inc. (1976). *Breakout.* [Video game]. Sunnyvale, CA: Atari Inc.

Beat Games. (2018). *Beat Saber.* [Video game]. Prague, Czech Republic: Beat Games.

Bethesda Game Studios. (2008). *Fallout 3.* [Video Game]. Rockville, MD: Bethesda Softworks.

Bethesda Game Studios. (2011). *The Elder Scrolls V: Skyrim.* [Video Game]. Rockville, MD: Bethesda Softworks.

Bjorklund, D.F. and Pellegrini, A.D. (2002). Homo ludens: The importance of play. *Developmental Review*, 22(3), pp. 261–302.

Blizzard Entertainment. (2004-ongoing). *World of Warcraft.* [Video Game]. Irvine, CA: Blizzard Entertainment.

Bogost, I. (2016). The Tragedy of Pokémon Go. The Atlantic, 11 July. Available at: https://bogost.com/writing/the-tragedy-of-pokemon-go/

Capcom. (2017). *Resident Evil: Biohazard.* [Video game]. Osaka, Japan: Capcom.

Chair Entertainment and Epic Games. (2010). *Infinity Blade.* [Video game]. Cary, NC: Epic Games.

Chalk, A. (2023). Electronic Arts is closing the servers for even more old games, including Dead Space 2, Crysis 3, and Mirror's Edge Catalyst. PC Gamer. Available at: https://www.pcgamer.com/electronic-arts-is-closing-the-servers-for-even-more-old-games-including-dead-space-2-crysis-3-and-mirrors-edge-catalyst/

Core Design. (1996). *Tomb Raider.* [Video game]. Derby, United Kingdom: Eidos Interactive.

Electronic Arts. (n.d.). 'Service updates'. Electronic Arts. Available at: https://www.ea.com/en-gb/legal/service-updates

Epic Games. (2023). *Cropout*. [Video game]. Cary, NC: Epic Games.

Facepunch Studios. (2006). *Garry's Mod*. [Video game]. Walsall, UK: Facepunch Studios. Available at: https://store.steampowered.com/app/4000/Garrys_Mod/

FromSoftware. (2019). *Sekiro: Shadows Die Twice*. [Video game]. Santa Monica, CA: Activision.

Fincher, D. (1995). *Seven [film]*. Los Angeles, CA: New Line Cinema.

Gearbox Software. (2009). *Borderlands*. [Video Game]. Plano, TX: 2K Games.

id Software. (2016). *DOOM*. [Video game]. Rockville, MD: Bethesda Softworks.

Imangi Studios. (2011). *Temple Run*. [Mobile game]. Raleigh, NC: Imangi Studios.

Infinity Ward and Raven Software. (2020). *Call of Duty: Warzone*. [Video game]. Santa Monica, CA: Activision.

Infinity Ward. (2007). *Call of Duty 4: Modern Warfare*. [Video Game]. Santa Monica, CA: Activision.

Insomniac Games. (2023). *Marvel's Spider-Man 2*. [Video Game]. Burbank, CA: Sony Interactive Entertainment.

Kietzmann, L. (2016). Half-minute halo: An interview with Jaime Griesemer. Engadget. Available at: https://www.engadget.com/2011-07-14-half-minute-halo-an-interview-with-jaime-griesemer.html

Living TV. (2002–2019). *Most Haunted*. London: Living TV Group.

Kinetic Games. (2020). *Phasmophobia*. [Video game]. United Kingdom: Kinetic Games.

Moon Studios. (2015). *Ori and the Blind Forest*. [Video game]. Redmond, WA: Microsoft Studios.

Naughty Dog. (2007). *Uncharted: Drake's Fortune*. [Video game]. Foster City, CA: Sony Computer Entertainment.

Nguyen, D. (2013). *Flappy Bird*. [iOS/Android]. Hanoi, Vietnam: GEARS Studios.

Niantic. (2016). *Pokémon GO*. [Video game]. San Francisco, CA: Niantic, Inc.

Nintendo. (1985). *Super Mario Bros*. [Video game]. Kyoto, Japan: Nintendo.

Nintendo. (2020). *Animal Crossing: New Horizons*. [Video game]. Kyoto, Japan: Nintendo.

Nutt, C. (2013). Raph Koster on 'play' - the possibility space for games. Game Developer. Available at: https://www.gamedeveloper.com/design/raph-koster-on-play---the-possibility-space-for-games

Portkey Games. (2023). *Hogwarts Legacy*. [Video Game]. Burbank, CA: Warner Bros. Interactive Entertainment.

Psyonix. (2015). *Rocket League*. [Video game]. San Diego, CA: Psyonix.

Reflections Interactive. (2000). *Driver 2*. [Video Game]. Lyon, France: Infogrames.

Retro Hawk. (2016). Driver (first mission training tutorial) Sony PlayStation PS1. YouTube. Available at: https://www.youtube.com/watch?v=8iCPzDEkkII

Robinson, M. (2015). Video: Miyamoto on how Nintendo made Mario's most iconic level. Eurogamer. Available at: https://www.eurogamer.net/video-miyamoto-on-how-nintendo-made-marios-most-iconic-level

Rocksteady Studios. (2011). *Batman: Arkham City*. [Video game]. Burbank, CA: Warner Bros. Interactive Entertainment.

Saltsman, A. (2009). *Canabalt*. [Video game]. Austin, TX: Semi Secret Software.

Sandham, A. (2015). Are game mechanics mappable to learning taxonomies? In *Proceedings of the 9th European Conference on Games Based Learning* (Vol. 1, pp. 753–761). Steinkjer, Norway.

Steam. (n.d.). *Garry's Mod*. [Online] Available at: https://store.steampowered.com/app/4000/Garrys_Mod/

Taito. (1978). *Space Invaders*. [Video game]. Tokyo, Japan: Taito.

Team Cherry. (2017). *Hollow Knight*. [Video game]. Adelaide, Australia: Team Cherry.

Team Meat. (2010). *Super Meat Boy*. [Video game]. Austin, TX: Team Meat.

The Coalition. (2015). *Gears of War: Ultimate Edition*. [Video game]. Redmond, WA: Microsoft Studios.

The Unreal Takeaway. (2023). 'Grand Theft Auto V' (Rockstar North, 2013). YouTube. Available at: https://tiny.cc/GTAV_Tutorial

Thatgamecompany. (2012). *Journey*. [Video game]. Foster City, CA: Sony Computer Entertainment.

TSR Hobbies. (1974). *Dungeons & Dragons*. [Role-Playing Game]. Lake Geneva, WI: TSR Hobbies.

Ubisoft Montreal. (2009). *Assassin's Creed 2*. [Video Game]. Montreal, QC: Ubisoft.

Ubisoft Montreal. (2020). *Assassin's Creed: Valhalla*. [Video game]. Montreal, QC: Ubisoft.

Valve Corporation. (2007). *Portal*. [Video game]. Bellevue, WA: Valve Corporation.

Visceral Games. (2011). *Dead Space 2*. [Video game]. Redwood City, CA: Electronic Arts.

Yu, D. (2008). *Spelunky*. [Video game]. Independent.

Zynga, A.D. (2009). *FarmVille*. [Video game]. San Francisco, CA: Zynga.

Core Techniques
Teaching the Player

2

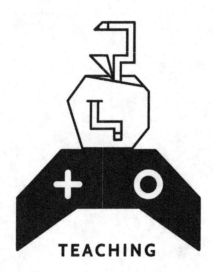

TEACHING

LECTURE OVERVIEW

In this lecture, we're going to look at another key facet of game design – **Teaching**.

Usually built into the initial section of any game or experience, this is a hugely important part of introducing the player to how to play your game.

DOI: 10.1201/9781032644721-2

GAME COMPONENTS

FIGURE 2.1   Game component types. Illustration by Andrew Thornton.

As discussed previously, teaching is a game component, and we'll be looking at each of these throughout the duration of the course. But first – let's get the ball rolling with an **Exercise**:

IN CLASS EXERCISE 2.1: USP CORNER!

Lecture reference: slide 2
Notes for Educator:
   Here's an exercise I run at the start of each lecture: Find a game trailer or clip with an identifiable USP, or "unique selling point." We'll look at USP's in more detail in the following chapters, but as an initial introduction, this exercise could feature a unique mechanic, such as "Time moves when you do" in *Superhot* (SUPERHOT Team, 2016); or an art style – for example, the "Sin City"-esque graphic novel style of *Madworld* (PlatinumGames, 2009); or some other identifiable unique element that makes the game stand out, such as flipping the classic player role of hero to "playing the bad guy" or the "reverse horror experience" in a game like *Carrion* (Phobia Game Studio, 2020).

USP's or "Unique Selling Points" are a core element of maximising the employability of your students. As a general rule in game development, for design roles, you won't hire without evidence of something playable. And to get the interview for the job, you need something *unique* to catch the eye of the employer. From a Game Design educator's perspective, the thinking is that regular exposure to unique game elements breeds the creation of unique game elements. Try it – you may be surprised!

Game video Discussion: Unique Selling points

FIGURE 2.2   "The Unfinished Swan." Illustration by Andrew Thornton.

Question:
Play the clip, and task the class with attempting to identify the USP element.

EXERCISE 2.1 VIDEO LINK:

"The Unfinished Swan" (Giant Sparrow, 2012)
https://bit.ly/EX2_1_SWAN

Exercise 2.1 Answers

So, a couple of USP's here: both the mechanics and the art style, which are synergistically linked – the player starting in a completely white environment where they use paint to reveal the world around them and can then navigate their way through it. The reward here is that you are effectively "creating" the game around yourself, and as we know, the element of creating (or feeling as if you are creating) can be a powerful motivator. The narrative in the game also offers its own rewards, but I won't spoil that – go and play it yourselves!

SECTION 2.1: TEACHING – THE PLAYER "USER GUIDE"

Lecture reference: slide 5

Here's a thing — The player won't automatically learn your game mechanics – you need to introduce them. And if you overload them with these mechanics at the outset, your players will become confused, will lose interest and, in the worst-case scenario, will drop your game. This is not so dramatic if your player has invested big money in your meticulously crafted AAA project and want value for money out of their title (or can't quite muster the energy required to return it to the shop *just yet*) but somewhat of a death knell if, for instance, you've created a free to play mobile title that relies on DAU's (see Box 2.1) and advertising revenue for your income. So, it's important that you take care guiding the player through these initial mechanics.

Regardless of if the teaching process is hidden or relatively opaque to the player, such as the physics mechanics in *Half Life 2* (Valve Corporation, 2004) being introduced in areas where the player learns them organically in order to progress, or fully exposed such as the narrator explaining the underlying design features of the level as in *The Stanley Parable* (Galactic Cafe, 2013) almost all games will teach you their mechanics. Even the most hardcore games, such as *Dark Souls*, will guide the player very carefully through their mechanics one by one (but being *Dark Souls*, also allows other users the ability to troll you via faux didactic messages left in the environment). As discussed in the previous lecture, the initial steps in teaching the player how to play your game can also be called onboarding. If you design your initial game sequences poorly and drop the player in to a hot mess, it will cause issues with onboarding them into the rest of the experience.

Box 2.1   DAU's

DAU stands for "Daily Active Users," widely used in game design and development to measure the number of unique users who will play your game in a 24-hour period. DAU is a hugely important analytic within social and mobile game development because it shows how well the game attracts and retains players on a day-to-day basis. Primarily, this not only can be utilised from a marketing perspective (leading to a revenue stream), but also allows game designers to make informed decisions about updates, bug fixes, new features, or promotional strategies that will keep the DAU (hence revenue!) high.

FIGURE 2.3   Tutorial example. Illustration by Andrew Thornton.

Let's start looking at the teaching component in more detail. There are many design ele-ments within this component – as an introduction, let's have another look at an example of teaching that is frequently just that – an introduction to the game:

Teaching: Tutorials

Lecture reference: slide 6

TUTORIAL CASE STUDY

Video Link 2.1: Far Cry 3: Blood Dragon
  https://bit.ly/EX2_1_BLOOD

So, that's an amusing riff on something which has fallen out of favour: the regimented on-screen tutorial, similar to the *Driver 2* example from last week's lecture. You do still see it in games as the quickest way to convey your control system, but at the risk of alienating hardcore players who don't wish to be handheld. Certainly, in something like a first-person shooter, for the most part, we are all familiar and fairly adept with these control systems now. And here's a tip: if you don't need to change a common control system, and there isn't a good reason to do so, **DON'T**. Things like clicking your left stick down on a console controller to sprint (in an FPS) are now ingrained in our muscle memory, and players won't welcome you fiddling with them, thank you kindly.

So as a further introduction, let's have a look at how a mechanics heavy game tackles the issue of introducing mechanics.

Introducing Mechanics

Lecture reference: slide 7

Here's a clip from a portal so you can start getting an idea of how this works.

VIDEO LINK 2.2: *PORTAL 2* TEACHING CASE STUDY

https://bit.ly/EX2_2_PORT

That clip included the narration from valve giving us an insight into some of the key issues they had scaffolding the player into the more complex mechanics in *Portal 2* (Valve Corporation, 2011). This is a clear example of how you've got to be super clear when you're introducing mechanics. In this case the valve designer, **Christopher Chin** is talking about how they've moved some of the chambers around and they've iterated around QA feedback – they've taken the game to the testers and the testers have become frustrated and confused at the mechanics as they've been introduced, resulting in a rethink from the design department. Again, we are seeing here about how important **iteration** (see Box 2.2) is in the process of Game Development. The actual portal system is in itself a hugely complex mechanic to introduce, and they spend a lot of time at the beginning of *Portal 2* getting the player to understand how to use it. They introduce fixed "in" portals before training the player in using these, before finally allowing the player free rein with the portal gun and the "in" and "out" mechanics. The portalling mechanic can be enormously confusing, even when you know exactly what you're doing, so it's a very good example of how you must be very careful with onboarding, or gradually introducing your mechanics.

Box 2.2   Iteration and Methodology

As described in the quote from Shigeru Miyamoto in Chapter 1, design iterations based on QA/user feedback are at the core of development. Are you introducing your mechanics too quickly? Or not quickly enough? A good QA department or user testing will highlight these flaws and allow for iteration. From a student perspective, documenting iteration is key to showcasing a junior designer's methodology and should be an essential part of any assignment within the curriculum. If a student or junior designer has a clear roadmap of how they progressed from a flawed mechanic/level flow/etc. to a functional, playable prototype, they have not only learned some of the tools of their day-to-day trade as a game designer (making changes and the purpose behind them apparent to the team) but also moved towards meeting the requirements of a typical game designer interview process (i.e., "How did you get from *there* to *here,* and *why?*").

Overloading Mechanics

Lecture reference: slide 8

FIGURE 2.4   Illustration by Andrew Thornton.

Let's have a look at the example of *Cut the Rope 2* (ZeptoLab, 2013) The original *Cut the Rope* (ZeptoLab, 2010) is a really clear example of using a couple of very simple mechanics, and it's the combination of these that create gameplay strategies. In *Cut the Rope 2*, it appeared that almost every single level introduced a new mechanic – this is fantastic from the perspective of content for your money – but perhaps at the risk of confusing the onboarding of your player into the core puzzle mechanics.

VIDEO LINK 2.2: *"CUT THE ROPE 2"* **ONBOARDING CASE STUDY**

https://bit.ly/EX2_3_ROPE

Instead of designing around their core set, they have continued to add new mechanics, which confused the living daylights out of the younger players I was watching take their initial steps into the game. (Disclaimer: my grandkids.) I should note that I'm not attempting to single out *Cut the Rope 2* – there are plenty of examples of games that increase the difficulty curve with a flurry of new mechanics. (Disclaimer 2: I've designed a few of them!)

A puzzle game should rely on two or three great mechanics, ideally with a synergy between them that allows for increasingly complex combinations and strategies. *Portal 2* (Valve Corporation, 2011) introduces the *gel* mechanics (see Box 2.3) about halfway through, after onboarding the player with a series of particularly complex mechanics from the very start of the game. And it paces these introductions very gradually and carefully to ensure the player is not overwhelmed.

Box 2.3   Puzzle Mechanics – Less (Gel) Is More!

In *Portal 2*, the paint (or gel) mechanics introduce three distinct types of gels that players can use to solve the increasingly complex puzzles. Each gel has its own unique colour and properties. The blue Repulsion Gel makes surfaces bouncy, enabling the player (and objects) to reach higher areas. Orange Propulsion Gel reduces friction, allowing players and objects to move faster across surfaces and achieve greater momentum. White Conversion Gel, the most complex from a design perspective, makes surfaces "portal-able," enabling new entry and exit points across the level.[1] When combined with the game's existing portal mechanics, the synergy between these different gel types creates an incrementally increasing variety of challenges that translate into a smooth onboarding process and a carefully managed difficulty curve.

SECTION 2.2: HOW TO TEACH THE PLAYER – A TOOLBOX

Lecture reference: slide 9

There are many methods of teaching the player. Let's have a look at some examples:

Teaching Technique Example 1: Embedding

Lecture reference: slide 10

FIGURE 2.5   Card design by Andrew Thornton. Illustration by Jack Hollick.

So, looking at the example card image describing "embedding," quite a common technique in video games, we see the *Dead Space* (EA Redwood Shores, 2008) example of "Cut off their Limbs." Someone, while in the process of expiration through bleeding to death, has thoughtfully decided to be helpful to anyone else in their predicament by using their bloodied stump to scrape out a useful set of instructions on how to defeat whatever horror it was that nobbled them in the first place. Thank you, dismembered spaceman!

Embedding information within the environment can be a useful tool for instructing players on how to play your game. *Portal* (Valve Corporation, 2007) is another example, embedding information telling you visually what you should be doing in each chamber. Unfortunately, the only real downside of this is that most players will miss this. Players, for the most part, unless you're talking about specific games (such as role-playing games) that rely on narrative or lore, will do their utmost to avoid reading anything you've put into the environment – so you should really treat this as a kind of backup system to what I would suggest is your primary method: *"Teaching through doing."*

Exercise 2.2 Example Answers

Example Answer 1:

Lecture reference: slide 11

FIGURE 2.6   Illustration by Shutterstock/Warm Tail.

Dark Souls (FromSoftware, 2011) utilises its own in-game message system to highlight mechanics and game systems to players, but FromSoftware adds its own unique take on this by allowing players to use this system to also create their own messages to guide the player, or in many cases, lead them to their death.[2]

Example Answer 2:

The Last of Us (Naughty Dog, 2013) Embeds personal notes (often in proximity to the long-dead and/or mummified author of the note) and "safe rooms" filled with graffiti, often emphasising the danger and despair within the post-apocalyptic setting (as well as giving out safe code combinations, as you would expect in a video game)

Example Answer 3:

Bioshock (Irrational Games, 2007).

FIGURE 2.7 Embedding in "Bioshock Infinite." Illustration by Jack Hollick.

The original *BioShock* incorporates a lot of embedding, which perhaps isn't the greatest example, as much of it isn't actually teaching gameplay at all. It's about imbuing "Rapture" (the world of *BioShock*) with a sense of "place," and introducing a version of the author Ayn Rand's ideology (echoed in the name of Raptures founder, Andrew Ryan) of objectivism and capitalism within this world. It showcases the collapse and dark consequences of these systems within the underwater city, illustrating how, when taken to the extremes, these systems can result in societal collapse. This embedding adds a dark subtext to the corrupt world, arguably making for more considered gameplay within (for example) sections such as the little sisters "moral choice" (see Box 2.4).

Box 2.4   The Introduction of "Moral Choice"

In "BioShock," one of the first games to utilise "moral choice" as a clear in-game mechanic, players are given an early moral choice in the form of the childlike Little Sisters: harvest them for large amounts of ADAM, crucial for upgrading your character's abilities, but which results in their death. Alternatively, rescue them for less ADAM with the ethical (and less psychopathic) satisfaction of choosing *not* to kill a child for assumed later game potential rewards, although clearly with a slower opportunity to upgrade your character leading to the possibility of a tougher gameplay experience. This choice also serves as a narrative device to encourage reflection on the game's greater themes of choosing yourself over others, tying into the overarching theme of Ayn Rand's objectivism and capitalism. For further, more recent, and arguably more complex examples of moral choices in games, see *The Witcher 3: Wild Hunt* (CD Projekt Red, 2015), *Mass Effect 2* (BioWare, 2010), and *Life is Strange* (Dontnod Entertainment, 2015).

Teaching Technique Example 2: Creating

Lecture reference: slide 12

CREATION

Creation fosters ownership and "stickiness" and is one of the most powerful ways to introduce and train the player in complex game systems.

FIGURE 2.8   Card design by Andrew Thornton. Illustration by Michelangelo.

Creating is one of the most elegant ways of teaching players. Allowing players to leave their personal stamp on some element of the game is enormously powerful from a psychological perspective, fostering re-engagement and "stickiness" (see Box 2.5) both of which we'll discuss in later lectures regarding motivation techniques.

Creation works from the perspective of re-enforcing the mechanics leading up to it, e.g. learning how to craft an axe, through to cutting down trees, through to making your first shack and surviving your first night in *Minecraft* (Mojang, 2011). Once you're allowed to put your own creative personal stamp on a game, and even better, receive peer review from others that will see this piece of work ("Mum Factor!") you've created then it's one of the best ways of re-enforcing or teaching the players those mechanics.

Creation, or self-expression in the case of your Minecraft shack, clearly acts as the "Reward" in the Objective/Challenge/Reward cycle.

Box 2.5 "Stickiness"

"Stickiness" generally refers to a variety of in-game systems or mechanics that either attract or re-engage players on a regular basis, making them want to keep playing. Some example systems that may help to foster this are personalisation and customisation options, ideally with a social or community element allowing for peer review, extensive character personalisation (or "ownership"), frequent reward and upgrade systems, and social features which allow for easy accessibility with a view to creating and managing a dedicated player base and community. It should be noted that social elements (e.g., playing with friends) are generally recognised as one of the strongest elements or systems with regard to promoting re-engagement.

Unfortunately, although creativity is an important and efficient way of teaching players, it's quite difficult to implement into games, and in many cases, "Chicken and egg" – are you using creative elements to emphasise your core mechanics, or are the core mechanics creative? In less complicated cases, you are effectively handing over at least some mechanics or systems within your game to the player. For example, the various systems within *Little Big Planet* (Media Molecule, 2008) such as the level editor, and game logic implementation (triggers, states, etc.) effectively allow players "under the hood," which is hard to police from the perspective of how the game plays, and, with large communities, certainly much harder to police from an obscenity perspective (*Little Big Planet* employed automated, community and a dedicated moderation team). Alternatively, you design your product from the ground up around creativity, agency, and player expression such as *Minecraft* (Mojang, 2011), in which case, the actual "game" element takes a back seat as Minecraft itself is effectively a sandbox – although notably, prior to its purchase and aggressive expansion and monetisation my Microsoft, Mojang expanded the game modes and added a climactic boss, the Ender Dragon to satisfy the communities request for a satisfying game conclusion.

Or do you go down the *Dreams* (Media Molecule, 2020) route and effectively create a game *engine* on a specific console such as the PS4 and PS5? Then there you have the issues of managing servers large enough to host the community creations that will further advertise the original product and sell more copies – again, not to mention moderator-type roles to police content. And why, as a user, would you invest time in learning a console-specific game engine when you could invest this time in a less platform agnostic and more commonly used game engine such as "Unity" or "Unreal Engine"? I imagine at least some of these reasons have led to the discontinuation of live support and active development for the game, which, although the servers are still open for user creations, came to a halt in 2023. Alternatively, you allow player creativity by handing over the same editor that the development team has used to create the original game (see *Doom*, id Software, 1993; *Half-Life 2*, Valve Corporation, 2004; or our own *Tomb Raider IV: The Last Revelation*, Core Design, 1999, etc.) and simply allow the community to organise their own spaces in which to host these "mods," (see Box 2.6) effectively handing over the keys of the game to the fans but with the issue of limiting the created content more specifically around the game and assets that the editor was originally used for. I should note, at the time of writing I'm still frequently asked to look over various Tomb Raider mods from dedicated and passionate designers utilising the engine within the community, and long may that continue.

Box 2.6 "Modding"

Modding is the process of altering or adding new content to video games, typically using the engine or editor in which the games were originally created (such as the "Creation Kit" released by Bethesda for *Skyrim* Bethesda Game Studios, 2011, in 2012). This enables modders to adapt and create new gameplay scenarios by affecting elements such as narrative, gameplay, environments, and level design. Some of these creations can be enormously important for amateur or junior designers hoping to secure a job in the industry, offering playable portfolio pieces without the need for extensive asset creation or coding knowledge. Modding is generally recognised within the industry as a talent pool for companies, as demonstrated by a number of modders securing jobs as designers within the companies whose games they have modded, such as Adam Foster, the creator of the "Minerva" mod for *Half-Life 2* (Valve Corporation, 2004), and Duncan Harris, who was hired by BioWare for the *Mass Effect* series (BioWare, 2007–2012) due to his previous work on Doom 3 mods (id Software, 2004). From the perspective of the original game developer, modding also serves various purposes, not only fostering a creative community but in many cases extending a game's lifespan. Beyond game-specific mods, I should note many "modded" levels have led to entirely new games. See *Counter-Strike* (Valve Corporation and Minh Le and Jess Cliffe, 2000), *Dota* (Eul, 2003), *PUBG* (PUBG Corporation, 2017).

IN CLASS EXERCISE 2.3

Teaching Component Discussion: Creation
Question:
    Other than those we've already discussed; can you think of any other examples of games that use "creation" as a core method of teaching the player?
(Discuss)

Exercise 2.3 Example Answers

Example Answer 1:
Kerbal Space Program (Squad, 2015)

FIGURE 2.9   Illustration by Shutterstock/FlashMovie.

Kerbal Space Program introduces us to the cute, technically focused Kerbals from the planet Kerbin – small green aliens with a penchant for science, engineering, and an overarching and infectious enthusiasm for space exploration that drives the game's core creation mechanics. The player employs complex aerospace and physics concepts to build increasingly complicated rockets and spacecraft to try and get the brave little Kerbals out onto planets in the solar system. The Kerbals act as an important gameplay anchor through their passion, bravery, and general incompetence, leading to a sense of "nurturing" allowing us to empathise with a more human (or in this case, human-esque alien) side of what might otherwise be perceived as more of an educational tool than a game.

Other Example Answers:

The Sims series (Maxis/Electronic Arts, 2000-present) utilises creativity to re-enforce "stickiness" mechanics such as nurturing and ownership, allowing players the opportunity to create and customise their own avatar Sims, build homes, and manage and experiment with the careers and lives of these Sims. It should be noted that ***Animal Crossing*** (Nintendo EAD, 2001) also echoes many of these design techniques.

Terraria (Re-Logic, 2011) features a complex and perfectly balanced crafting curve and progression system that allows the player to gradually access new materials and crafting stations (the "objective"), enabling them to build better equipment and tackle more difficult challenges, and further their exploration (the "reward").

Teaching Technique Example 3: Sandbox

Lecture reference: slide 13

SANDBOX

Allow the player time and space to learn through play.

FIGURE 2.10   Card design by Andrew Thornton. Illustration by Jack Hollick.

"**Sandbox**" is another way of teaching – and is really a clear example of humanity's innate need to play to learn, as described in the book *"Homo Ludens: A Study of the Play-Element in Culture"* (Huizinga, 1949). As we grow up, we learn through play, so sandbox is very much a clear example of this – as a child you play in the sand with freedom and without any real sanctions (other than perhaps, your parents complaining about the mess you're making). You learn how to build things, you learn how to find things, and in some cases, you learn how to interact with other people within this environment. These are all useful tools for successful human existence. In a very similar fashion, a sandbox is very useful in games to allow people to learn without penalising them. As a rule, from a game designer perspective, you don't generally go around killing your player in zones where you need to teach them your game mechanics – although some games do this with glee[3] – but we'll go into that in more detail shortly.

IN CLASS EXERCISE 2.4

Teaching Component Discussion: Sandbox
Question:
　　　Are you able to think of any other examples of games that use "Sandbox" as a method of teaching the player?
(Discuss)

Exercise 2.4 Example Answers

Example Answer :
Garry's Mod (Newman, G., 2006)

FIGURE 2.11   Illustration by Shutterstock/Franklin Brown.

Garry's Mod (Facepunch Studios, 2004), originally a mod for *Half-Life 2*, is a physics-based sandbox that entirely sidesteps any preset game rules or objectives and instead allows the player to manipulate elements, objects, and physics within the world in any way they see fit, effectively creating a giant, chaos filled playground. This freedom encourages learning through trial and error, creativity, problem-solving, and teaching via application as players learn through the immediate impact of their actions and creations. The addition of multiplayer and a large community introduces many new game modes, both cooperative and competitive, with players effectively creating their own objectives in a quest for fun, amusement, peer review, and the kudos of outdoing each other's collective insanity.

Other Example Answers:

Minecraft (Mojang, 2011)
The quintessential sandbox game that allows players to mine and farm resources, build structures, and craft a huge variety of objects with a core gameplay loop that rewards the players with the ability to completely customise and personalise their own unique world.

No Man's Sky (Hello Games, 2016)
Originally focused on exploration, survival, and resource gathering, introducing players to an (originally solo player) sandbox experience, learning through interaction, with a subtle narrative thread of alien lore and the pursuit of the mysterious "Atlas" at the universe's centre. Following community feedback, later updates introduced a clearer narrative path, shifting away from the game's initial sandbox emphasis.

Fortnite (Epic Games, 2017)
Blends sandbox elements, notably through its building mechanics, in its core Battle Royale mode. The addition of "Fortnite Creative Mode" fully embraces sandbox creativity, offering a platform for player-driven design and construction, as described by Epic as allowing you to *"freely create content on your own Creative Islands. Your islands offer you a place where you make the rules, filled with your favourite things and your favourite people!"*[4]

Teaching Technique Example 4: Safety First

Lecture reference: slide 16

FIGURE 2.12 Card design and illustration by Andrew Thornton.

The basic premise of the teaching component" Safety first" is that if you're attempting to teach a player mechanics – don't kill them in the process. Death, for the most part in games, is not a reward (although there are exceptions to this which we'll look at). If you're teaching a player, rewards are a good way of re-enforcing correct actions such as learning game mechanics – discussed in psychological and behavioural terms as "reward schedules" and "positive re-enforcement." It should be noted that, conversely, there is also "negative re-enforcement" an example of which is trial and error leading to death, and in this case, my almost automatic knee-jerk crisis memory here is *Dark Souls*, more specifically the "Sens fortress" section and the pattern recognition of environmental hazards. Basically, the drill here is that you learn through death via being squished by a ball every single time you go around a corner until you learn the pattern and timing of them to progress further up the level. I'd suggest that it could be argued that trial and error and negative re-enforcement isn't really good design as your reward is death, but I'd also suggest that in games such as *Dark Souls*, you're getting a kind of deferred gratification which makes all the death so much sweeter due to the time and effort you've put into overcoming the particular challenge – "High risk, High Reward" gameplay. Ideally, depending on the type of game you're making (i.e., not a "Soulslike") I would generally suggest creating an initial safe environment in which the player learns the initial mechanics without jeopardy.

IN CLASS EXERCISE 2.5

Teaching Component Discussion: Safety First!
Question:
Other than those we've already discussed; are you able to think of any other examples of games that use **Safety First!** as a method of **teaching** the player? **(Discuss)**

Exercise 2.5 Example Answer

The Legend of Zelda: Breath of the Wild (Nintendo EPD, 2017)

FIGURE 2.13   Illustration by Shutterstock/Channar.

In *The Legend of Zelda: Breath of the Wild* at the start of the game the player is introduced to an area known as the Great Plateau, which serves as a masterclass in presenting a safe sandbox for learning the game mechanics. This area is a microcosm of the game that, through a series of mini quests, guides the player to obtaining the para-glider, enabling them to glide off the plateau and into the "main game." From the first moments, the player is skill-gated ("gating" discussed shortly) – you must learn your initial traversal moveset (or skill) to leave the Shrine of Resurrection and then venture out into the world, with an abundance of teaching techniques scattered across it to guide the player. These range from environmental cues, such as paths that guide you, and orientation points and landmarks like the derelict Temple of Time, to the shrines that gradually teach the players how to use their skillset before travelling out into the game as a whole. It should be noted that this initial area is not entirely "safety first!" as it also introduces combat mechanics, but these are relatively safe as the player is onboarded into combat through the introduction of a selection of low-level mobs. This initial area is a familiar design trope of Zelda games and is echoed in the arguably more complex initial teaching area in *The Legend of Zelda: Tears of the Kingdom.* (Nintendo EPD, 2023)

Teaching Technique Example 5: Humour

Lecture reference: slide 18

FIGURE 2.14   Card design by Andrew Thornton. Illustration by Jack Hollick.

Humour is seldom used in games, and when it is, it often falls short of being genuinely funny, primarily, because as any stand-up comedian would agree, humour is very challenging to execute effectively – or, in layman's terms "get a laugh." *If* used correctly (i.e., if it amuses or entertains you) humour is a vital tool in our toolbox for teaching the player.

Several academic and psychological studies discuss how humour can enhance the learning process, making it more effective and engaging for students, and also, as game designers, our players. In his 2006 article "Humor in Pedagogy: How Ha-Ha Can Lead to Aha!" Houston State University psychologist Randy Garner, PhD, found that students were more likely to recall a statistics lecture when it was interjected with jokes about relevant topics. Garner adds, "Well-planned, appropriate, contextual humor can help students ingrain information." (Garner, 2006)

If you want to teach your players, the same rules apply – context is key. The *Fallout* series of games (Interplay Productions/Bethesda Softworks, 1997-present) showcases very dark humour throughout, thematically based around the idea of satirising 1950s Americana, and Cold War-era politics amidst the backdrop of retro-futuristic design, quirky characters, and absurd scenarios that contrast sharply with the grim realities of the game world. This, again, contrasts with the one-off jokes, quips, and cartoon characterisation of *Borderlands*, (Gearbox Software, 2009) which contextually fit into its crazy game world. Either way. If you can work a sense of humour into your game, you'll be amazed at how it can broaden its appeal across a much wider audience – and if you impart important game information in a humorous way people will remember it more readily, and, I will argue, increase its appeal across the broadest gamer demographics. All gamers remember the *Portal* cake meme, right?

IN CLASS EXERCISE 2.6

Teaching Component Discussion: Humour!
Question:
Other than those we've already discussed; are you able to think of any other examples of games that use **Humour!** as a method of **teaching** the player?
(Discuss)

Exercise 2.6 Example Answers

Example Answer 1:
Goat Simulator (Coffee Stain Studios, 2014)

FIGURE 2.15   Illustration by Shutterstock/Marius456.

Much of the humour in *Goat Simulator* is based around the ragdolling physics-based player controller (see Box 2.7) and systems within the game that create hilarious emergent situations in the sandbox environment. For example, try headbutting a gas station, causing a massive explosion, and then immediately taking off into the sky wearing your goat jetpack, only to crash into a low-flying helicopter. This kind of chaos is also re-enforced by the deliberately idiotic quests, such as the "ritual" quest where you snag as many humans as you can with your super long rubbery sticky tongue in an effort to drag them into a pentagram. Once the correct number is reached, a ritual then endows the goat player with even more absurd demonic powers (don't ask). The game also embraces it's rough and ready unpolished nature (echoing its inception from an internal gamejam at coffee stain studios), with glitches aplenty, which somehow adds to the unplanned chaos and hilarity.

Box 2.7   "Physics-Based Controllers"

Physics-based controllers in games refer to how game entities interact with the game world according to physics or physics-like rules. An early example of this would be "Ragdoll physics," frequently utilised in games around the early 2000s to create more realistic death or collision animations that interacted with the world more dynamically as opposed to "canned animations" (see Box 1.7) which often wouldn't fit the environment in a realistic way. Around this period, game engines were created in-house on a per-project basis ("Insanity!", I hear you cry. "Correct!" I answer, sagely.), and a game could very much fail based on your physics programmers/

engineers. A notable step forward in both physics systems (using dynamic inverse kinematics) and, unfortunately with a side order of much hilarity, was the game *Trespasser* (DreamWorks Interactive, 1998). The game pushed its real-time physics systems to the absolute max on what were, at that time, relatively low-spec PCs – a valiant effort, only undercut by physics glitches that allowed for much memorable mischief, such as using your Uzi bullets to spin a velociraptor corpse in mid-air for 20 minutes. This game has been cited (Kennedy, 2021) as a direct inspiration for the deliberate idiocy of the control scheme in *Surgeon Simulator* (Bossa Studios, 2013) and at some point, developers such as Bennett Foddy, creator of *QWOP* (Foddy, 2008) seized on the idea of the unpredictability of physics-based controllers as a core game pillar, leading to the continued popularity of the frustration and hilarity of this genre of games today.

Other Example Answers:

Grand Theft Auto series (DMA Design, now Rockstar North, (1997–2023)
From its inception humour has been a core element of the GTA series, teaching mechanics and game systems through various ludicrous and exaggerated characters, missions, and environments, as well as offering a satirical commentary on American culture.

FIGURE 2.16   Glados from "Portal." Illustration by Jack Hollick.

Portal (Valve Corporation, 2007)
A pioneering game for humorous antagonists, with the AI GLaDOS guiding players through the game, her dark humour and witty dialogue serving both as an obstacle and an aid to solving the in-game puzzles

The Stanley Parable (Galactic Cafe, 2013)
Humour in the Stanley Parable utilises an in-game narrator to teach and guide the player through the levels, using irony and unexpected outcomes to up-end typical player expectations.

Untitled Goose Game (House House, 2019)
You are tasked with playing as a mischievous goose, learning mechanics and game systems via a feedback system that rewards the creation of being as irritating as possible in a sleepy English village, with an outcome of comedic chaos.

Fall guys (Mediatonic, 2020)
A hilarious competitive multiplayer experience based around physics-based controllers and challenges.

Teaching Technique Example 6: Chunking/Scaffolding

Lecture reference: slide 20

FIGURE 2.17 Card design by Andrew Thornton. Illustration by the Author.

Chunking

George A. Miller introduced the world to "chunking" back in 1956 with his paper, "The Magical Number Seven, Plus or Minus Two: Some Limits on Our Capacity for Processing Information." His research uncovered the cognitive limitations of the human mind to only hold a certain amount of information in short-term memory at one time – which he famously estimated to be somewhere around five to nine items, or "chunks."

Now, imagine you're teaching mechanics to a player within the context of a game. If you introduce these "chunks" or mechanics sequentially, you reduce the cognitive load, and by carefully managing how you introduce (or scaffold) more of these chunks or mechanics, you allow the players to build on their knowledge step by step, allowing you, as the designer, to scaffold their knowledge into more complex related concepts (such as combining mechanics). If this starts to sound familiar, it's perhaps due to the fact that some of the most well-known and best-loved games of all time utilise exactly this method. Let's have a look at some examples.

FIGURE 2.18   Collectible card games. Illustration by the Shutterstock/Karlovserg.

As explained, if you're providing information you want the player to retain, you want to chunk it into "pieces" that are more readily absorbed into the short-term memory.

A good example of where this is useful in games is a "Main Menu" or "options" screen. Working on the digital game *Magic: The Gathering: Duels of the Planeswalkers 2012* (Stainless Games, 2011), I took it upon myself to redesign the front end, primarily because the previous version of the menu had, in my humble opinion, too many options. Prior to becoming lead on this project, I hadn't played the collectible card game *Magic: The Gathering* (Garfield, 1993), around which the digital version was based, and being faced with that number of choices at the outset on the original main menu screen was enough to promote an aneurysm. While designing this new menu screen there was a lot of concern among the *Magic* die-hards that I was diluting the core experience, part of which revolved around the vast amount of player agency offered in the game, down to a series of reduced choices that dumbed down the experience.

FIGURE 2.19 Proposed CCG game main menu screen. Illustration by Andrew Thornton.

I argued that three visible options struck a balance by being easy to remember and not overwhelming, chunking these into the short-term memory, and allowing players to quickly process and make their decisions without getting lost in excessive choices, or "not being able to see the wood for the trees." Did this "chunking" work? I'll leave that up to you to decide!

IN CLASS EXERCISE 2.7

Teaching Component Discussion: Chunking and Scaffolding
Question:

Other than those we've already discussed; are you able to think of any other examples of games that use **Chunking/Scaffolding** as a method of **teaching** the player?

(Discuss)

Exercise 2.7 Example Answers

Example Answer 1:

The Legend of Zelda: Ocarina of Time (Nintendo EAD, 1998)

FIGURE 2.20   Illustration by Jack Hollick.

Some of the clearest examples of chunking and scaffolding are contained across the *Zelda* series of games (Nintendo, 1986–2023) where they lock you in a room and then feed you mechanics one at a time, gradually scaffolding and layering the mechanics – let's have a look at a couple of clips here to see how Nintendo does this.

IN CLASS EXERCISE 2.8

Game Video Discussion: Chunking and Scaffolding
   Question:
   Watch the following clips, try to identify which mechanics Nintendo were chunking here, and how did they scaffold them? Write the answers down for discussion afterwards.

EXERCISE 2.8 VIDEO LINK:

The Legend of Zelda: Ocarina of Time (Nintendo EAD, 1998).
   https://bit.ly/EX2_81_ZELD

Exercise 2.8 Answers

The mechanics introduced were the use of blocks (see Box 2.8) as "helper tools" within the environment. Nintendo introduces the block within a tightly corralled channel – you can only push it in one direction. It drops into the water, and note that we have a little bit of a telegraph here when you stand on top of it – this is echoed when the player realises, they can actually push blocks onto other blocks, scaffolding the initial concept or mechanic with another, more complex one.

Other Example Answers:

Super Mario series (Nintendo, 1985–2023)
Each level chunks new mechanics or obstacles, and then scaffolds this knowledge into more complex mechanics or obstacles, gradually building up the player's skills and understanding.

Celeste (Extremely OK Games, Ltd., 2018)
   Uses level design to teach players advanced movement mechanics in a step-by-step manner (chunking), often isolating specific skills for practice before combining them. (scaffolding)

Overcooked series (Ghost Town Games, 2016)
   Divides cooking tasks into simple steps that players must manage and execute under time pressure (chunking), often increasing complexity with new recipes and kitchen layouts. (scaffolding)

Box 2.8   "Blocks" (Junior Designer Tip #1)

When designing an escape puzzle for a room, junior designers/students will often opt for one of two classic solutions:

Moving and climbing onto a block to reach an exit or gain access to an open window or vent. This is frequently combined with attempting to "stack" blocks (usually involving a physics system as the "challenge") as a slightly more complex solution.

Solving a combination puzzle based on clues found within the room, such as a sequence of patterns on the wall, or a faintly implausible password in an email ("if you've forgotten the code for >insert object or location here< then use this new code!")

These approaches are tried and true, and there's nothing wrong with them. Indeed, as we've just seen in our chunking examples, games frequently use these, such as *Zelda: Ocarina of Time* (Nintendo EAD, 1998) and *Skyrim* (Bethesda Game Studios, 2011), respectively. However, as I suggest to my students, it's always a good exercise to try and "flip" any common or easily recognisable mechanics into something new.

As an example, how about flipping the old "shadow on wall to make shape" (as seen in *Resident* Evil 7: biohazard by Capcom, 2017) into an invisible ink puzzle where you must heat paper (is the paper on the walls or in an ancient book?) using a light source (is it a candle, or cleverly redirected sun or moonlight?) to reveal the patterns required. DISCLAIMER: I never said designing puzzles was easy!

To Chunk or Not to Chunk? A Cautionary Tale

FIGURE 2.21   Arno overwhelmed. Illustration by Jack Hollick.

As a final note on chunking and scaffolding, we should note that as games grow larger, so does the necessity of feeding out information to the players, and it's our job as designers to make sure this is drip-fed to them as opposed to a cascade of information that washes their motivation away. A case in point is *Assassins Creed Unity* (Ubisoft., 2014), which, in its (successful) mission to upgrade the *Assassins Creed* game systems to a new level of interaction and immersion, unfortunately forget to feed these out in a manageable task usability format, resulting in many player complaints focused on the "bloated map" (Mohsin, 2024) littered with enough task icons to make even a seasoned Assassin consider jumping into a haystack and staying there, this lack of chunking undercutting some of the player motivation and enjoyment in what was arguably one of the greatest games in the series.

Teaching Technique Example 7: Application

Lecture reference: slide 22

FIGURE 2.22   Card design and illustration by Andrew Thornton.

Another useful weapon in the arsenal for designing around teaching players is Bloom's "Cognitive Domain" Taxonomy (Bloom, Engelhart, Furst, Hill, & Krathwohl, 1956), Designed to sequentially categorise learning levels in education to aid in curriculum development, delivery, and assessment.

These levels, from the lowest to the highest cognitive demand ("lower" and "higher" learning), form a learning ladder from "knowledge" (essentially rote learning) to "Evaluation," which involves some combination of all the other behaviours of *Knowledge, Comprehension, Application, Analysis, and Synthesis* (Bloom et al., 1956, p. 185).

This concept is similar to the game design processes of "Onboarding" and "Gating" (discussed shortly) and is also seen in the previously discussed "scaffolding," akin to Yusoff, Crowder, and Wills's 2009 study on serious games:

> One of the aspects of a game which supports 'learning and engagement' is 'scaffolding', or 'the support and help given by the game during the learning activities' (Yusoff, Crowder, Gilbert & Wills, 2009, p.22). This also a component of Blooms 'mastery learning', where a student or player achieves a certain skill or cognitive level before the next becomes accessible (Sandham, 2015.)

Translating this into game terms, it becomes more recognisable: Basically, to reach the next level, the player must master the level before it. And we find another direct translation in the third level of Bloom's taxonomy, **"Application,"** which (from an educational perspective) refers to *"where the student moves beyond basic comprehension in order to begin to apply what they have learned. Students are expected to use concepts or tools they have learned in new situations in order to show that they can use what they have learned in increasingly complex ways"* (Kelly, 2019). Or, from the game design perspective of teaching the player, gameplay that requires players to apply skills or knowledge learned in earlier levels to solve new challenges or puzzles. Examples should already be springing to mind, but before we look at more general examples of "Application" across games, let's look at how Nintendo frequently uses it through the technique of "locks-ins," effectively a microcosm of the game as a whole, teaching the player a set of gradually in an enclosed or "locked" areas that will only allow the player to progress when they have mastered a particular skill.

Application Case Study: "Lock-Ins"

Nintendo tends to build lock-in systems that require you to perform specific actions or combinations of learned mechanics before you can leave an area. For example, you're locked in a chamber where you must light a torch, which allows you to burn a cobweb. You can't burn the cobweb until you've utilised the block puzzle to get onto that platform, and then you need to apply your previously chunked knowledge of how to light the torch to burn the cobweb. There's more variation allowed, but it's still effectively chunked because you are in a section where they control how far the blocks can move and where they can move, limiting your options and guiding you within that space. This shows how you ramp up from the initial introduction of that crate, where it's locked into a groove in the floor, to the later puzzle where you must stack the blocks on top of each other to progress. The block stacking is a clear example of Bloom's "application." Player's use learned techniques in new and increasingly complex ways. I should note the lock-in approach also employs the game design technique of "gating," which we'll look at shortly.

IN CLASS EXERCISE 2.9

Teaching Component Discussion: Application
Question:
    Other than those we've already discussed; are you able to think of any other examples of games that use **Application** as a method of **teaching** the player? **(Discuss)**

Exercise 2.9 Example Answers

Example Answer 1:

The Witness (Thekla Inc., 2016)

FIGURE 2.23   *The Witness.* Illustration by Jack Hollick.

Designed by Jonathan Blow of Braid fame, (Number None, 2008) over a period of 7 years, ***The Witness*** is an excellent example of the game design teaching technique of "Application." This complex puzzle and exploration game does not explicitly teach mechanics but gradually allows the player to free-roam, building up a set of tools such as pattern recognition and rulesets, then requiring that the player apply this knowledge incrementally across various puzzle areas dotted across the island, facilitating the gradual unlocking of areas and game progression.

Other Example Answers

***Papers, Please** (Pope, 2013)* is an indie simulation game, in a setting reminiscent of an Eastern European communist/police state, where players take on the role of an immigration officer at a border checkpoint. Players observe and gradually learn the tools required to apply attention to detail and the quick decision-making skills required to balance humanity and empathy for others (the moral dilemma of letting immigrants through) with the survival of an income for themselves and their families.

In the ***SimCity*** Series (Maxis (1989 onwards), players apply urban planning and management skills to design and grow cities. This involves the gradual process of learning and applying such skills as zoning, resource management, infrastructure development, and dealing with crises like natural disasters.

SECTION 2.2: CORE TEACHING COMPONENTS

"Gating"

Lecture reference: slide 24

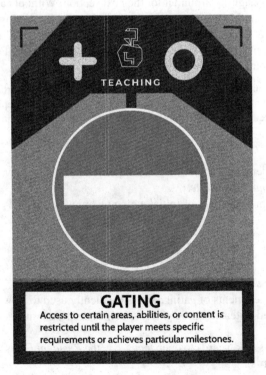

FIGURE 2.24   Card design by Andrew Thornton. Illustration by Author.

Gating, a subset of the teaching component, is utilised to prevent overwhelming the player and to specifically onboard mechanics, systems, or gameplay in a manageable fashion. Looking at the teaching card in the image, we see that the description is "Access to certain areas, abilities, or content is restricted until the player meets specific requirements or achieves particular milestones." There are many ways of gating the player, which we'll look at in detail in this section.

Gating 101

Lecture reference: slide 25

"Gating" is crucially important for the game *designer* as, when done correctly, it prevents the player from accessing certain areas or confines them within a specific area, forcing them to learn mechanics, such as the previously discussed "lock-ins," i.e., the player is unable to progress until they have fulfilled the specific requirements set by the designer. This is hugely important for designers, as a core element of game design is **knowing if and when the player has fulfilled and learned the specific set requirement**. For instance, if we, as designer make sure they can't leave the area until they've learned a mechanic, then we *know* that they've learned it, and we can design from that point on with the knowledge that they have that mechanic or skill in their toolset, incorporating and designing around it for the next section. Without carefully gating our mechanics or skills in this way, we risk overwhelming and frustrating the player. In my paper "Are Game Mechanics Mappable to Learning Taxonomies?" (Sandham, 2015), I give the example of Robin Walker, one of the game designers of Portal (2007), who discusses the introduction of the portal mechanic:

> Completing the puzzle requires walking through a minimum of five portals in a specific order. This kind of gating, in which a solid understanding of key gameplay concepts is required for success, helped standardize the learning curve of the game tremendously.
>
> *(The Portal Wiki, 2010)*

With that in mind, let's look at Gating as a kind of "chunking" of player progression and learning for *the game as a whole.*
So, let's explore some examples of initial gating techniques.

Gating Type 1: Key Gating

Lecture reference: slide 26
One of the simplest elements of gating, and is frequently used to slow and manage progression, as opposed to teaching the player specifics. Some examples of this might be:

- Finding keys or keycards to open locks, e.g. the *Resident Evil* series (Capcom, 1996-onwards).
- Required sequences or specific objects, i.e., cubes and pressure pads opening doors in the *Portal* series (Valve Corporation (2007–2011.)

- Simple puzzles, such as missing items, e.g., cogs in *Tomb Raider* (Core Design & Crystal Dynamics, 1996-onwards.) or levers or switches being activated in the correct order, e.g. *Skyrim* (Bethesda Game Studios, 2011.)

IN CLASS EXERCISE 2.10

Gating Discussion: Key Gating
Question:
    Other than those we've already discussed; are you able to think of any other examples of games that use **Key Gating**?
(Discuss)

Exercise 2.10 Answers

Example Answer 1:

Silent Hill (Konami, 1999)

FIGURE 2.25   Illustration by Shutterstock/Stasia04.

The original *Silent Hill* utilises a number of key gating techniques. One example puzzle, located in the Midwich Elementary School in the Otherworld (for the Otherworld, think "the Upside Down" in "Stranger Things," Duffer, & Duffer, 2016), directs the player to use a rubber ball to block water drainage, forcing a key out of a blocked faucet.

This key opens a previously inaccessible door, gating the player until they have navigated (and learned) a series of relatively complex logical systems. It should be noted that the Otherworld allows for a more complex layering of simple puzzles, i.e., objects and environmental elements you are able to find in the real world aren't there in the Otherworld, and vice versa, similar to a "detective mode" overlay/subgame. Although not used in this example puzzle, this technique is a useful form of "obfuscation" in puzzle design, which we'll discuss in the relevant section.

Other Examples

In the original *Dark Souls*, (FromSoftware, 2011) the door to the Artorias Crest area (located in Darkroot Garden) is opened by a simple key in the form of a Crest. The obtaining of this crest is gated in two specific ways, both designed to ensure that once it is opened, you are of sufficient skill level to progress through the area. The first method is to purchase the Crest of Artorias from a vendor (Blacksmith Andrei) for 20,000 souls, the acquisition of said souls requiring plentiful and extensive gruelling combat. The second method involves using an alternate back entrance into Darkroot Basin. "Wow!" you might think – "This sounds like an easy solution!" Not so. This is Dark Souls, and as such, will also require plentiful and extensive gruelling combat. In fact, possibly even more so, as a penalty for attempting to take the easy way round.

Now Let's move on to more specific examples of gating.

Gating Type 2: Skill/Gear Gating

FIGURE 2.26   Collecting the morph ball. Illustration by Jack Hollick.

Skill (or gear) gating refers to the design choices pioneered in the original *Metroid* (Nintendo, 1986) game and further popularised after the release of *Castlevania:*

Symphony of the Night (Konami, 1997) when the term (Met+Vania=Metroidvania!) came into common use. This design philosophy favours a style of gating where the player needs a particular type of gear, power-up, or skill before they are granted access to the next area. An example of this is the "Morph Ball," in *Metroid* which allows Samus, the player avatar, to curl into a ball, enabling the player to access narrow tunnels and areas inaccessible in her "normal" form. The core and unique element of this design choice is that the player must remember where the previously impassable areas are and frequently backtrack extensively to reach them, adding the learning element of becoming familiar with the layout of the level.

Skill/Gear Gating Case Study

Assassins Creed 2 (Ubisoft Montreal, 2009)

FIGURE 2.27   Illustration by Shutterstock/Hoika Mikhail.

An example here of how perhaps *not* to skill/gear gate is in the otherwise flawless *Assassin's Creed 2* (Ubisoft Montreal, 2009). This involved attempting to traverse a particular tower to reach an obviously accessible platform. The problem being that I couldn't access the obviously accessible platform. Had I missed a carefully hidden handhold somewhere in the brickwork which would launch me to the top? Perhaps some minor protrusion that I could somehow swing on to gain extra height? After many hours of this, and beginning to question my sanity, I abandoned the tower and continued into the game. Imagine my delight when, later in the game, I met up with my unlikely chum, Leonardo DaVinci, who provided me with a "climbing glove" which, as he described, allowed for an "extended leap." Thanks Leo!

Although the dopamine hit of receiving that specific piece of gear may have been worth the wait, from a design perspective, the issue here may be that the platform that I could now reach looked *exactly the same as any other platform in the game*. If it had been flagged or marked in some specific way that differentiated it from a normal plat-form (i.e., painted bright fluorescent yellow), then perhaps I would have understood it was somehow "special" and left well alone. This type of design is often referred to as "affordances" or "readability" and we'll look at these in following lectures.

I should note Ubisoft removed this particular "silent" (as in, I didn't know about it until it was given to me) upgrade mechanic from later versions of Assassin's Creed, possibly because they received extensive messages from players spending much of their weekends jumping up and down attempting to reach the top of a tower they could never reach the top of.

IN CLASS EXERCISE 2.11

Gating Discussion: Skill/Gear Gating
Question:
Other than those we've already discussed; are you able to think of any other examples of games that use **Skill/Gear Gating**?
(Discuss)

FIGURE 2.28   *"Big Daddy."* Illustration by Jack Hollick.

Lecture reference: slide 29

Exercise 2.4 Example Answers

Example Answer 1:

EXERCISE 2.11 VIDEO LINK

Bioshock (Irrational Games, 2007).
   https://bit.ly/EX2_11_BIO

In reference to introducing skill or gear gating in *Bioshock*, let's have a look at some comments from the focus group testing, as described by the game director, Ken Levine; *"Overly dense, confusing, and not particularly engaging. Players would acquire new powers and not know how to use them, so they stuck to using more traditional weapons and became frustrated."*

"We changed the medical pavilion from having sandbox style gameplay to having a set of locks and keys that were set up to ensure that the player knew how to use at least a few key plasmids" (Finley, 2023).

Plasmids, as I'm sure you know, are a kind of special power or skill that you discharge from your hand and you select them dependent upon the task you need them for (which is, in many cases, combat). In the case of the locked door example, the level has been re-designed specifically so the player will learn how to use plasmids. The benefit of skill gating the player with that door is that once the player leaves that area, as a designer you can be certain the player understands and is able to use plasmids. There are some questions if this is entirely successful, as for much of the game I used the same physical weapon (see Box 2.9) and mostly ignored the plasmids, other than when specifically required for a task, a bit like having a toolbox and only ever using the hammer.

Box 2.9   A Note on Weapons Upgrades

One of the issues with designing difficulty curves and variety into an FPS is that as a player, you do tend to stick to the same weapon unless it's something really, obviously advantageous – if you're upgrading a weapon throughout the game, and you find a much more powerful late game weapon, you'll note a sense of "ownership" over the weapon you've spent all that time levelling up, and wherever possible, will tend to stick with it. "Ownership" particularly incorporating XP systems, is powerful, and finding ways to design the player out of using their favourites, is difficult. In which case, I would always ask, do you need to dissuade them from using their favourites? Or do you just make their favourites more interesting as the game progresses? You're the designer, you decide!

Gating Type 3: Area Gating

Lecture reference: slide 30

"Area gating" refers to the method of barring access to a region of the game's world until the player has reached a given point in the main storyline or acquired a specific skill or experience level.

FIGURE 2.29   Image by Shutterstock/Kiselev Andrey Valerevich.

A good example of this is the Skellige Isles in *The Witcher 3: Wild Hunt* (CD Projekt Red, 2015). Although the player could theoretically access these areas earlier in the game, they are level-gated through narrative (Geralt, the player character, is tasked to find a way to Skellige in search of Ciri, after completing various quests) and also via the cost of hiring the boat, which requires the commitment of at least a few hours of gameplay. As a final area gating technique, on the sea trip to Skellige, you are attacked by pirates at levels 15 and 16, preventing players from accessing the island until they are sufficiently levelled up to handle these enemies effectively.

IN CLASS EXERCISE 2.12

Gating Discussion: Area Gating
Question:
    Can you think of the design reasons why CD Projekt red is utilising **area gating** to gate the Skellige isles?
(Discuss)

Example Answers:

Narrative coherence.
By assigning this quest automatically through the unfolding events of the story, the game provides narrative coherence, chunking plot elements into gated areas, ideally avoiding a character popping up in a conversational reference that doesn't quite align with the fact you murdered said character 2 weeks previously (see Box 2.10). Another way of avoiding this issue is to entirely de-populate an entire area of any important plot characters (or any characters at all) until it is needed in the plot, causing much confusion to the player as to where everyone has disappeared to (see *FarCry 6* Ubisoft Toronto, 2021, Where I wandered around an empty sea fort for 3 hours).

Content bingeing
Allowing players access to all areas of your open world game at once, can provide issues with player motivation. As exploration often needs some type of challenge (In the Objective/challenge/reward cycle), being allowed to go anywhere without it, often feels like it has removed the reward. In addition, without chunking objectives, the player may feel that they have too many options, which as previously discussed, can feel like there are no options at all. Even vast, seemingly fully accessible open world games such as *World of Warcraft* (Blizzard Entertainment, 2004) will utilise some form of area gating, in this case in the form of high-level MOB areas that will soon dissuade you from venturing into them. Which leads to:

Underpowered player in overpowered area
If your low-level player has access to high-level areas too early, this will upset the difficulty curve in your game or level, and in many cases cause frustration, as anyone who has attempted to return to their body as a ghost when it is in a particularly difficult to get to location in *World of Warcraft* will attest to. This is why the pirates attack the ship on the way to the Skellige isles, or door to the Artorias Crest area (in *Dark Souls*, FromSoftware, 2011) requires so many souls to gain entrance.

Fund gating
Although really another element of area gating (where your level or XP is represented by in game currency), this can often be a simple way of managing your difficulty curve or narrative coherence. A specific example in *Grand Theft Auto 5* (Rockstar Games, 2013) is that you wouldn't want your low-level character having access to a penthouse in the hills of Vinewood at the start of the game. This is an objective that the player aspires to, driving them through the game structure and narrative to the clearly visible affluence of a multimillion-dollar house in the Vinewood hills area, and the satisfaction of a reward well earned. In a similar way, Fund gating is used in the *Witcher 3* example via the payment required to the captain of the ship, ensuring the player has earned passage via in-game experience.

**Box 2.10 "How Doesn't He Know that I've
Already Killed Him?" Syndrome**

This problem can frequently evolve out of the "branching narrative" system. This gives the player a much greater feeling of "agency" and also goodwill of the player feeling that the developer has maximised value for money with the vast amount of options and replayability available to the player (see *Mass Effect 2*) The issue here is that each branch in your narrative will add more dialogue options geometrically until three or four branches in, the amount of writeable/recordable dialogue becomes untenable. When designing and writing branching narratives (in the early designs for "Tomb Raider 6," (which became the entirely unrelated *Tomb Raider: Angel of Darkness*), the core element to remember is to guide the narrative back in from any tributaries to the main trunk. Your core trunk is sacrosanct and written to take the player through to the end of the game regardless of which branch they take – so probably best not to reference minor characters in this trunk, unless you want to find yourself in the predicament highlighted in the title of this boxout!

Gating Type 4: Arena/Boss Gating

Lecture reference: slide 31

This is the design practice of enclosing a player in an area (or arena) until they have defeated a boss or enemies, at which point, the entrances will miraculously open. Specifically in the case of the boss fight arena, you will find there is usually a pattern to learn, or a required skill set to progress. This is a very useful technique for not only forcing your player to attain the level of skill required, but also as a way of clearly denoting choke points that are recognisable as required challenges that the player must beat to progress into the next section of the game (see *Dark souls*)

FIGURE 2.30   *Dark Souls*. Illustration by Jack Hollick.

It should be noted that other than the somewhat artificial lock-in techniques used for bosses, as designers we do find ways to cover up this "artificiality" – we saw it in the lecture one *Gears of War* clip where the player is gated into an area until they have eliminated all the enemies, until, suddenly, and with perfect timing, something cuts through the door or smashes through the wall and you've suddenly got access to a massive hall with which you can continue your progression through the game.

IN CLASS EXERCISE 2.13

Gating Discussion: Arena/Boss gating
Question:
    Can you think of any games that feature boss fights with a pattern to learn, or that require a specific skill set?
(Discuss)

Exercise 2.13 Answers

Lecture reference: slide 33
Example Answer 1:
Metal Gear Solid (Konami, 1998)

FIGURE 2.31   Illustration by Shutterstock/Roberto Marantan.

As an example of a "specific skill set," the boss fight against Psycho Mantis in *Metal Gear Solid* requires the player to understand and utilise a particular object that resides outside of the game world, forcing the player to think outside the box (and controller port).

In the battle, Psycho Mantis can initially "read your mind," which in gameplay terms means he can predict and counter your controller moves. To beat him, the player must physically unplug their controller from the first port and replace it in the second port on their gaming console. Psycho mantis is now unable to predict your moves, and vulnerable to attacks. Sounds like a few sandwiches short of a picnic? It's often cited as one of the most memorable boss battle moments in gaming history. If it helps, it may also be worth noting this battle was designed by Hideo Kojima, never one to shy from "unique" gameplay choices.

Example Answer 2:

The Legend of Zelda: Ocarina of Time (Nintendo, 1998)
As an example of a "Required pattern to learn," a classic example is the boss fight against Ganon in *The Legend of Zelda: Ocarina of Time*. The player finds themselves in a dark arena, where the master sword is initially knocked away and they must use

timing and anticipation to avoid Ganon's sword strikes, while targeting the visible weak point of his tail. Surviving this section leads to retrieval of the Master sword, allowing reflection of Ganon's magic attacks, stunning him, and once more allowing attacks on his weak point, eventually leading to victory (or possibly, in my case, giving up).

Gating Type 5: Observation Gating

Lecture reference: slide 34

The technique of introducing a mandatory pause in the action to make the players stop and notice a particular event or key mechanic.

FIGURE 2.32 The "portal" gun. Illustration by Jack Hollick.

This is really the designer forcing the player to watch something in-game or watch another player or NPC performing a particular action. The purpose of this is an effort to teach the player the required process ahead of time. Let's have a look at an example from the *Portal* series.

OBSERVATION GATING VIDEO LINK:

Portal (Valve Corporation, 2007)
https://bit.ly/EX2_4_PORT

Here's a transcript of the developer commentary from the video, with some important points:

> In early versions of this map the play testers charge down the stairs without noticing what was creating the portals. we introduced a mandatory pause in the action – what we call a gate -to help ensure that players stop and notice the portal gun making a blue portal. A particle effect and a loud noise help draw their attention.

> *(Jason Brashill, 2007)*

The concept here is that before you pick up the Portal gun, you're forced to watch it shooting holes in walls. Control is not actually removed from the player in this sequence, so theoretically, you don't have to watch this happening; it's not foolproof, but the designers have kept what the player must look at in this area to a minimum in an effort to direct them towards observing the portal room. This is a common game design challenge. As a rule, outside of a cutscene, it is particularly difficult to actively force the player to look at a specific aspect or element within the environment, and even more so if that aspect or element is above or behind the player. This is exacerbated in VR games or experiences, where you are able to basically look anywhere. Tips or techniques for attracting player attention include (as described in the developer example) noises or particle effects (e.g., a laser bolt from over the shoulder would generally make the player turn, unless they are waiting patiently to be shot in the back) and, as in the *Portal* example, constricting them into a small, featureless environment where the player basically has nothing else to look at other than the featured aspect or element you're directing them towards. There are still no real tried and tested solutions to this design problem, so, if you're attempting to teach the player through visual cues, Observation gating may be a solution. Good luck!

Gating: A Conclusion

Lecture reference: slide 35

As we've seen, there are many different types of gating, and uses for the technique – indeed, many more than listed here. Keep an eye out for them and note any particularly successful examples – you will always need ways of directing and teaching players, and as such, you'll never know when you'll need a new gating technique!

To conclude this chapter, let's have a look at an example and discuss some of the other various types of gating techniques involved. The example in Figure 1.23 is "Father Gascoigne," the brutal first gatekeeper boss in *Bloodborne* (FromSoftware, 2015), who, in true FromSoftware style, prevents you from proceeding into the main body of the game without first learning the core combat system to an aptitude level that, with my gradually calcifying reflexes, I would generously refer to as "above average."

FIGURE 2.33   Father Gascoigne. Illustration by Jack Hollis.

IN CLASS EXERCISE 2.14

Gating Discussion:
Question:
    Other than "Arena/Boss" what type of gating do you think the designers have used in this case, and why?
(Discuss)

Exercise 2.14 Answers

Example Answers:

Skill Gating – the "Regain system"
With such an unforgiving difficulty curve, the designers need to ensure that the player is ready for the varied and unrelenting enemy types that gradually ramp up from this point into the rest of the game. The Gascoigne encounter solidly sets up *Bloodborne's* unique "Regain System." When players take damage, they have a brief window in which to strike back at the enemy to regain lost health. This encourages aggressive combat (over the generally defensive combat favoured in previous Soulslikes), making sure the player understands this system before sending them out into the dark and generally brutal and unpleasant world.

Content gating

You will frequently find gating in games to prevent the player from consuming all your content in one fell swoop and then losing the motivation of exploration, which is often designed as the "reward" in the objective-challenge-reward cycle. The inherent difficulty of *Bloodborne* prevents bingeing on content, but you'll find FromSoftware has carefully managed open-world access in their more recent title, *Elden Ring* (FromSoftware, 2022). Various gatekeepers and environmental hazards prevent the player from rushing through all available content, but it is still designed in a manner that promotes the excitement of exploration (e.g., "Where does that jumbo jet-sized lift shaft lead to?").

Narrative gating

One of the reasons designers frequently implement gating is because they want to control the game's narrative. Although *Bloodborne* is not primarily narrative-focused, it has a strong narrative component controlled through the levelling of the character, and thus, access to new areas of the city. Arguably, in *Elden Ring*, allowing the player access to various areas from the onset can, in some cases, muddy the narrative. Similarly, with a game like *Grand Theft Auto IV*, (Rockstar North, 2008) it's very difficult for designers and scriptwriters to control the narrative if you suddenly move into a completely new zone and open up all kinds of new subquests and narrative elements when you still haven't completed all of these in the previous part of the island, leading to a "narrative dislocation." An example of this is when you find characters in subquests talking about other characters that either haven't been introduced yet or characters that you've previously killed, like a TV soap opera where the cast has forgotten who's been written out of the series (See Box 2.10).

And with that brief look at some of the various other gating techniques available, let's move on to the end of the lecture!

Conclusion

Lecture reference: slide 37

In this chapter, we've learned that teaching the player is essential for guiding them through the early stages of the game, onboarding them into the necessary processes and skills while chunking these skills to avoid overwhelming them. Additionally, mastering techniques to gate the player helps game designers manage content effectively. In the next lecture, we'll explore game components further, focusing on one of the core elements of the gameplay loop – objectives – and how to motivate players to achieve them.

LECTURE TWO "TEACHING": RESOURCE MATERIALS

Lecture Two in PowerPoint Format
Lecture Two Working Class
    Edit and upload to a shared drive of your choice!
(Chapter 2 instructor resources can all be downloaded from the **Instructor Hub**. For further information, please see the chapter "How to Use This Book.")

NOTES

1 With the possible player options available here, as a game and level designer, this is the sort of challenge that would keep me awake at night with the "Player agency sweats."
2 *The messages in the undead asylum were really helpful and taught you controls and everything. but the messages in every other zone in the game are like completely random and hardly helpful.*" (Rdmqwerty, 2013)
3 See "Sens fortress," in *Dark Souls*, discussed in more detail in the "Safety First" teaching technique.
4 *Whatiscreativemodeinfortnite? howdoesitwork?* Availableat: https://www.epicgames.com/help/th/c-Category_Creative/c-Creative_Gameplay/what-is-creative-mode-in-fortnite-how-does-it-work-a000084986

REFERENCES

2KGames. (2013). *BioShock Infinite*. Irrational Games, USA: 2K Games.
Bethesda Game Studios. (2011). *The Elder Scrolls V: Skyrim*. Rockville: Bethesda Softworks.
BioWare. (2007–2012). *Mass Effect Trilogy*. Edmonton: Electronic Arts.
BioWare. (2010). *Mass Effect 2*. Edmonton: Electronic Arts.
Blizzard Entertainment. (2004–present). *World of Warcraft series*. Irvine, CA: Blizzard Entertainment.
Bloom, B.S., Engelhart, M.D., Furst, E.J., Hill, W.H. and Krathwohl, D.R. (1956). *Handbook I: Cognitive Domain*. New York: David McKay.
Bossa Studios. (2013). *Surgeon Simulator*. London: Bossa Studios.
Capcom. (2017). *Resident Evil 7: Biohazard*. Osaka: Capcom.
CD Projekt Red. (2015). *The Witcher 3: Wild Hunt*. Warsaw: CD Projekt.
Coffee Stain Studios. (2014). *Goat Simulator*. Skövde: Coffee Stain Publishing.
Core Design. (2003). *Tomb Raider: The Angel of Darkness*. Eidos Interactive.
Core Design and Crystal Dynamics. (1996-present). Tomb Raider Series. Various Publishers.
Dead Space. (2008). *EA Redwood Shores*. Los Angeles: Electronic Arts.
DMA Design (now Rockstar North). (1997–2023). *Grand Theft Auto series*. New York: Rockstar Games.
Dontnod Entertainment. (2015). *Life is Strange*. Tokyo: Square Enix.
DreamWorks Interactive. (1998). *Trespasser*. Los Angeles: Electronic Arts.
Duffer, M. and Duffer, R. (2016-present). *Stranger Things*. Los Angeles, CA: Netflix.
Eul. (2003). *Defense of the Ancients (DotA)*. Mod for Warcraft III: Reign of Chaos. Irvine, CA: Blizzard Entertainment.
Extremely OK Games, Ltd. (2018). *Celeste*. Vancouver: Matt Makes Games Inc.
Finley, A. (2023). *Postmortem: 2K boston/2K Australia's Bioshock*. Available at: https://www.gamedeveloper.com/design/postmortem-2k-boston-2k-australia-s-bioshock
Foddy, B. (2008). *QWOP*. N.p.: Foddy.net.
FromSoftware. (2011). *Dark Souls*. Tokyo: Namco Bandai Games.
FromSoftware. (2015). *Bloodborne*. Japan: Sony Computer Entertainment.
FromSoftware. (2022). *Elden Ring*. Japan: Bandai Namco Entertainment.
Galactic Cafe. (2013). *The Stanley Parable*. Renton: Galactic Cafe.

Garfield, R. (1993). *Magic: The Gathering*. Renton: Wizards of the Coast.

Garner, R. (2006). Humor in pedagogy: How Ha-Ha Can Lead to Aha! *College Teaching*, 54(1), pp.177–180.

Gearbox Software. (2009). *Borderlands*. Novato, CA: 2K Games.

Ghost Town Games. (2016). *Overcooked*. London: Team17.

Giant Sparrow. (2012). *The Unfinished Swan*. Santa Monica Studio, Sony Computer Entertainment, Santa Monica, CA.

Hello Games. (2016). *No Man's Sky*. Guildford: Hello Games.

House House. (2019). *Untitled Goose Game*. Melbourne: Panic Inc.

Huizinga, J. (1949). *Homo Ludens: A Study of the Play-Element in Culture*. Haarlem: Tjeenk Willink & Zoon.

id Software. (2004). *Doom 3*. Mesquite: Activision.

Irrational Games. (2007). *BioShock*. Novato: 2K Games.

Kelly, M. (2019). Bloom's taxonomy - application category and examples, ThoughtCo. Available at: https://www.thoughtco.com/blooms-taxonomy-application-category-8445

Kennedy, V.P. (2021). How Jurassic Park unintentionally inspired Octodad and surgeon simulator, ScreenRant. Available at: https://screenrant.com/jurassic-park-trespasser-arms-octodad-surgeon-simulator-physics/

Konami. (1997). *Castlevania: Symphony of the Night*. Tokyo: Konami.

Konami. (1998). *Metal Gear Solid*. Tokyo: Konami.

Konami. (1999). *Silent Hill*. Tokyo: Konami.

Maxis. (1989-present). *SimCity* Series. Various Publishers.

Media Molecule. (2008). *LittleBigPlanet*. Tokyo: Sony Computer Entertainment.

Media Molecule. (2020). *Dreams*. Tokyo: Sony Interactive Entertainment.

Mediatonic. (2020). *Fall Guys: Ultimate Knockout*. London: Devolver Digital.

Miller, G.A. (1956). The magical number seven, plus or minus two: Some limits on our capacity for processing information. *Psychological Review*, 63(2), p. 81.

Mohsin, S. (2024). I played assassin's Creed Unity almost 10 years later. It's (kinda) spectacular, GameLuster. Available at: https://gameluster.com/i-played-assassins-creed-unity-almost-10-years-later-its-kinda-spectacular/

Mojang. (2011). *Minecraft*. Stockholm: Mojang.

Naughty Dog. (2013). *The Last of Us*. Tokyo: Sony Computer Entertainment.

Newman, G. (2006). *Garry's Mod*. Bellevue: Valve Corporation.

Nintendo. (1985–2023). *Super Mario series*. Kyoto: Nintendo.

Nintendo. (1986–2023). *The Legend of Zelda series*. Kyoto: Nintendo.

Nintendo. (1998). *The Legend of Zelda: Ocarina of Time*. Kyoto: Nintendo.

Nintendo EAD. (2001). *Animal Crossing*. Kyoto: Nintendo.

Nintendo EPD. (2017). *The Legend of Zelda: Breath of the Wild*. Kyoto: Nintendo.

Nintendo EPD. (2023). *The Legend of Zelda: Tears of the Kingdom*. Kyoto: Nintendo.

Nintendo R and D1. (1986). *Metroid*. Kyoto: Nintendo.

Number None. (2008). *Braid*. San Francisco, CA: Number None.

Phobia Game Studio. (2020). Carrion. London: Devolver Digital.

PlatinumGames, 2009. *MadWorld*. New York: Sega.

Pope, L. (2013). *Papers, Please*. 3909 LLC.

Re-Logic. (2011). *Terraria*. Indianapolis: Re-Logic.

rdmqwerty. (2013). R/darksouls on reddit: Whats the deal with messages? Available at: https://www.reddit.com/r/darksouls/comments/1cv7q0/whats_the_deal_with_messages/

Rockstar Games. (2013). *Grand Theft Auto V*. New York: Rockstar Games.

Rockstar North. (2008). *Grand Theft Auto IV*. New York: Rockstar Games.

Sandham, A.. (2015). Are game mechanics mappable to learning taxonomies?. In *Proceedings of the 9th European Conference on Games Based Learning* (Vol. 1, pp. 753–761).

Squad. (2015). *Kerbal Space Program*. Mexico City: Squad.

Stainless Games. (2011). *Magic: The Gathering - Duels of the Planeswalkers 2012*. Renton: Wizards of the Coast.

Stambor. (2006). How laughing leads to learning. *College Teaching*, 54(1), pp. 177–180.

Superhot Team. (2016). *Superhot*. Lodz, Poland: SUPERHOT Team.

The Sims series. (2000–present). Maxis/Electronic Arts.

Thekla, Inc. (2016). *The Witness*. San Francisco, CA: Thekla, Inc.

Theportalwiki.com. (2010). Portal developer commentary - Portal Wiki. Available at: https://theportalwiki.com/wiki/Portal_developer_commentary

Ubisoft. (2014). *Assassin's Creed Unity*. Montreal: Ubisoft.

Ubisoft Montreal. (2009). *Assassin's Creed II*. Montreal: Ubisoft.

Ubisoft Montreal. (2013). *Far Cry 3: Blood Dragon*. Montreal: Ubisoft.

Ubisoft Toronto. (2021). *Far Cry 6*. Montreal: Ubisoft.

Valve Corporation. (2000). *Counter-Strike*. Bellevue: Valve Corporation.

Valve Corporation. (2004). *Half-Life 2*. Bellevue: Valve Corporation.

Valve Corporation. (2007). *Portal*. Bellevue: Valve Corporation.

Valve Corporation. (2007–2011). *Portal Series*. Bellevue, WA: Valve Corporation.

Valve Corporation. (2011). *Portal 2*. Bellevue, WA: Valve Corporation.

ZeptoLab. (2010). *Cut the Rope*. Moscow: ZeptoLab.

ZeptoLab. (2013). *Cut the Rope 2*. Moscow: ZeptoLab.

Core Techniques

Objectives and Motivators

3

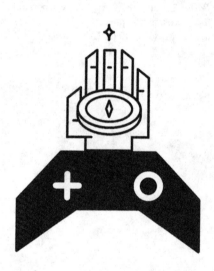

LECTURE OVERVIEW

Lecture reference: slide 2

In this lecture we'll be looking at some of the most important elements of any game, **Objectives and Motivators**. With reference to the Objective/Challenge/Reward gameplay loop, this is (as you may have guessed) the **Objective** element of the loop.

DOI: 10.1201/9781032644721-3

GAME COMPONENTS

FIGURE 3.1   Game Components. Illustration by Andrew Thornton.

Objectives are a **Game Component** – always keep your game component list in mind when creating your games, and always try to refer to this list to ensure you are aware of which element of the game you are focusing on, and indeed, which elements are required for your particular project.

Objectives and motivators are about *Guiding, leading, corralling and persuading* the player – so ethically we must be aware of how we approach this from a design perspective – a good example of this would be "Loot boxes" (see Box 3.1) – we need to be very aware of our responsibility as game designers.

Box 3.1   Loot Boxes

Perhaps no term within the game industry still[1] ignites such ire within players as "Loot Boxes." They generally refer to the practice of randomised pickups, "drops," or rewards (e.g., for completing a quest) within a game that can lead to a variety of benefits (e.g., skins, weapons, cosmetics). Powerful psychological processes are in effect, such as variable ratio reinforcement schedules and operant conditioning (that we'll look at in more detail later in this lecture), driving us to want to acquire these Loot Boxes, since in many cases we don't know what is inside, but the anticipation leads us to believe that perhaps it is not only what we want, but exactly what we *need*. Many of these games would have sub systems designed in to work towards collecting these rewards and benefits legitimately by around allowing players to "grind," or alternately simply pay for the benefits to avoid this grind in a system known as "cash rich, time poor." Fair enough, yes? Problems began to arise when Loot Boxes contained items that began to unbalance gameplay, such as more powerful weapons or items, and then the players that were previously paying to save time then became seen to be "paying to win." Unscrupulous companies were seen to be taking advantage of this system, providing more and more epic items at higher costs, that would often be far out of the reach of "grinding" to achieve (unless you chained yourself to your computer for 6 months). Comparisons to gambling, particularly among younger players and financial outlay/addiction also drew attention from researchers, parents, and regulators, questioning the ethics of such practices (Zendle & Cairns, 2018; Drummond & Sauer, 2018), leading to a backlash that not only led to countries such as Belgium and the Netherlands banning them outright as a form of gambling (BBC, 2018), but also to the game industry re-evaluating the design of monetisation methods within games around regulatory guidelines geared towards securing more ethical practices in the industry.

As an endnote to this initial section, I should point out that a core element of designing most games is the inclusion of reward systems, and as such, it could be argued that games will *always* have an element of behavioural and psychological motivators designed in, which could be cynically linked to the "addiction" elements of gambling. Although it's very difficult to design a game that's so addictive, compulsive, or persuasive that it causes life-changing issues, we should take note of extreme examples of this. For instance, excessive playtimes in Massively Multiplayer Online Role-Playing Games (MMORPGs), caused by in-game reward systems exacerbated by social obligations, leading to cases such as the teenager in Norway collapsing after playing *World of Warcraft* (Blizzard, 2004) for 24 hours without a break (The Guardian, 2012). Although not currently officially recognised, the American Psychiatric Association has considered "Internet Gaming Disorder" as a potentially diagnosable condition (American Psychiatric Association, DSM-5, 2013). This again highlights the need to consider the ethical implications of game design, such as building in systems to promote time away from the computer. An example is "Rest XP" in *World of Warcraft*, which encourages the player to periodically stop at inns overnight or for a set real-world duration, with the reward of double XP for a short time when they resume play.

Now Let's have a look now at our regular introductory exercise – "USP Corner!"

Lecture reference: slide 4

IN CLASS EXERCISE 3.1: USP CORNER!

Game Element Discussion: USP's
Question:
Name the unique selling point (or points!) in the following clip!

EXERCISE 3.1 VIDEO LINK

SuperLiminal (Pillow Castle, 2019)
    https://bit.ly/EX3_1_PILL

Exercise 3.1 Example Answer

Players are able to adjust the shape and size of an object depending on their position in the world.

This unique core mechanic was initially formulated during a 2013 gamejam, the 7DFPS (Seven-Day First-Person Shooter) Gamejam, also the origin of the original prototype for *Superhot* (SUPERHOT TEAM, 2016). This highlights how the pressurised "try it and see if it sticks" nature of gamejams can lead to totally original (sometimes accidental) mechanics that may not surface in a normal, planned game development environment, and would suggest why many game companies have now adopted "in-house" game jams at regular times throughout the year.

SECTION 3.1: MACRO (OR "MAIN") OBJECTIVES AND MOTIVATORS

Lecture reference: slide 6

We've talked about Macro objectives in games before so let's just have a bit of a closer look at how these work. We're beginning to have to think along narrative lines here, i.e., classic story systems such as the "three act structure" which we will be looking at in more detail in the narrative lecture, but just to give you an introduction of how objectives cross over between movies and games, the *objective* of the main character (or protagonist) in movies is usually called "*Drive*" or "*Motivation*."

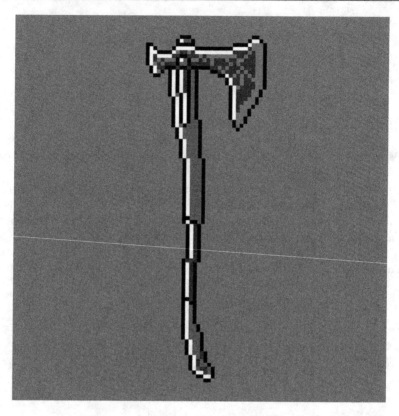

FIGURE 3.2   Kratos's clear and overarching motivation in the early "God of War" games is "revenge." Illustration by Shutterstock/Roberto Marantan.

Lecture reference: slide 7

This "drive" is something that should be introduced relatively early in the runtime to get you to become interested in or empathise with the character or certainly to actually want to sit in the movie theatre without your mind drifting off to the choc ice counter or your smartphone every few seconds. 20 minutes is usually the "sweet spot" for when you've been introduced to the characters and the initial premise, and now the main character needs a gripping drive or motivating event to push them forward into the second act, which is commonly known in scriptwriting parlance as "the inciting incident."

FIGURE 3.3   The "Ark of the covenant," Indiana Jones "Macro" objective in the first film. Image by Shutterstock/P Maxwell Photography.

The "Inciting Incident"

Lecture reference: slide 9

This not only introduces the drive for the protagonist but also propels them forward into the second act. I'd note the "three-act structure" is one of the simplest narrative structures, but still frequently utilised and relatively easy to spot – look out for it, starting with the inciting incident![2]

IN CLASS EXERCISE 3.2: OBJECTIVES AND INCITING INCIDENTS

In class narrative Discussion:
Question:
   Can you name the *Objectives* and *inciting incidents* in the following game and movie examples?

Lecture reference: slide 10

Example 1:
The Last of Us (Naughty Dog, 2013)

FIGURE 3.4   Image by Shutterstock/FXQuadro.

Exercise 3.2 Example Answers

Example 1 Answer: (Spoilers!):

Objective and Inciting Incident:
In the original *The Last of Us* game, the player character, in an early *"inciting incident,"* witnesses the death of his daughter during a prelude that describes the initial stages of the "Fungal-pocalypse." Skipping forward in time, Joel is reintroduced as a burnt-out sociopath with little motivation to continue living, until his *objective* is introduced in the shape of the young girl, Ellie, apparently immune to the infection, who must be escorted across the infected no-man's land of America to a research centre where scientists may be able to use her to craft a possible antidote that could save mankind. This is the Macro/main objective in the game and drives the player through the entire playtime. As a byproduct, In the process, the initially hesitant Joel is perceived to "arc" from "crusty burnt-out sociopath" to "father figure with extremely strong sociopathic tendencies." Welcome to the wonderful world of video game scriptwriting!

Example 2:
Lecture reference: slide 12

Star Wars (Lucas, G., 1977)

FIGURE 3.5 Illustration by Shutterstock/Algol.

Example 2 Answer: (Spoilers!):

Objective and Inciting Incident:

In the first 20 minutes of *Star Wars*, we're introduced to Luke Skywalker, a relatively happy farm boy (albeit a farm boy that craves adventure), living with his aunt and uncle, tending crops and shovelling galactic gruel into his face without so much as a care in the world. And then? The *inciting incident* – something happens that drives him headlong into the plot, in this case, the seemingly motiveless slaughter of his aunt and uncle at the hands of the Empire. In a way, from this point on, it becomes a kind of a revenge plot, which is often used as a very quick shorthand for a clear, unambiguous (usually male) character motivator. Luke's next objective is to find transport off the planet – which becomes his *sub-objective*. (or in game terms, the next part of the main quest)

The macro/main *objective* in *Star Wars* is to blow up the Death Star (and, to some degree, to destroy Darth Vader). The Death star is effectively the ultimate weapon which has now been evidenced to have the power to destroy worlds. And what do you do to an ultimate weapon that is able to destroy worlds? To balance the force, you must, of course, DESTROY IT! Aunt and Uncle (and numerous other Empire mithered innocents) avenged, Objective complete!

It should be noted that *Star Wars* was arguably one of the first films to employ elements from Joseph Campbells book *The Hero with a Thousand Faces* (Campbell, 1949), describing how heroic tales are mirrored across all cultures. This was allegedly distilled down to a simplified one-page memo described as, "The Hero's journey" by Hollywood development executive Christopher Vogler, where purportedly it was seen and used by Lucas during the early scriptwriting stages of "Star Wars," and has since become widely influential across both the movie and game industry. We'll discuss the "Hero's journey" scriptwriting system more in the narrative lecture.

Exercise 3.3 Example Answer

Half Life (Valve, 1998)

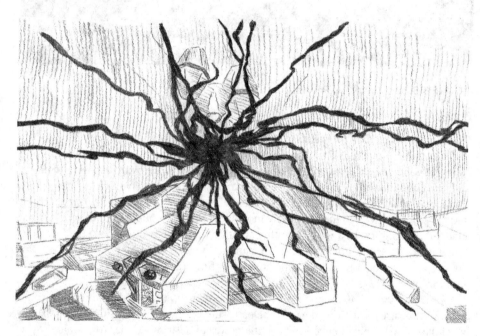

FIGURE 3.6   The lab incident, Half Life. Illustration by Jack Hollick.

At the start of the game *Half Life*, the player is introduced to the Black Mesa research facility via a series of interactive cutscenes and cinematic events that eventually lead the player to the test chamber, where they must perform an experiment that goes disastrously wrong, opening a portal to another dimension which allows hostile alien creatures to enter earth. This also sets up the Macro/Main objective, i.e., "Save Earth." It should also be noted, as one of the first games to create a believable, interactive cinematic narrative, Valve also placed this inciting incident in at around the first 20–30 minutes of the game (depending on playstyle) mirroring the structure of the cinematic experiences it was attempting to emulate.

SECTION 3.2: OBJECTIVES AND MOTIVATORS – CORE CONCEPTS

Lecture reference: slide 16

FIGURE 3.7   Illustration by Jack Hollick.

Lecture reference: slides 17–18

In non-narrative focused titles, for example, *Doom* (id Software, 1993) we usually aren't afforded the time or opportunity to introduce characters (or indeed, an act structure), so objectives must be introduced at the outset. It's crucial to introduce at least one objective at the outset of the game, as without this initial objective, players are likely to quickly become confused and frustrated, two words I'd suggest, as a game designer, you'd want to avoid in your players.

In the case of *Doom*, the in-game UI tells you everything you need to know from the outset – a large pistol poking out of the centre of the screen above the head of an angry, buzz-cut soldier type. When the first enemy arrives, I'd suggest the objectives are fairly unambiguous. It should be noted the *Doom* reboots (id Software, 2016), stray little from this formula. If we go back even further into the misty annals of game design, you'll find even simpler examples. *Space Invaders* wears its objective on its sleeve – in this case, the sleeve being the illustrations on the arcade cabinet, featuring a hulking alien shambling towards a massive industrial-sized ground-to-air missile launcher. *Super Mario Bros.* introduces Princess Peach and her predicament in the game *manual*, leaving her (and the "real" Bowser's) actual appearance until the last level of the game.

In narrative-based games, you also have the issue of cutscenes introducing the objectives at the start of the game. Skippable or Unskippable? Unskippable may frustrate players who want to get straight into the action of the game, whereas skippable may result in player confusion and a diminished narrative experience. It's a difficult balancing act.

Difficulties in introducing Objectives and Motivators in games are alleviated somewhat by a set of *core concepts*, that are pretty ubiquitous in games, and without guidance, will often be assumed by the player – usually, these are:

> **Survive.**
> **Destroy threats. (Kill everything!)**
> **Explore/Escape.**
> **Reach a location/Fetch quest.**
> **Narrative or Plot conclusion.**

Let's have a look at some examples of these "core concepts" in action.

IN CLASS EXERCISE 3.4

Lecture reference: slide 19
Objective/Motivator Discussion: "Core Concepts"
Question:
   Can you recognise the core concept objectives from our provided list in the following examples?
(Discuss)

Lecture reference: slides 20–21
Example 1:
Journey (thatgamecompany, 2012)

EXERCISE 3.4 VIDEO EXAMPLE

https://bit.ly/EX1_6_JOUR
Journey (thatgamecompany, 2012)

FIGURE 3.8   Illustration by Andrew Thornton.

Exercise 3.4 Answer 1

The objectives and motivators in this case are:

> *Explore.*
> *Reach a location.*

If we look at the first few seconds of *Journey* you'll find that your primary objective is to "get to the mountain." This objective is clear throughout the majority of the game, exploring areas as you progress, with the almost ever-present silhouette of the mountain to guide you.

Narrative *is* an objective in *Journey*, but the genius of the game is that the narrative emerges from interactions with other players and changes with each playthrough, making it an "emergent narrative" outside of strict narrative structures or regulations. Much of how your own story unfolds is based on the empathy you develop towards your co-op players whom you've picked up and accompanied along the way. Indeed, a random player and I both completed the game together, achieving (what certainly used to be deemed) the holy grail of "emotional design," with me in a flood of tears (see Box 3.1, "the cry test").

Example 2:

Lecture reference: slides 22–23
Tomb Raider (Core Design, 1996),

FIGURE 3.9 Image by Shutterstock/Marcin Roszkowski.

Exercise 3.4 Answer 2

If we look at the original *Tomb Raider* (Core Design, 1996), even without the introductory cutscene, the objective is clear. Starting the game proper inside a sealed temple, there is only one way forward – and you quickly realise your objective is to explore and escape. When bats, bears, wolves, and other endangered species need to be rapidly culled (in classic TR fashion) to clear the route ahead, a second objective becomes quickly apparent: Survival. Or perhaps, depending on your playstyle, "kill everything." So, the immediately apparent core concepts here are:

> *Survive.*
> *Destroy threats. (Kill everything.)*
> *Explore/Escape.*

I'd note, unfortunately, "Killing everything" is still probably one of the most prevalent and common objectives in the game industry. As a game designer, if you're able to avoid that particular design choice, give yourself extra points. I should note that I'm not really one to comment – during a recent playthrough of my London levels in *Tomb Raider 3* (Core Design, 1998.) I was somewhat horrified to find that my younger self seemed to think it was fine for Lara to rampage through a water filtration plant murdering innocent security guards. Not sure what the Met would make of that one.

Box 3.1 – "The Cry Test"

Part of designing games is also about creating the emotions you want the player to feel at any particular point during playtime. Around the first decade of the 21st century, games were becoming noticeably more sophisticated, with more complex narratives, greater graphical fidelity, techniques for motion-capturing actor performances, and more memory to include expansive cinematic scores and sound effects. The industry responded by attempting to provoke tangible, measurable emotions within games – and the easiest initial target seemed to be "trying to make the player cry." There has been much debate among designers and critics about this early focus on one particular emotion, which can mostly be summed up with an agreement that narrowing the focus to sadness or tragedy prevents developers from exploring other meaningful and complex emotional experiences such as joy, fear, surprise, or relief (Lankoski & Björk, 2015). The modern industry looks to game designers to create a wide spectrum of emotions across a diverse range of human experiences that resonates with a broad audience. Although possibly also with a good cry included.

The early *Tomb Raider* series of games usually had the clear Macro objective of completing or escaping the level, whereas micro-objectives would form the "challenge" (in the objective/challenge/reward cycle) preventing you from achieving this. Usually, this would take the form of puzzles, environmental hazards (traversal) or enemies hampering your path.

Let's have a closer look at Micro objectives.

SECTION 3.3: MICRO OBJECTIVES AND MOTIVATORS

Micro objectives are the smaller "moment to moment" objectives and feedback required to keep the player moving forward or progressing in your game.

FIGURE 3.10 Third person platforming. Image by Thomas White/ Synty Studios/Epic Games UE5.

Figure 3.10 depicts a simplified whitebox for a third-person action-adventure traversal/platformer in the *Tomb Raider* or *Uncharted* mould. As you're entering the chamber you can see multiple routes which may offer a view to the exit, the exit being your "Macro" objective, but which route to choose? There's another pointer there to help you, a "Micro" objective in that some of you may have spotted, which is quite common for guiding players in this type of game.

IN CLASS EXERCISE 3.5: MICRO OBJECTIVES

Lecture reference: slides 26–27
In class Discussion: Micro objectives
Question:
Can you name the "Micro" objective in Figure 3.9 that helps to guide the player?

Exercise 3.5 Answer

Micro objective example: enemy placement

The answer is the enemy on the platform in front of the player. In a third-person action-adventure game situation, the possibility space can often appear quite expansive, but the actual metrics of how the level is designed mean there are often not really a lot of places you can go – it's "illusion of choice." Jump distance metrics will prevent you from reaching certain areas, and the water means that the platforms are out of reach from below. However, with the enemy placement, you're fairly certain that is the correct path – why else would an enemy be placed on a platform if you're not meant to defeat it? It should be noted that our little bad-guy would have had to have been previously introduced as a melee, not a ranged character, otherwise, this would alter the dynamics of the design (i.e., the enemy would shoot at you from a distance). Enemy placement to guide the player is quite a common game design technique. Think of the number of times you've been lost in a game only to find that a spawned enemy is the "Aha!" moment that helps you realise you are back on the right track.

Micro objectives: other examples

Lecture reference: slide 28

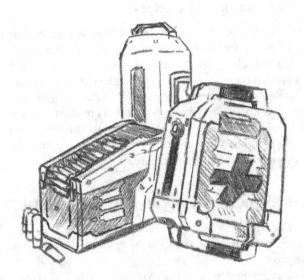

FIGURE 3.11   Health packs and pickup items. Illustration by Jack Hollick.

Micro objective example: health packs

Pickups such as health packs or weapons are another way of guiding a player through the level. Pickups are also very useful if you're creating a horror game, or at least to surprise the player through misdirection, quite a common technique in these titles. Think of the time that you spotted a fantastic new weapon illuminated at the end of a corridor, and then ran down to snatch it, when suddenly out of the shadows next to you (that you hadn't noticed due to overwhelming excitement at the possibility of the pickup) something GRABS at you and makes you jump out of your skin. Or something jumping out to eat your brain when you're picking up a medi pack. Or even the walls collapsing around you to reveal a swathe of enemies ready to give you a beating. And don't even get me started on *Dark Souls* mimic chests!

Micro objective example: traversal design

Traversal design is a massive element of action/adventure game design which takes a lot of trial, error, and iteration to do well – some of the techniques of traversal design are really to do with hiding the route in plain sight without frustrating the player to the point where they want to drop the game. There are several elements you can use to guide the player through more complex routes, which we'll discuss at the end of the lecture, but one of the core tenets of traversal design is that if you've set up the metrics (e.g., jump distances, height to grab, etc.) clearly for the player in a safe environment, and re-enforced these through the early stages, it will become "second nature" for a player to scan various environmental hazards you put in front of them (i.e., a precipitous cliff) and, if you've done your job well, recognise a possible route through it.

Micro objective example: puzzles

In the early *Tomb Raiders* (Core Design, 1996–2000), we incorporated a lot of puzzle elements where you're frequently backtracking to find objects (e.g., missing cogs required to complete a mechanism). We utilised puzzle design in some ways to slow the player down and prevent them from rushing through content, but also because finding the solution to a well-designed puzzle, along with the relevant "Eureka!" moment, gives the player a huge dopamine rush. I'd also note that there must be a careful balance of pacing between puzzles, combat, and exploration. Puzzle rooms often pace the level out as required downtime between combat. We'll discuss (specifically first and third person) puzzle design in the "challenge" lecture.

IN CLASS EXERCISE 3.6: MICRO AND MACRO OBJECTIVES

Lecture reference: slides 29–30
 Let's look at some further examples of Micro *and* Macro objectives.
In class discussion:
 Can you describe the Micro or Macro element in the following example?

EXERCISE 3.6 VIDEO LINK:

Example 1: Super Mario Bros (Nintendo, 1985): World 1-1
 https://bit.ly/EX1_3_MAR

FIGURE 3.12   Illustration by Shutterstock/BlackWhiteMouse Design.

Exercise 3.6 Answer 1

MACRO: Rescue the Princess
MICRO: There are lots of options here, navigation through the level, scoring and collecting points, or simply describing the usual platform progression from left to right.

**IN CLASS EXERCISE 3.6: MICRO AND
MACRO OBJECTIVES (PART 2)**

Lecture reference: slides 31–32
In class discussion:
Question:
    Can you describe the Micro or Macro elements in the following example?
Example Two: Portal (Valve Corporation, 2007)

FIGURE 3.13   Illustration by Jack Hollick.

Exercise 3.6 Answer 2

Macro

Escape from Glados!

Micro

Again, there are a lot of micros here. One of the clearest micros, which is beautifully designed, is that you must exit the room. You're (usually) in a small, enclosed environment where you're working towards a very clear objective that is visible in the environment – the exit. You work towards it in small, manageable stages ("chunking," see Lecture 2). From a gameplay perspective, you're rewarded, and you see clear progress. It's a simple, robust piece of game design that helps the player understand what they're doing and makes them want to keep playing towards the next micro-objective, and that's why *Portal* has stood the test of time as a classic piece of game design.

**IN CLASS EXERCISE 3.6: MICRO AND
MACRO OBJECTIVES (PART 3)**

Lecture reference: slides 33–34
In class discussion:
Question:
    Can you describe the Micro or Macro elements in the following example?
Example Three: Minecraft (Mojang, 2011)

FIGURE 3.14   Illustration by Shutterstock/Doc_js.

Exercise 3.6 Answer 3

Macro

In initial versions of *Minecraft*, there was no real "Macro" objective other than a cycle of Micro objectives such as surviving and building. Later versions have split these modes, tacking on a "kill the ender dragon" Macro objective for "survival mode," and splitting out a "Creative mode" allowing users unlimited access to resources while removing the jeopardy of survival completely, making this mode more akin to a user "sandbox" where users are able to explore, build, and show off creations to the world. (An important motivator!)

Micro

In the original *Minecraft*, the initial Micro objective was to survive the first night. This is interesting as these mechanics are effectively introducing us to an inverse "Difficulty curve" (see Box 3.2). The first night is a real challenge, as players struggle to find resources with which to build a shelter and protect themselves, whereas from that point on, the player accumulates knowledge and resources rapidly, increasing in strength and power at a rate of knots until they become almost godlike in their invulnerability, allowing them to farm and collect resources with relative impunity.

Box 3.2 – "Game Difficulty Curves"

A game difficulty curve is a design element that determines how the challenge level of a game evolves as the player's skill increases[3] keeping them engaged without overwhelming, or "spiking" at any point to a degree which causes the player to drop the game. Using teaching mechanics as described in lecture two should allow onboarding of mechanics to not overwhelm. Later game difficulty can be balanced by such game design techniques as in-game avatar improvement (better stats and skills, i.e., *Skyrim*) or alternately avoiding buffing the player in anyway, but instead training them gradually in learning combat and health management (i.e., *GTA 3-5*) – albeit, in the case of GTA, with a side helping of (fund and mission gated) gradually improving weapons, and vehicles to help you in your mission objectives. In general, the difficulty curve should also provide increasing rewards to match the increasing level of the challenge – i.e., increasing XP amounts or improved loot as your level or skill increases to promote continued player engagement – you don't want to end up having to bring a knife to a gunfight!

IN CLASS EXERCISE 3.6: MICRO AND MACRO OBJECTIVES (PART 4)

Lecture reference: slides 35–36
In class discussion:
   Can you describe the Micro or Macro element in the following example?

EXERCISE 3.6 (PART 4) VIDEO LINK:

Example Four: Assassins Creed 2 (Ubisoft, 2009)
   https://bit.ly/EX3_6_ASSC

FIGURE 3.15   Illustration by Shutterstock/ SK_Artist.

Exercise 3.6 Answer 4

Macro

A good example of a macro-level objective in "Assassin's Creed II" is to assassinate the prominent politician and banker Francesco de' Pazzi. The plot and gameplay objectives cleverly build up to and mirror the actual assassination of this real-world historical figure in 15th-century Florence.

Micro

Part of the micro-objectives involves strategically working your way through the level to position yourself for the assassination. This includes many of the core mechanics and game systems from the original series, such as blending in with crowds, stealth combat, avoiding line of sight, and verticality – your player character gradually evolving into a fine-tuned killing machine, reflecting a core element of many triple A titles – what I like to call "Badassery" (see Box 3.3)

Box 3.3 – Set Course for "Badassery"!

Big AAA franchises have often been designed around simple power fantasies for their ongoing appeal. And franchises don't come much bigger than *Assassins Creed*, with an intriguing amount of design adjustments, course corrections, and improvements throughout the series history, but always striving to keep the core player character, for the most part "Badass." Although retracing its roots with *Assassin's Creed Mirage* (Ubisoft, 2023), with *Assassin's Creed Origins* (Ubisoft, 2017), Ubisoft attempted to reboot the series. This reboot focused on combat, XP, and RPG systems, allowing for extensive character customisation. However, in the process, I'd suggest it removed one of the core level design pillars of the Assassin's Creed series: verticality and dominating the skyline like a – you guessed it – badass. How could you not miss charging around the rooftops, chaining parkour moves while casually decimating oblivious guards, while the blissfully unaware plebs potter about absent mindedly far below? Admittedly, from a design perspective, it is noticeable that at a certain point in the series, it became too easy to run about on the street without being penalised, leading to players not utilising the rooftops as much, and leading to what effectively became large pedestrianised zones. This issue was addressed in *Assassin's Creed Syndicate* (Ubisoft, 2015), where the introduction of the "rope launcher" prevented the perceived unnecessary tedium of climbing up walls, by allowing players to launch themselves onto the rooftops instantaneously. And, in the process, once more feeling like Badasses.

FIGURE 3.16 An environmental feature. Illustration by Shutterstock/Sensvector.

EXERCISE 3.6: MICRO AND MACRO OBJECTIVES (PART 5)

Lecture reference: slides 37–38
In class discussion:
Question:
    Can you describe any games that have a clear Macro objective from the start
of the game, such as the mountain in Figure 3.16?

Exercise 3.6 Answer 5

Macro

Examples here would be the signature mountains that dominate the start of the game in both
Journey (thatgamecompany, 2012) and *FarCry 4* (Ubisoft, 2014.) Another urban example
would be the combine tower in *Half Life 2* (Valve Corporation, 2004.) As discussed previously, it's rare to find these in games – these landscape features are macro-objectives
which are clearly visible at key, regular moments in the game to re-enforce these as core,
Macro objectives– a prominent landscape feature that you see frequently and you know
you're heading towards it, and that is your ultimate objective. It's a good, clear motivator
for the player, but frequently difficult to design in. Try it and see!

SECTION 3.4: MAXIMISING MOTIVATION

Lecture reference: slide 39

Other Important Motivators and How to Use Them

A good designer will layer many different types of game design motivators into their
levels.
    Chris McEntee, one of our former students from the school of "International Game
Architecture and Design" at Breda University of Applied Sciences (BUas) and a designer
at Ubisoft during the development of *Rayman Origins*, discusses various player motivations in his article "*Rational design: The core of Rayman Origins*" (McEntee, 2012.)
    *"Motivation involves understanding different player types and what drives them. It
includes integrating various motivators into the environment that lead players toward
a state of flow and intrinsic motivation."*
    Drilling down to understanding different player types and what motivates them,
McEntee mentions flow and intrinsic motivation. Let's have a closer look at these
important elements that should be clearly understood and utilised frequently within a
good game designer's toolbox.

Design Toolbox 1: "Flow"

Lecture reference: slide 40

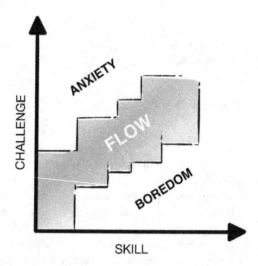

FIGURE 3.17   Basic flow state. Illustration by Andrew Thornton.

The concept of "Flow" is the theory of a psychological state, introduced by Hungarian American psychologist Mihaly Csikszentmihalyi in the 1970s. It describes a state where a person is fully and completely absorbed in and focused on an activity, enjoying it to the point where there is a general loss of self-consciousness accompanied by a lack of perception of time passing, where nothing else seems to matter other than the activity at hand.

Csikszentmihalyi's extensive research on happiness and creativity led to the identification of flow as a highly productive and satisfying state. His foundational work on this topic is detailed in his 1990 book, *Flow: The Psychology of Optimal Experience.* (Csikszentmihalyi, 1990) From a game perspective, it is recognised (as per Figure 3.17) that flow is "triggered" by a perfect balance of game difficulty and player skill (or abilities), and that this state can be maintained by the difficulty curve perfectly matching the player's increasing skill and prowess as they play through this curve.

I found the concept of flow somewhat dubious, until, during what I believed to be a brief session grinding for some XP in my latest game purchase, my wife tapped me on the controller and said, "why have you been playing the same bit of that game for 4 hours"?

It's really a case of balancing out your skill exactly with the increasing difficulty level of the game, which is quite a challenge to design. It's more a case again of iterating until you find flow – watch users playing your game or level, make notes, and keep tweaking the balance until you find the player approaching that elusive flow state.

And before you ask – the 4-hour farming session was in *Dark* Souls (FromSoftware, 2011). Being a relatively bad player (always beneficial from a game design point of view, as you tend to design upward from the lowest possible entry level – or that's my excuse), I had discovered an exploit online. Basically – run out into some woods, find a load of high-level mobs, get them to chase, and then scramble out onto a very thin ledge. The Mobs, in theory, would pursue me onto it, and due to the size of their collision boxes not matching the size of the ledge, would all fall off into an abyss, rewarding me with abundant, and not particularly hard-earned souls. Rinse and Repeat. For 4 hours.

The balance between difficulty and challenge in this situation being that following almost *exactly* the same route into the high mob area each time was paramount. If I strayed even slightly from this "correct" route, i.e., following a particular "desire line" through the trees, I'd get a *little* too close to one of these mobs and then either they'd blast me with a high-level spell or run up behind me and impale me on a giant spike. So the difficulty versus the skill here was focusing entirely on keeping to that line, and memorising the optimal route through the trees, with the enemy AI providing the difficulty as if you strayed, they would correct their attack route on line of sight, and cause – difficulties. And that, in a nutshell, is how flow can lose you 4 hours of your life.

Design Toolbox 2: Intrinsic and Extrinsic Motivators

Lecture reference: slide 41

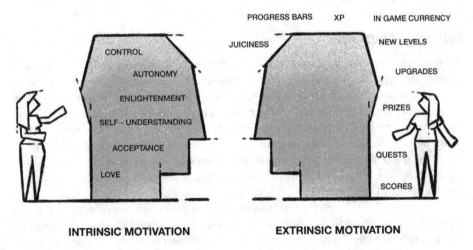

FIGURE 3.18   Intrinsic and extrinsic motivators. Illustration by Andrew Thornton.

Background

The concepts of extrinsic and intrinsic motivation were developed and popularised by Edward L. Deci and Richard M. Ryan via their Self-Determination Theory (SDT), which they began formulating in the 1970s and 1980s culminating in the book "*Intrinsic Motivation and Self-Determination in Human Behavior*" (Deci & Ryan, 1985).[4] SDT elaborates on previous theories and research into different types of motivators to create a "taxonomy" of how human motivation is often driven by a need for autonomy, competence, and relatedness, and differentiates between *extrinsic* motivation that is driven by external rewards, and *intrinsic* motivation that arises from within the individual, driven by interest and enjoyment in the task itself. In the book *"Gamification by Design: Implementing Game Mechanics in Web and Mobile Apps"* (Zichermann & Cunningham, 2011). Zichermann discusses the concepts of intrinsic and extrinsic motivation from a game or "gamification" perspective. Extrinsic relies on external rewards or incentives, such as badges, points, or achievements, which supply short-term interest which must be carefully balanced from a design perspective so as to not dilute or undermine any deeper intrinsic motivators.

Extrinsic: overview

If we look at extrinsic, and the game perspective of points, levels, and skills, an example might be skill trees, quests for points or XP, or winning in a multiplayer match. These are some of the elements that are motivating you to continue playing and are effectively "layered" on top of the game. They're quite easy to design in, fulfilling the "reward" element of the objective/challenge/reward cycle. In some cases, such as Esports, there are also real-world rewards to be won, providing further, tangible reward systems. All these extrinsic elements will motivate you, but the really hard one to design, and certainly the most influential on what we might call addiction or stickiness in games, are the intrinsic motivators.

Intrinsic: overview

As discussed, Intrinsic is really to do with enjoying the activity itself for the sake of it, in many cases leading to a feeling of self-improvement. Elements like autonomy (being in control of your own choices), belonging, power, mastery, love – Feeling as if you've bettered yourself, or feeling as if you've changed or developed as a person – and as you can imagine, it's quite hard to build that into games. But some games do it – and do it really well. As we see from the diagram, an example of an intrinsic motivator is "love." So, if we're having trouble designing in and prompting the emotion of "crying" from a game (see Box 3.1, "The Cry Test"), how do we, as designers, manage to prompt or direct a player to feel "love"?

I'd suggest this falls into two categories – loving your character or avatar, or, in the second category, observing or being involved with a narrative that illustrates love in a way that prompts the player to recognise that emotion and how it might affect them.

FIGURE 3.19 A young couple meet. Illustration by Shutterstock/Nopparat Techapreechawong.

Box 3.4 Case Study: *Florence* (Mountains, 2018)

Lecture reference: slide 42

Florence (Mountains, 2018) was originally a mobile title that presents a realistic, or at least recognisable, playable depiction of a relationship. Players may be able to relate to events in this relationship, and to some degree, this may lead to intrinsic rewards – i.e., how you improve yourself in your own relationships. However, I'd suggest it doesn't trigger intrinsic love in you as a player who actively "falls in love" with these characters. Are we able to design systems that promote players actually "loving" a character within a game? A carefully crafted avatar you have spent many hundreds of hours with while playing an MMORPG? Or a love for an NPC like you love a pet, e.g., your horse from *Red Dead Redemption 2* (Rockstar Games, 2018)? As artificial intelligence progresses, perhaps in the future we'll see these types of relationships between players and player characters, similar to those depicted in the film *Her* (directed by Spike Jonze in 2013). But currently, with regard to designing this type of emotion, the jury is still out.

Elements of intrinsic: creativity

Lecture reference: slide 43

As we've discussed in our "Teaching" lecture, Creativity is a big one – Creativity is an intrinsic motivator, and games such as *Minecraft* (Mojang, 2011), *Dreams*, (Media

Molecule, 2020) and *Little Big Planet* (Media Molecule, 2008) have creativity "Designed in." Part of the pleasure of utilising the systems in these games is through being able to express yourself through creativity, and even more so if that creativity allows for "peer review" allowing you to share (and show off) your creations with other like-minded gamers, in some cases leading to collaboration on larger projects together. The creative systems within these games also allow players to set their own goals, engaging in activities that they themselves find personally meaningful or enjoyable, re-enforcing the core intrinsic motivator of autonomy, specifically control over their own choices and development within the game world.

Elements of intrinsic: self-knowledge/learning

Lecture reference: slide 44

Some games will invite or encourage further learning outside of the core game systems.

Anyone who has played the *Assassins creed* series (Ubisoft, 2007-present) may want to further explore the history of the real worlds, environments, people and culture they are playing within. Recognising this, Ubisoft introduced the "Discovery Tour" mode in in *Assassin's Creed Origins* (Ubisoft, 2017) and *Assassin's Creed Odyssey*, (Ubisoft, 2018), an educational sandbox where players are able to explore these worlds in a combat-free environment curated by voiceovers from historians and educators, with a view to not only being utilised by players, but also in class or learning settings. Games such as *Kerbal Space program* (Squad, 2011), with its focus on a physics-driven universe in which players must build and fly spacecraft, have inspired numerous players to pursue careers in aerospace, engineering, and other STEM fields (BuzzFeed Multiplayer, 2022). Playing *This War of Mine* (11 bit studios, 2014) promotes a deeper understanding of the consequences of war, influencing players to learn more about global conflicts and humanitarian issues, whereas *That Dragon, Cancer* (Numinous Games, 2016), an autobiographical interactive drama exploring the terminal cancer of a child, encourages players to reflect on themes of life, loss, and coping with grief. All these examples are promoting intrinsic learning that may alter the player's knowledge of, or outlook on the world, or in some cases, prompt them to equip themselves for difficult life situations. If you are able to build some of these systems into your game, you will probably find a loyal audience hungry for what you have created.

IN CLASS EXERCISE 3.7: EXTRINSIC AND INTRINSIC MOTIVATORS

Lecture reference: slide 46
In Class Discussion:
Question:
    Are you able to think of any extrinsic and at least *one* intrinsic motivator in games you've recently played?

FIGURE 3.20   Illustration by Shutterstock/Algol.

Exercise 3.7 Example Answers:

Example One: "Eve Online" (CCP Games, 2003)

This MMORPG launches players out into a vast universe where they can choose their own unique path from day one, allowing them to engage in activities from mining and piracy to governing entire star systems.

Extrinsic: points or "money"

Players can earn in-game currency, known as ISK, to purchase and upgrade ships and equipment, allowing access to further exploration and resources, which can then be ploughed back into improvements – a classic progression curve and reward loop.

Intrinsic: power and responsibility

As one example of intrinsic motivators within the Eve universe, individual players can lead large alliances or corporations within the game, which translates into significant power, respect, and social standing within the Eve community. Activities "out of game," such as participating in real-world forums, conferences, and social media, can impact important decisions within the game world, such as influencing its player-driven economy, affecting vast numbers of players.

FIGURE 3.21   Building in animal crossing. Illustration by Jack Hollick.

Example Two: "Animal Crossing: New Horizons" (Nintendo, 2020)

Extrinsic: points or "money"

"Nook Miles" are an in-game currency that are rewarded for completing tasks listed in the Nook Miles app, such as catching a certain number of fish, and allow the player to buy exclusive items and tickets for travelling to mystery islands, allowing access to further exploration and resources, these rewards motivating the player to progress further into the game.

Intrinsic: autonomy

Autonomy describes the ability to make your own decisions without being coerced, and the autonomy in *Animal Crossing* can be reflected in in-game tasks such as gardening, interior decorating, and other aspects of "ownership" over your own space in the virtual world. Outside of the game, players will often take inspiration from their in-game creations to apply to home improvement projects in the real world (Play, 2021). For Further reading, see[5]

SECTION 3.5: (SOME) BEHAVIOURAL MODIFIERS

As discussed, there are many methods of designing behavioural modifiers in video games to influence and encourage specific player actions and habits – psychological motivators such as Skinner's box and Maslow's hierarchy of needs, which we'll look at in more precise detail in later lectures, but as brief introduction for the purposes of this section let's look at "operant conditioning" as part of the psychological techniques investigated by the aforementioned B.F. Skinner, and their perceived use in game design.

Design Toolbox: Operant Conditioning

Lecture reference: slide 48

Background:

B.F. Skinner first described operant conditioning in his 1938 book titled *"The Behaviour of Organisms,"* expanding on Thorndike's law of effect (Thorndike, 1933), and outlining the basic principles of how behaviour can be influenced and, to some degree, controlled by positive and negative reward systems.

The concept of the "Skinner box" is integral to the study of these positive and negative reward systems and is known collectively as "operant conditioning." In a typical Skinner box setup (see Figure 3.22), an animal, like a rat or pigeon, presses a lever or a button to receive a food reward or, in some cases, a "punishment" such as an electric shock, which prompts the reinforcement of specific behaviours. Examples of positive reinforcement involve adding a stimulus to increase a behaviour (i.e., "press button & get more food"), whereas negative reinforcement involves removing an unpleasant stimulus to increase a behaviour (i.e., "press button quickly to stop getting electrocuted"). Bear in mind many of these experiments took place in the 1950s, when animal welfare was, perhaps, not at the forefront of the experimenter's mind.

FIGURE 3.22   "Skinner box" operant conditioning. Image by DataBase Center for Life Science (DBCLS), CC BY 4.0 (<https://creativecommons.org/licenses/by/4.0>, via Wikimedia Commons Illustration by Wikimedia commons).

You may view these systems as too crude to fool our highly developed Homo sapiens minds, but unfortunately, that's not the case. A simple example of how this works in humans is the "one-armed bandit" (see Figure 3.23) commonly used in Vegas casinos. "Intermittent reinforcement," or the concept of receiving rewards at irregular intervals, has been found to be one of the most powerful ways to reinforce behaviour (Kendall, 1974). In this case, despite numerous losses, the act of feeding coins into the machine continues until the reward, and the dopamine rush of it finally coughing up, occurs (despite the fact you've probably put more money into it than it has paid out). Add to this the visual feedback that some machines provide of "near misses," and the "juiciness" of the flashing lights and sounds despite the fact you may actually be losing, and you have a perfect example of a human Skinner box system. We keep pulling that lever, chasing that dopamine hit, proving that even when we know the psychological processes behind it, we can still be reduced to drooling Pavlovian dogs.

FIGURE 3.23   One armed bandit. Image by casino, CC0, via Wikimedia Commons.

Similarly, in video games, psychological techniques along these principles can be used to modify player behaviour by using rewards and punishments that are applied based on the player's actions, often by rewarding them with extra points or XP, new levels, equipment upgrades, gear, and other simple extrinsic rewards.

Let's have a look at some further video game examples of behavioural motivators.

Design Toolbox: Behavioural Modifiers in Video Games

In his book "Fun Inc.: Why Games are the 21st Century's Most Serious Business" (2010), Tom Chatfield not only explores the impact and potential of video games in modern society, but also the psychological effects of gaming, including some core motivators. In his presentation at the International Game Architecture and Design school (IGAD), entitled "Learning to fail better" Chatfield (2013), gave some examples of these various behavioural motivators and how they work in games. Let's look at examples and variants of these in more detail and expand on them with game examples.

Behavioural modifier 1: visible progress

Lecture reference: slide 49

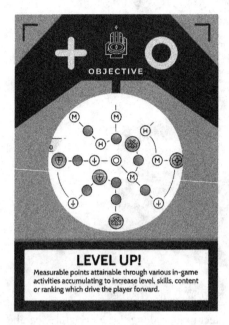 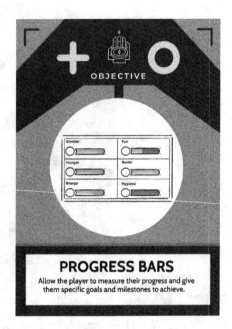

FIGURE 3.24   Example objective gamecards. Illustrations by Andrew Thornton.

Here's a couple of examples of simple extrinsic motivators in games, "Levelling up" and "Progress bars." As previously discussed, these elements are designed to clearly show players their progress, provide positive feedback, and give them a sense of ongoing achievement. From a behavioural perspective, this is important for maintaining engagement and motivating them to continue playing, making the player feel there is a visible purpose to their efforts.

Behavioural modifier 2: micro and macro objectives

Lecture reference: slide 50

FIGURE 3.25   Example objective gamecards. Illustrations by Andrew Thornton.

To re-iterate, if a game's main (or Macro) quest objective feels a little too confusing, time consuming or intimidating, developers will often incorporate smaller, manageable sub-quests or *Micro objectives* that allow players to engage with the game without extensive commitment. Games like the *Grand Theft Auto* series, *World of Warcraft*, and *Skyrim* offer mini quests that players can complete in about 10 minutes. Players can frequently explore and encounter NPCs who provide these shorter quests or engage in simple sub-games like cooking or fishing to gain experience points. For *long-term aims*, an example would be a completionist – a player who wants to get all the achievements, etc., and make sure they have "rinsed" the game for everything it has to offer.

Behavioural modifier 3: who dares wins!

Lecture reference: slide 50

FIGURE 3.26   Example objective gamecards. Illustrations by Andrew Thornton/Stuart Atkinson.

As a by-product of our inclination towards operant conditioning and reward schedules, our brains are naturally stimulated by the uncertainty of random outcomes. This taps into our innate risk-taking behaviours, the uncertainty triggering the release of dopamine in the brain, a deeply ingrained response in human psychology (Clark, Averbeck, Payer, Sescousse, Winstanley & Xue, 2013). An example is the V.A.T.S. system[6] in *Fallout 3* (Bethesda Game Studios, 2008) – a classic piece of design, that reveals the "under the bonnet" complex probabilities of hitting your target, including calculations of distance, projectile type, and player weapon skill. Players might face a choice between a high probability of hitting a larger target area like the enemy's chest for minimal damage, versus a smaller chance of a critical headshot that delivers much greater damage. Which do you go for? Human psychology would suggest more often than not, we go for the high risk/high reward choice. It seems we are frequently unable to untangle the possible dopamine hit of the big prize, with the increased possibility of failure.

Storylines are another example of how we want resolution from uncertainty. This is particularly evident when plot twists, such as those in *Bioshock* (Irrational Games, 2007) introduce us to new layers of unpredictability, heightening our anticipation of what might happen next. Similarly, in games like *Heavy Rain* (Quantic Dream, 2010) or *Detroit: Become Human*, (Quantic Dream, 2018) the excitement is often based around the myriad choices presented to the player, each of which can lead to different, unexpected outcomes that entirely alter the course of the game.[7]

This element of reward systems built into uncertainty is also evident in our drive to explore, or "what's around the next bend?" Driven by a pursuit of intrinsic rewards in an effort to enhance our personal growth and fulfilment (Lopez, Pedrotti & Snyder, 2018), or perhaps, in a more primitive fashion, and adhering to the systems within Maslow's hierarchy of needs (Maslow, 1943), as what's around the next corner may offer a better chance of survival.

Behavioural modifier 4: teamwork makes the dream work!

Lecture reference: slide 52

FIGURE 3.27   Example objective gamecards. Illustrations by Andrew Thornton.

In co-operative gaming, such as the "friend in need" gamecard illustration depicting *It Takes Two* (Hazelight Studios, 2021) assisting your teammates or friends is a core design strategy for re-engagement. In games like *Draw Something*, (OMGPOP, 2012) invitations are used re-engage players by prompting them to respond to challenges from their friends, a strong psychological motivator (Luton, 2013). Similarly, games like *Forza Horizon* (Playground Games, 2012) employ features like "Drivatars," which simulate your friends' driving behaviours on the track, inviting you to beat their best times. This mix of competition and cooperation taps into the social dynamics of MP gaming, leveraging our innate desire to connect and compete with others.

Additionally, in games like *Monster Hunter* (Capcom, 2004–present) or *World of Warcraft* (Blizzard Entertainment. 2004–present), displaying achievements like the elite status of the Death Knight allows players to show off their achievements and gear to their peers, an important element of demonstrating social status and mastery, and again enhancing our innate need not only for connection with others, but also, in many cases, to compete with them.

To finalise our toolbox of more specific examples of game-based motivators, let's have a look at some level design-specific techniques.

SECTION 3.6: MAKING OBJECTIVES CLEAR – LEVEL DESIGN TOOLBOX

Lecture reference: slide 53

There are a variety of core techniques we can utilise to corral, guide, and lead a player through a level. Before our more in-depth study of level design later in the course, let's look at an overview of some of the basic level design motivators.

IN CLASS EXERCISE 3.8: LEVEL DESIGN TOOLBOX

Lecture reference: slides 54–55
In class discussion: LD objective techniques
Example one: The Last of us (Naughty Dog, 2013)
Question:
Imagine the image in Figure 3.28 is from a post-apocalyptic title such as The Last of Us – You are lost in a large, enemy-infested warehouse. Which level design technique visible in the image would guide you out of the area?

FIGURE 3.28 Level Layout example. Image by Shutterstock/Michel Stevelmans.

Exercise 3.8 Answer

Light

Lighting is one of the simplest and clearest methods for directing players through a level. If you often find yourself lost, you'll naturally head towards the nearest source of light. In a game like "The Last of Us," dark interiors will usually have clear exits marked by daylight, tapping into our innate desire to reach the outside.

IN CLASS EXERCISE 3.9: LEVEL DESIGN TOOLBOX

Lecture reference: slides 56–57
In class discussion: LD objective techniques
Question:
     Watch the clip and attempt to identify the level design technique that guides the player:

EXERCISE 3.9 VIDEO LINK

Example two: Super Mario 64 (Nintendo, 1996)
     https://bit.ly/EX3_9_MA64

FIGURE 3.29   "Breadcrumbing." Illustration by Jack Hollick.

Exercise 3.9 Answer

"Breadcrumbing"

We can observe the coins in *Super Mario 64* guiding the player around the level, and pickups are a common way of Breadcrumbing, although it doesn't always require a continuous trail of pickups as we see in the clip. For instance, in the *Tomb Raider* games, I frequently placed pickups such as health packs not only to guide the player, but also in positions where I could then trigger an unexpected monster to jump out on them as they were picking it up – an addition that could become the height of hilarity when you've been sitting watching your tester/QA play the same section of game for 72 hours straight (see also, Micro Objective Example: Health Packs).

FIGURE 3.30   Illustration by Shutterstock/ustas7777777.

IN CLASS EXERCISE 3.10: LEVEL DESIGN TOOLBOX

Lecture reference: slides 58–59
In class discussion: LD Objective techniques
Question:
    Watch the clip and attempt to identify the level design technique that guides the player:

EXERCISE 3.10 VIDEO LINK

Example three: Mirrors Edge Catalyst (DICE, 2016)
    https://bit.ly/EX3_10_MIRR

Exercise 3.10 Answer

"Readability"

This concept, which is a little tricky to figure out before it's explained, is called "readability." It involves having a clear, visible route, path, or goal denoted by some type of visual cues. In titles like *Batman* or *Assassin's Creed*, this will be via tools such as detective mode or "Eagle vision" that highlight your objectives in distinct colours, clarifying your next steps. In *Mirror's Edge*, readability is based around how colours guide you through a level. In this game, red indicates paths, like pipes, that you can safely run along (a slightly odd choice, as red typically signals danger, not safety.) Similarly, yellow is used to denote elements you can jump to and grab onto. This colour coding that guides you through the level is readability.

FIGURE 3.31   Destination marker in "Death Stranding." illustration by Jack Hollick.

IN CLASS EXERCISE 3.11: LEVEL DESIGN TOOLBOX

Lecture reference: slides 60–61
In class discussion: LD Objective techniques
Question:
    Watch the clip and attempt to identify the level design technique that guides the player:

EXERCISE 3.11 VIDEO LINK

Example four: Dead Space (EA Redwood Shores, 2008)
https://bit.ly/EX3_11_DEAD

Exercise 3.11 Answer

"Objective distance marker"

This concept is similar to "breadcrumbing." In *Dead Space*, for example, pressing the left stick down on your console controller reveals the path to your next objective, which is incredibly useful, as the ship in *Dead Space* has a modular design. This means many corridors appear identical and it's easy to get lost. This navigational guide is a genius piece of design, which avoids frustration in what is a complex, dark and repetitive ship, and allows the designer to focus more on the complexities of horror design. Concealing the route or designing a complex and confusing maze generally doesn't benefit the player; it frustrates them – something I *eventually* learned designing *Tomb Raider* games over a period of 5 years.

FIGURE 3.32 A maze, yesterday. Illustration by Purpy Pupple, CC BY-SA 3.0 Wikimedia commons (https://creativecommons.org/licenses/by-sa/3.0, via Wikimedia Commons).

With this in mind, I'd suggest minimising the use of mazes – while some games still incorporate them, navigating a complex maze without any form of signposting often becomes a matter of trial and error, where you are as likely to find a dead end as you are an exit. This may lead players to abandon the game out of irritation. Mazes can be effective in certain contexts, but I'd suggest using them carefully, and with at least some form of navigational guidance for the player.

IN CLASS EXERCISE 3.12: LEVEL DESIGN TOOLBOX

Lecture reference: slides 62–63
In class discussion: LD objective techniques
Example five: "Open World game"
Question:

Imagine the image in Figure 3.33 is from a vast open-world game such as *Breath of the wild*, *Skyrim*, or *World of Warcraft*. Which technique visible in the image may help the player to choose where to go next?

FIGURE 3.33   Open world level layout. Illustration by Shutterstock/Gorodenkoff.

Exercise 3.12 Answer

Motion/Enemies

Motion can be a very effective tool in game design. For instance, if you find yourself lost in an environment, particularly in an open-world setting – motion, such as moving elements or enemies, can help to direct the player towards where they should be going – or indeed, going away from. I'm sure you've all played a game where you've been in an environment, got lost, and then, as you turn a corner, you encounter a live enemy – and then you know you're back on the right path. Using an enemy as a dynamic level design element helps reassure players that they are heading in the correct direction.

IN CLASS EXERCISE 3.13: LEVEL DESIGN TOOLBOX

Lecture reference: slides 64–65
In class discussion: LD objective techniques
Example Six: Everybody's gone to the rapture (The Chinese Room, 2015)
Question:
　　Which level design technique, as depicted in Figure 3.34, and used frequently in the game *Everybody's gone to the rapture,* helps to guide the player towards their objectives?

FIGURE 3.34　Level Layout example. Illustration by Shutterstock/Victoria_Hunter.

Exercise 3.13 Answer

Corralling

Corralling is a common game design technique used to keep players confined within certain areas of the environment, preventing them from exiting specific, designer set boundaries. This can cause issues in games that ape reality – you might find that you can't climb over fences, even though that might be perfectly feasible in reality. In the game world, because you're unable to jump/climb, you'll need to follow along the fence for a gate.

　　Corralling in its original form is a hangover from the dark ages of game development – you would put invisible barriers up on either side of the level that stopped the player jumping out of the game world (usually that the player could just bounce up and down against.)

Modern examples such as *Assassin's Creed* incorporate and integrate corralling effectively and seamlessly as part of its narrative. The game restricts access to certain areas by hitting the limits of the "Animus" simulation displaying a message that the memory period has not been unlocked. Similarly, in *The Legend of Zelda*, an agility meter corrals the player, although this is more a case of area denial based around skill gating.

FIGURE 3.35   The Washington Monument. Illustration by Jack Hollick.

IN CLASS EXERCISE 3.14: LEVEL DESIGN TOOLBOX

In class discussion: LD objective techniques
Lecture reference: slides 66–67
Example seven: Fallout 3 (Bethesda Game Studios, 2008).
Question:
   Which level design technique, as depicted in the image of the Washington Monument in Figure 3.33, as used in the game *Fallout 3*, helps to guide the player towards their objectives?

Exercise 3.14 Answer

Framing, hero buildings, and orientation points

A classic example of an orientation point is the Washington Monument in *Fallout 3*. Set in a post-apocalyptic version of Washington D.C., the Washington Monument serves as a highly visible landmark due to its height and shape, allowing the player to quickly orient themselves in the "Capital Wasteland" and act as a marker for navigation and progression in the game. While other big single-player open-world games such as (for example) *Assassin's Creed: Origins* (Ubisoft Montreal, 2017) benefit from orientation points like the Great Pyramid, these orientation points are even more essential in multiplayer scenarios. For example, if you respawn in a team deathmatch and don't quickly recognise where you are, you're at a high risk of receiving a well-placed headshot. That's why popular multiplayer games like *Call of Duty* (Infinity Ward and Treyarch, 2003–ongoing) or *Halo* (Bungie, 343 Industries, 2001–ongoing) feature well-defined landmarks in their maps to aid players in quickly locating themselves after respawning, helping them to strategise more effectively around their (or their teams) preferred gameplay tactics.

And with that brief look at some of the various level design techniques to guide the player towards their objectives, let's move on to the end of the lecture!

CONCLUSION

Lecture reference: slide 68

In this lecture, we've learned clearly defined game objectives and motivators are crucial in guiding and driving the player forward, while retaining their engagement. By establishing clear goals from the outset and incorporating compelling motivators, while understanding the psychological drivers behind driving player behaviour, game designers can utilise their skills to not only engage and absorb the player, but also take into consideration the ethical implications of their design choices to create more dynamic and fulfilling gaming experiences.

LECTURE THREE "OBJECTIVES & MOTIVATORS": RESOURCE MATERIALS:

Lecture Three in PowerPoint Format:
Lecture Three Working Class:
    Edit and upload to a shared drive of your choice!
(These included instructor resources can all be downloaded from the **Instructor Hub**. For further information, please see the chapter "How to Use This Book.")

NOTES

1 "Still" meaning "Until the latest industry mishap replaces it."
2 Watching a 1.5–2-hour film? Check your watch at around 20 minutes. Give or take a minute or two, you'll usually recognise the inciting incident is bang on time!
3 See Section 3.4: Maximising Motivation: "Flow state"
4 Further reading on this subject Ryan and Deci (2000).

5 Whalen, (2020).
6 "Vault-Tec Assisted Targeting System."
7 Usually, in my case, choices that lead to *drastically* altering the course of the game due to general QTE ineptitude leading to me losing the majority of the playable characters.

REFERENCES

11 bit studios. (2014). *This War of Mine*. [Video game]. Warsaw: 11 bit studios.

American Psychiatric Association. (2013). *Diagnostic and Statistical Manual of Mental Disorders (DSM-5)*. Washington, DC: American Psychiatric Association.

BBC. (2018). Belgium says loot boxes are gambling and wants them banned in Europe. *BBC News*.

Bethesda Game Studios. (2008). *Fallout 3*. [Video game]. Rockville, MD: Bethesda Softworks.

Blizzard Entertainment. (2004). *World of Warcraft*. [Video game]. Irvine: Blizzard Entertainment.

Bungie, 343 Industries. (2001–ongoing). *Halo Series*. [Video game]. Microsoft Game Studios (now Xbox Game Studios).

Campbell, J. (1949). *The Hero with a Thousand Faces*. New York: Pantheon Books.

Capcom. (2004–present). *Monster Hunter Series*. [Video games]. Osaka: Capcom.

Chatfield, T. (2010). *Fun Inc.: Why Games are the 21st Century's Most Serious Business*. London: Virgin Books.

Chatfield, T. (2013). 'Learning to Fail Better'. *Presented at IGAD School of International Game Architecture and Design, NHTV University of Applied Sciences, 25 March 2013*, Breda, Holland.

Clark, L., Averbeck, B., Payer, D., Sescousse, G., Winstanley, C.A. and Xue, G. (2013). Pathological choice: the neuroscience of gambling and gambling addiction. *Journal of Neuroscience*, 33(45), pp.17617–17623.

Core Design. (1996). *Tomb Raider*. [Video game]. Derby: Eidos Interactive.

Core Design. (1998). *Tomb Raider III: Adventures of Lara Croft*. [Video game]. Derby: Eidos Interactive.

Core Design. (1996-2000). *Tomb Raider I-V*. [Video games]. Derby: Eidos Interactive.

Csikszentmihalyi, M. (1990). *Flow: The Psychology of Optimal Experience*. New York: Harper & Row.

Deci, E.L. and Ryan, R.M. (1985). *Intrinsic Motivation and Self-Determination in Human Behavior*. New York: Plenum.

DICE. (2008). *Mirror's Edge*. [Video game]. Stockholm: Electronic Arts.

Drummond, A., & Sauer, J.D. (2018). Video game loot boxes are psychologically akin to gambling. *Nature Human Behaviour*, 2(8), pp.530–532.

EA Redwood Shores. (2008). *Dead Space*. [Video game]. Stockholm: Electronic Arts.

FromSoftware. (2011). *Dark Souls*. [Video game]. Tokyo: Namco Bandai Games.

Hazelight Studios. (2021). *It Takes Two*. [Video game]. Stockholm: Electronic Arts.

id Software. (1993). *Doom*. [Video game]. Richardson, TX: id Software.

id Software. (2016). *Doom*. [Video game]. Dallas, TX: Bethesda Softworks.

Infinity Ward and Treyarch (2003–ongoing). *Call of Duty Series*. [Video game]. Mesquite: Activision.

Irrational Games. (2007). *BioShock*. [Video game]. Novato, CA: 2K Games.

Kendall, S.B. (1974). Preference for intermittent reinforcement. *Journal of the Experimental Analysis of Behavior*, 21(3), pp.463–473.

Lankoski, P., and Björk, S. (2015). *Game Research Methods: An Overview*. Pittsburgh, PE: ETC Press.

Lionhead Studios. (2004). *Fable*. [Video game]. Washington, DC: Microsoft Game Studios.

Lopez, S.J., Pedrotti, J.T. and Snyder, C.R. (2018). *Positive Psychology: The scientific and Practical Explorations of Human Strengths*. New York: Sage publications.

Lucas, G. (1977). *Star Wars: Episode IV - A New Hope*. [Film]. Los Angeles, CA: 20th Century Fox.

Luton, W. (2013). *Free-to-Play: Making Money From Games You Give Away*. Berkeley, CA: New Riders.

Maslow, A. H. (1943). A theory of human motivation. *Psychological Review*, 50(4), 370–396.

McEntee, C. (2012). Rational design: The core of Rayman Origins. *Game Developer*. Available at: https://www.gamedeveloper.com/design/rational-design-the-core-of-i-rayman-origins-i-

Media Molecule. (2008). *LittleBigPlanet*. [Video game]. Guildford: Sony Computer Entertainment.

Media Molecule. (2020). *Dreams*. [Video game]. Guildford: Sony Interactive Entertainment.

Mojang. (2011). *Minecraft*. [Video game]. Stockholm: Mojang.

Mountains. (2018). *Florence*. [Video game]. Melbourne: Annapurna Interactive.

Nintendo. (1985). *Super Mario Bros*. [Video game]. Kyoto: Nintendo.

Nintendo. (1996). *Super Mario 64*. [Video game]. Kyoto: Nintendo.

Nintendo. (2020). *Animal Crossing: New Horizons*. [Video game]. Kyoto: Nintendo.

Naughty Dog. (2013). *The Last of Us*. [Video game]. Santa Monica, CA: Sony Computer Entertainment.

Numinous Games. (2016). *That Dragon, Cancer*. [Video game]. Colorado: Numinous Games.

OMGPOP. (2012). *Draw Something*. [Video game]. New York: Zynga.

Pillow Castle. (2019). *Superliminal*. [Video game]. Seattle, WA: Pillow Castle.

Playground Games. (2012-2021). *Forza Horizon Series*. [Video game]. Redmond, WA: Microsoft Studios/Turn 10 Studios.

Rockstar Games. (2018). *Red Dead Redemption 2*. [Video game]. New York: Rockstar Games.

Ryan, R.M. and Deci, E.L. (2000). Self-determination theory and the facilitation of intrinsic motivation, social development, and well-being. *American Psychologist*, 55(1), pp.68–78.

Skinner, B.F. (2019). *The Behavior of Organisms: An Experimental Analysis*. Cambridge, MA: BF Skinner Foundation.

Squad. (2011). *Kerbal Space Program*. [Video game]. Mexico City: Squad.

SUPERHOT Team. (2016). *SUPERHOT*. [Video game]. Lodz, Poland: SUPERHOT Team.

The Chinese Room. (2015). *Everybody's Gone to the Rapture*. [Video game]. Japan: Sony Computer Entertainment.

The Guardian. (2012). Teenager collapses after playing World of Warcraft for 24 hours straight. http://news.sky.com/skynews/Home/Technology/World-Of-Warcraft-Player-Collapses-Teenager-Played-Online-Role-Playing-Game-For-24-Hours-Non-Stop/Article/2008 11315153928?lpos=Technology_News_Your_Way_Region_9&lid=NewsYourWay_ARTICLE_15153928_World_Of_Warcraft_Player_Collapses%3A_Teenager_Played_Online_Role-Playing-Game_For_24_Hours_Non-Stop.

Thorndike, E.L. (1933). A proof of the law of effect. *Science*, 77(1989), pp.173–175.

Ubisoft. (2007–present). *Assassin's Creed series*. [Video games]. Montreuil: Ubisoft.

Ubisoft. (2009). *Assassin's Creed II*. [Video game]. Montreuil: Ubisoft.

Ubisoft. (2014). *Far Cry 4*. [Video game]. Montreuil: Ubisoft.

Ubisoft. (2017). *Assassin's Creed Origins*. [Video game]. Montreuil: Ubisoft.

Ubisoft. (2018). *Assassin's Creed Odyssey*. [Video game]. Montreuil: Ubisoft.

Ubisoft. (2023). *Assassin's Creed Mirage*. [Video game]. Montreuil: Ubisoft.

Valve. (1998). *Half-Life*. [Video game]. Bellevue, WA: Sierra Studios.

Valve Corporation. (2004). *Half-Life 2*. [Video game]. Bellevue, WA: Valve Corporation.

Valve Corporation. (2007). *Portal*. [Video game]. Bellevue, WA: Valve Corporation.

Vogler, C. (1992). *The Writer's Journey: Mythic Structure for Writers*. Studio City, CA: Michael Wiese Productions.

Whalen, A. (2020). People are having their birthday parties in 'Animal crossing'. *Newsweek*. Available at: https://www.newsweek.com/animal-crossings-new-horizons-multiplayer-birthday-party-social-distancing-1495608.

Zichermann, G. and Cunningham, C. (2011). *Gamification by Design: Implementing Game Mechanics in Web and Mobile Apps*. Sebastopol, CA: O'Reilly Media.

Zendle, D., & Cairns, P. (2018). Video game loot boxes are linked to problem gambling: Results of a large-scale survey. *PLoS One*, 11(13), pp.e0206767.

Core Techniques
Game Mechanics

4

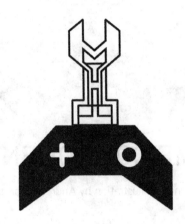

LECTURE OVERVIEW

In this lecture, we'll be looking at Game Mechanics. These are often at the heart of the game, dictating how players will interact with the systems within it (e.g., traversal, puzzle solving, stealth, deck management), and, importantly, defining the outcomes of these interactions (e.g., points, resources, narrative progression, avatar improvement).

DOI: 10.1201/9781032644721-4

FIGURE 4.1   Game Components. Illustration by Andrew Thornton.

Lecture reference: slide 3

Mechanics are a core element of our **Game Component** list. Try to refer to this list
to ensure you are aware of which element of the game design you are focusing on.
Mechanics cover a huge range of game elements but will frequently follow common
structures or rules. We'll look at these in more detail shortly, but in the meantime let's
get the ball rolling with a **Recap exercise**.

In Class Exercise Example: Recapping and Re-Iterating

Notes for Educator:
Recap exercises are a hugely effective way of re-enforcing the previous week's
learning (Roediger & Karpicke, 2006), and "warming up" the class for the new
material. At a certain point, you'll have enough material from your student exercises to utilise this within the taught material. A simple and effective example of
this is to take the previous week's working class/Game card exercise and translate
a few of the most effective cards into a "Which game component is this?" short
quiz.[1] Ideally, I'd also introduce one "wildcard" example at the end that I've created
myself to keep them on their toes. Finally, before starting the exercise, I'll offer
them a brief recap of my own examples from the previous lecture (see Figure 4.4)

in a couple of the initial slides and allow them to take pictures of them if they feel it will help them with the answers (again, reinforcing learning). In certain circles, this is known as "flipping the classroom," allowing students to shoulder some of the burden as a tool for reducing a lecturer's workload. From my own experience, I've found the benefit is more that students often react positively, with anticipation and an increased attention span, to the possibility of seeing their own work featured in front of the class. It also helps to increase opportunities for discussion, as if the example is student-created, they don't feel the answer is "set in stone" by the lecturer and will argue the case for or against the featured game/mechanic if they disagree with the students who have created it, usually fostering a lively debate.

Recap: Objectives and Motivators – New Examples

Lecture reference: slides 4–6

Let's have a quick recap of some of the examples of **Objectives and Motivators** from last week's lecture, using student examples from the in-class exercise. Before we start, let's take a look at a couple of additional objectives to give you an idea of the variety available within games:

FIGURE 4.2   Illustration by Andrew Thornton.

Objectives and Motivators: "Rapid Respawn"

If you die and there is a lengthy respawn time, you'll find player engagement waning – certainly much more of an issue in the "dark ages" (see Box 4.1) of gaming before the proliferation of solid state drives and super powered CPUs and GPUs, but there are still some modern culprits that will keep you waiting when you'd prefer to be diving back in to your last autosave. In arcade games, or games with a high frequency of death, players expect to be able to restart almost immediately, or you are in danger of the player dropping the game through frustration. With games like *Limbo* (Playdead, 2010) or (the original) *Resident Evil 4* (Capcom, 2005), despite relatively fast respawns, they also tackle this issue with an interesting (or, depending on how sadistic you are, amusing) animation when you die, utilising this as a reward which somehow makes the death, and consequent reload time, seem not quite so bad.

Box 4.1   The "Dark Ages" of Gaming

With regard to quick loads or respawns in games, I'd refer these people to the confusion and horror on my students' faces when I describe, circa 1982, sitting sweating in front of a screeching tape deck attached to my Sinclair Research ZX Spectrum 48K "home computer" for 15 sanity threatening minutes while waiting for a game to load. This would also involve occasionally squeezing the cassette down in the deck in some misconceived belief I was adjusting the pitch to better improve the chances of it actually working, before finally, 30 seconds before finally loading, invariably the screen would flash to grey, and display the message "R Tape loading error," causing a small but poignant amount of weeping. Before, somewhat optimistically, the 12-year-old version of me would rewind the tape, get my finger in position for squeezing, press play, and start the gruesome process all over again.

FIGURE 4.3   Illustration by Andrew Thornton.

Objectives and Motivators: Blissful Productivity

Lecture reference: slide 7

"Blissful productivity" is a term used by game designer and author Jane McGonigal, particularly in her book "Reality Is Broken: Why Games Make Us Better and How They Can Change the World." (McGonigal, 2011). She describes a version of the "flow state" (Csikszentmihalyi, 1990), discussed in detail within the last lecture, where, through constant feedback and "juiciness" (my terms), the player feels as if they are maximising their productivity, leading to feelings of deeper engagement, fulfilment, and satisfaction. If you look at a game like *Temple Run*, what we might call "juiciness," is effectively the process of being rewarded perpetually; it's a continuous cycle of rewards and progress. As human beings, we're hardwired to want to see clear progress for our endeavours, and "blissful productivity" is a positive reinforcement descriptor term with regard to this feedback being delivered constantly and efficiently. McGonigal argues that the game design principles behind "blissful productivity" could be harnessed (via "Gamification" - see Box 4.2) to make real-world tasks more engaging and meaningful. Regardless, blissful productivity is a very real element of video games, where, as a kind of flipside of "grinding," we can often find ourselves in a loop of collecting rewards that have no real meaning within the game world, famously satirised by author and developer Ian Bogost in his "game," *Cow Clicker* (Bogost, 2010). This "joke that became a viral" game has now spawned its own genre, often referred to as "clicker" or "idle" games. In this case, I'm not sure if the last laugh is on the players or Bogost.

Box 4.2   "Gamification"

Gamification describes the application of game design principles and systems, such as point scoring, leaderboards, and competition, to non-game contexts like websites, product marketing, education, and workplace productivity, with the aim of making tasks more enjoyable and rewarding. Somewhat of a "buzzword" in the early twenty-tens, it became big business at the time, sought out by many companies as a miracle technique for snagging new demographics, loyalty, and re-engagement for their products or services. The term itself has fallen out of favour in recent years mostly due to the fact that almost everything we now use on a daily basis contains some form of game design elements, from points on your supermarket loyalty card to XP points and a smiling face on your toothbrush for brushing correctly (see game designer, author and educator Jesse Schell for his prescient, and highly amusing, description of many predicted gamification processes we now take for granted).[2]

Recap: Objectives and Motivators – Taught Examples

Lecture reference: slides 8–9

Now, before looking at the student examples from last week's working class, let's have a look at some of the examples from last week as a reminder.

SUBQUESTS

Too many choices causes confusion, too few causes frustration. Ideally allow the player a variety of graded options for downtime or extra XP.

COMPLETIONIST

The players desire to "rinse" the game for all content

FIGURE 4.4   Illustration by Andrew Thornton.

Here are some of our objectives – not an exhaustive list, but some examples, such as "sub-quests," describing how if you're overwhelmed with the main quest, you can wander off and take on some smaller ones to keep you playing and engaged with the game, and "Completionist," the itch some players find themselves having to scratch by cleaning out every corner of the map of collectibles, achievements, sub quests, secret areas, plot, and whatever else may be required by the game to afford a perfect score or rating.

Notes for Educator

NOTE: To further expand this exercise, cover the title of the example card while tasking the class with guessing what it may be (as per Figure 4.5.)

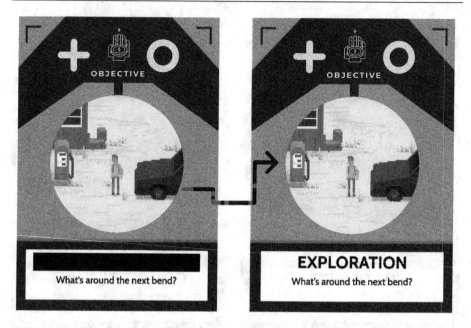

FIGURE 4.5   Illustration by Andrew Thornton and Stuart Atkinson.

Now let's drill down, examine and discuss some of your own examples from last week's exercise.

(**Please note**, in the absence of actual student examples from last week's working class, illustrations representing games/techniques have been used instead.)

IN CLASS EXERCISE 4.1

Lecture reference: slides 10–11
Recap discussion: Objectives and Motivators
Question:
      Are you able to identify the possible Objectives and/or Motivator from the following game/image?
(**Discuss**)

Example 1: TRIALS HD (RedLynx, 2009)

FIGURE 4.6   Illustration by Jack Hollick.

EXERCISE 4.1 ANSWER

"Rapid Respawn"

As per the example *Super Meat Boy* objective/Motivator discussed at the start of the lecture, when you die and have a super quick respawn, you're not only finding amusement in the way your character dies (the reward) but also can carry on from where you left off within seconds.

IN CLASS EXERCISE 4.2

Lecture reference: slides 12–13
Recap discussion: Objectives and Motivators
Question:
   Are you able to identify the possible Objectives and/or Motivator from the following game/image?
(Discuss)

Example 2: Assassin's Creed: Unity (Ubisoft, 2014)

FIGURE 4.7   Illustration by Jack Hollick.

EXERCISE 4.2 ANSWER

"Sub Quests"

This illustration depicts some of the perceived issues with *Assassin's Creed Unity*, which faced backlash due to bugs upon its initial release, e.g. characters involved in vigorous conversations with floating eyeballs and/or teeth due to the rest of the model not loading, etc. I'd suggest this didn't impact the core gameplay systems, which were as robust as any of the preceding Assassin's Creed games, but one change that was not welcomed was the increase in quests and "busy work," which leave the player with quite a hectic and confusing looking map.[3] This is certainly one of those cases where the map can intimidate and overwhelm. In fact, when playing the game, it is often quite difficult to locate yourself as a player on the map due to the number of icons, and there are additional issues with attempting to work out where the next step in your main quest, or critical path lies. In this example, we can refer back to the game design component "Teaching," and particularly the element of "chunking" – overwhelming the player with too many options confuses and demotivates – although in the case of *Unity*, the frequency of running into a new sub-quest every 30 or so seconds can still motivate by tapping into our inherent urge to collect[4] and "tidy" – you try to mop up quests in an effort to clean up the confusion of the map. This element failed to some degree in later games such as *Assassin's Creed Odyssey* (Ubisoft, 2018) due to the map approximating the terrifying size of the entirety of Greece. This overabundance of content is part and parcel of the triple A "content race" at the time,[5] where the larger publishers felt that more content would make a game more appealing to the player. In more recent games in the series, such as *Assassin's Creed Mirage*, Ubisoft has sensibly scaled this back to less busy work and more prominent, carefully "chunked" subquests to guide the player through the content.

IN CLASS EXERCISE 4.3

Lecture reference: slides 14–15
Recap discussion: Objectives and Motivators
Question:
    Are you able to identify the Objectives and/or Motivator from the following game/image?
(Discuss)

Example 3: *Skyrim* (Bethesda Game Studios, 2011)

FIGURE 4.8   Illustration by Shutterstock/Vector Radiance.

EXERCISE 4.3 ANSWER

"Exploration"

Skyrim uses exploration as a motivator – you're looking at a mountain or a tower in the distance, and there are gameplay benefits associated with exploring and reaching these objectives. The mountain may offer distant views of settlements and further objectives, and the tower in the middle distance might involve conflict resulting in XP, which leads to avatar improvement, more skills, and game progression. So, you'll be heading towards these, and in the process, progressing deeper into the game. The landscape itself motivates you to keep playing.

IN CLASS EXERCISE 4.4

Lecture reference: slides 16–17
Recap discussion: Objectives and Motivators
Question:
    Are you able to identify the Objectives and/or Motivator from the following game/image?
(Discuss)

Example 4: The Last of Us (Naughty Dog, 2013)

FIGURE 4.9   Illustration by Shutterstock/HappySloth.

EXERCISE 4.4 ANSWER

"Storyline"

So, this is *The Last of Us*. Many people have talked about this being one of the most coherent and well-written plots or narratives in games – which was reworked as a popular TV series (Mazin & Druckmann, 2023). I say "reworked" because not only the main characters, but many minor characters were fleshed out to give it a little more depth, and indeed, one of the more popular episodes, "Long Long Time"[6] focused specifically on characters other than Joel or Ellie, in this case, the gay couple Bill and Frank, showcasing a gentle and life-affirming relationship, and their character arcs over the duration of an episode, in a break from the "core narrative" which could have been very difficult to create within a game (although Naughty Dog, did, to some degree attempt this with the 2014 DLC *The Last of Us: Left Behind*). From a game perspective, the narrative of *The Last of Us* is gripping and well written, and beautifully paced over its duration, the narrative twists and tight plotting feeding directly into gameplay forming a very clear motivator for the player. Although I'd suggest the scriptwriters at Naughty Dog aren't always as frugal, sometimes extending plots well beyond the purposes of gameplay: See the extensive "patting the dog" beach scene from the end of *Uncharted 4: A Thief's End* (Naughty Dog, 2016).

IN CLASS EXERCISE 4.5

Lecture reference: slides 18–19
Recap discussion: Objectives and Motivators
Question:
    Are you able to identify the Objectives and/or Motivator from the following game clip?

EXERCISE 4.5 VIDEO LINK

Lecture reference: slides 18–19
    Example 5: A Way Out (Hazelight Studios, 2018)
    https://bit.ly/EX4_5_AWAY

EXERCISE 4.5 ANSWER

"A Friend in Need" – Supportive Co-Op

A Way Out is an excellent example of a cooperative game that fully exploits the advantages of couch co-op, i.e., sitting next to the person you are playing with. The game director, Josef Fares, further advanced this design with the studio's next title,

It Takes Two (Hazelight Studios, 2021), which really highlights the joy of playing games together within a proximity space. You both play together sometimes in split screen, with a lot of synchronised and mimetic tasks to perform together, resulting in a hugely entertaining experience through emergent interactions, and also, in many cases, due to watching the person next to you performing ridiculous movements or tasks. Having a friend in close proximity again taps into a strong sense of teamwork and peer review which motivates and keeps you playing. Co-op or supportive multi-player is frequently a strong motivator in itself and, considering how effective it is, is used surprisingly rarely.

IN CLASS EXERCISE 4.6

Lecture reference: slides 20–21
Recap discussion: Objectives and Motivators
Question:
    Are you able to identify the Objectives and/or Motivator from the following game/image?
(Discuss)

Example 6: Fortnite (Epic Games, 2017)

FIGURE 4.10   Illustration by Jack Hollick.

EXERCISE 4.6 ANSWER

Swag (or "Gear" or "Bling" or "Drip" or "Shinies" – See Box 4.3)

It's hard to say what terminology your class will be using for avatar outfits and cosmetics on the particular day you teach this, but one of the motivators in playing some of the less serious, leaderboard-based multiplayer games is *showing off*. *Fortnite* is very much about peer review; you want other players to see your bling, your outfit, and any rare or unique items you may have. Obviously, there are several game strategies that need to be employed to actually *win*, but a huge part of the game, I'd even suggest one of the pillars, is players running about in these ridiculous costumes. This is part of the fun of showing off – seeing who's got the funniest or coolest costume. With your own chosen gear or look, there's also a huge element of personalisation, ownership and instilling a sense of identity in your character. This can be further emphasised with updated skins or cosmetics, or the various seasonal or time-sensitive items that are released, not to mention specific items from collaborations with current, trending, cultural icons to add to your kudos.

Box 4.3   Video Game Slang & Lexicon: Skins and Cosmetics

Video game slang evolves as quickly as the industry it is based around, and even attempting to pen some of the most current examples will end up with them being outdated (or, as we might have said back in the noughties, "old skool") before the ink dries on the page. Terms for skins and cosmetics follow this pattern, and it's interesting to examine the timelines of how some of these terms and systems have evolved. From the late 1990s, across games such as the *Quake* series (id Software, 1996–2000), players began to alter the appearance of texture files on characters and game objects (e.g., guns) to change appearances. These became known as "skins," which evolved during the 2000s in games such as *World of Warcraft*, where cosmetic items were designed into the game, often to showcase unique achievements or status, with some items categorised by rarity levels such as "Legendary" or "Epic." Moving through to the twenty-tens, these items were monetised in games such as *Team Fortress 2* (Valve Corporation, 2007) and *League of Legends* (Riot Games, 2009), where skins and cosmetic items could be purchased directly. And through to the current mainstream popularity of character customisation, where skins and cosmetic items are now deeply embedded in the culture of games such as *Fortnite* and *Overwatch*, with myriad terms for these cosmetic items, e.g., Drip, Bling, Swag, Flex (Nature, 2022), and their applications, e.g., "skin flexing," "decked out," and "OG skins" (Dev & Ayers, 2023), are expanding at an almost exponential rate. (Apologies to anyone reading this boxout currently cringing at my inclusion of slang terminology that may already seem horrifically archaic.)

After that comprehensive recap, let's now move on to our regular introductory exercise – "USP Corner!"

IN CLASS EXERCISE 4.7: USP CORNER!

Lecture reference: slide 23
Game Video Discussion: Unique Selling Points
Question:
    Try to identify one (or more) unique selling points in the following video clips. Imagine you are pitching them to a publisher and need a hook to reel them in!

EXERCISE 4.7 VIDEO LINK

Example 1: Outer Wilds (Mobius Digital, 2019).
    https://bit.ly/EX4_7_WILD

FIGURE 4.11 Illustration by Jack Hollick.

EXERCISE 4.7 EXAMPLE 1 ANSWER

The "20-Minute Life Cycle"

It's quite hard to work out the USP from such a brief trailer, but I'd suggest the USP in this case is the 20-minute play cycle. It's a world where the sun goes supernova every

20 minutes and then it resets (with the player respawning), but everything remains intact as the player left it, hence it being known, in game terms, as a "persistent world." Perhaps also a bit of an early *Minecraft* vibe here, as, with *Minecraft* in its infancy before it became the world-dominating game we know now, the initial players really didn't have much idea what they were supposed to do, and crafting was effectively a dark art. Similarly, with *Outer Wilds*, it's very much a case of working everything out for yourself – i.e., from a game perspective, you begin to realise that you're exploring worlds but also discovering how these worlds work, so it's really a huge voyage of discovery. You're choosing your own route through the game, making up your own rules and then gradually piecing together a giant jigsaw to understand exactly what the objectives are. It emerged from a gamejam, and as we've discussed previously, the pressure of game jams often brings interesting core mechanics, with the aim of them being fully playable within the short time provided. Very much like a geological era over aeons, where enormous pressure creates a rough-hewn diamond at the centre of a hunk of coal. The (only) difference here is that the "geological era" usually spans 24 hours, and the "diamond," in this case, is a game mechanic. (Watches tumbleweed rolling across classroom.)

EXERCISE 4.7 (USP CORNER!) VIDEO LINK 2

Lecture reference: slide 24
   Example 2: Minit. (Vlambeer, 2018)
   https://bit.ly/EX4_7_MINT

FIGURE 4.12   Illustration by Andrew Thornton.

EXERCISE 4.7 EXAMPLE 2 ANSWER

The "60 Second Life Cycle"

Are you noticing a trend? In *Minit,* each gameplay session only lasts 60 seconds before the player dies and respawns. In these one-minute play loops, the player must explore, gather items, speak to NPC's, fight enemies, and solve puzzles. Again, in this race against time, and as with *Outer Wilds,* the world is persistent, although, in a concession to making the map larger than the small start area, various checkpoints allow the player to progress without having to start from the beginning location each time they reset. This allows the player to gradually piece together objectives and rewards that lead towards completion in tiny, bite-sized chunks.

And now back to the main event!

SECTION 4.1: WHAT IS A GAME MECHANIC?

Lecture reference: slide 25

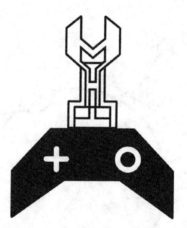

FIGURE 4.13   The Mechanics Game component. Illustration by Andrew Thornton.

Let's have a look at the core focus of this chapter – what a game mechanic is. Regarding the objective-challenge-reward cycle, the question really is: Where does the game mechanic fit in? The answer, really, is "anywhere you want it to." This is because mechanics can cover any of the game components. During the lecture we'll look at different definitions of what game mechanics are and examples of where they fit into gameplay. So, let's get started.

What is a Game Mechanic (1)?

Lecture reference: slide 26

Definition one (in no particular order):
Game mechanics are rule based systems/simulations that facilitate and encourage a
user to explore and learn the properties of their possibility space through the use of
feedback mechanisms (Sicart, 2008).

So that's one rather complex academic description of what game mechanics are,
notably mentioning *"through the use of feedback mechanisms."* This is important, as in
the majority of cases, for a mechanic to be recognised by the player, there needs to be
some form of in-game feedback (see Box 4.4) provided.

Box 4.4   Positive and Negative Feedback

In our previous boxout (Chapter 1, Box 1.1, Progression and Feedback), we discussed
how feedback such as visuals, sound, and haptics is a hugely important element
of Game Design. It provides the player with information about their performance,
allowing them to build on successes and correct mistakes. With that in mind, let's
look at some examples:

In *Super Mario Bros* (Nintendo, 1985), when Mario collects a coin, the coin
disappears with a sound effect, and the score increases. This is both visual and
auditory, providing positive reinforcement feedback that tells the player, "This is
correct – you're doing well." Conversely, feedback from Mario being hit by a Goomba
involves him spinning and dropping off the screen with a downward-pitched sound
effect and loss of a life – this is negative reinforcement feedback telling the player,
"This is bad – be more wary of these Goombas." In *Call of Duty: Modern* Warfare
(Infinity Ward, 2019) positive reinforcement includes feedback with a sound and
animation (of impact) when hitting an enemy with a weapon, as well as score feedback and on-screen messages (dependent on mode). Negative reinforcement feedback involves the sharp sound of an enemy shot, leading to a red flash around the
screen edges, and the haptic feedback of the controller vibrating, telling the player,
"You've been shot!" Another interesting example of haptic feedback, is in the *Forza
Horizon* racing series (Playground Games, 2012–2022) which uses haptic feedback
to simulate different terrains – but in keeping with the constant reward cycle of
that series of games, it steers more towards guidance as opposed to true negative
reinforcement, used outside of actual race situations to increase the "realness"
of the environment you are crashing through. On a side note, if you'd told your
co-designers in the nineties about an idea for a racing game where you got skill
bonuses and points for crashing your supercar repeatedly through stone walls at
140 MPH, they'd probably suggest (1) probably not telling the boss about it, and (2)
a holiday (effective immediately).

SECTION 4.2: GAMING – A (RELATIVELY) NEW MEDIUM

Lecture reference: slide 27

Gaming is a (relatively) new creative medium, and it follows that it is also a new academic field for study. Whereas film began to find its footing in the early 1900s with seminal works like *The Cabinet of Dr. Caligari* (Wiene, 1920) and *The Jazz Singer* (Crosland, A., 1927), video games only really began to find a commercial foothold in the early 1970s with games such as *Pong* (Atari, 1972) and *Space Invaders* (Taito, 1978). As such, with a 70-year head start, film studies have been firmly rooted as part of academic curricula since at least the mid-20th century, gaining a foothold in universities and influencing areas such as cultural studies, psychology, and sociology. Conversely, although with some notable examples in the 1980s such as early positive cultural studies such as *The Second Self: Computers and the Human Spirit* (Turkle, 1984), the academic study of video games didn't really start gaining traction until concerns over video game violence and gaming aggression prompted studies such as *Video Games and Aggressive Thoughts, Feelings, and Behaviour in the Laboratory and in Life* by Craig A. Anderson and Karen E. Dill, published in 2000. In more recent times, games and their positive effects (other than the odd loot box hiccup) have thankfully been recognised as a legitimate field of study, and although perhaps not quite as broad in its range as film, games are catching up quickly with research focused on areas like gaming culture, the psychology of gaming, educational use of games, and, most importantly from the perspective of this book, game design and its effect on players.

Let's have a look at an example of some of this new game design research, with some influential game designers attempting to put together a new taxonomy or lexicon of game design with **mechanics** as one of the core three pillars. As discussed in the previous chapter on motivation, we are only just beginning to understand the complex psychological processes that playing games utilise. I'll reference some of these important research resources as we move through the lecture, but in the meantime, let's have a look at the "Mechanics, Dynamics, Aesthetics (MDA) Approach" as created by three prominent game developers, programmers, and game theory focused academics: Robin Hunicke, Marc LeBlanc, and Robert Zubek.

MDA: A Formal Approach to Game Design and Game Research

Lecture reference: Slide 28

The MDA approach (Hunicke, LeBlanc & Zubek, 2004) is an early effort to clarify and standardise game terminology into a widely recognised and accepted lexicon – an admirable goal. To cite the authors "MDA is a formal approach to understanding games – one which attempts to bridge the gap between game design and development, game criticism, and technical game research. We believe this methodology will clarify and strengthen the iterative processes of developers, scholars and researchers alike, making it easier for all parties to decompose, study and design a broad class of game designs and game artifacts." Papers such as this are necessary, as you'll see that the way games are designed does not neatly fit into the usual structure of established design techniques and common methodologies. For example, the widely used "Double Diamond technique" (Council, B.D., 2005), created by the British Design Council in an effort to structure the creative process, and although used across various design disciplines such as product, graphic, and interior, it could be argued it falls short in addressing the comprehensive and diverse elements involved in game design – a unique field that by its nature inherently integrates elements from various disciplines including film, audio, and narrative. And, most importantly (lest we forget), through direct player or user interaction, Game Design necessitates an understanding of constant and adaptive behavioural or psychological player facing elements that must be built into the design from the ground up.

It should be noted that since the introduction of the MDA (Mechanics, Dynamics, Aesthetics) framework, there have been several significant advancements in game theory, such as recent research into as the aforementioned psychological and behavioural studies based around research into Player Experience Modelling (for an example, see endnote here[7]).

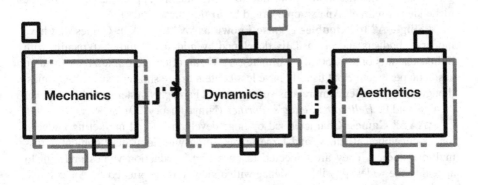

FIGURE 4.14   Illustration by Andrew Thornton.

As we see from Figure 4.14, at the core of the MDA framework is breaking down the components of "rules," "systems," and "fun" and translating them into the game design terms "Mechanics, Dynamics, and Aesthetics" – and so, with that, we have another definition to add to our list.

What is a Game Mechanic (2)?

Lecture reference: slide 29

Definition two:
"The particular components of the game, at the level of data representation and algorithms." (Hunicke, LeBlanc & Zubek, 2004)

Does that help from the perspective of designing mechanics into our games? Perhaps if we explain the further elements in the system, and how one leads into the other –

Dynamics "Describes the run-time behaviour of the mechanics acting on player inputs and each other's outputs over time."

Aesthetics "Describes the desirable emotional responses evoked in the player, when she interacts with the game system."

Using this system, we now have a benchmark for how mechanics drive gameplay ("Dynamics") and the emotional experience within the player. For example, if our mechanics are designed around stealth, i.e., hiding or moving silently – then the Dynamics become the run-time function of the opponents – perhaps not getting out of line of sight in time, means a guard breaks from patrol to investigate, creating the emotions of suspense and anticipation in the player.

Now let's look at the importance of mechanics across game "tiers" (see Box 4.5):

Box 4.5   Game Production "Tiers"

Although there are some arguments over the specificity of these terms, briefly:

"Indie": Typically developed by individuals or small teams with limited budgets, these games often stand out due to their "auteur" approach, i.e., a specific niche idea or market. An example would be *Braid* (Blow, 2008.)

"Single-A" to "Double-A" (also known as "A" to "AA"): Games that have moderate budgets and are usually developed by mid-sized studios, typically with in-house teams of 30–250 (my estimate). "AA" can often seem like AAA from an aesthetic perspective but usually have less content or are shorter than AAA games, though they still offer comprehensive and myriad gameplay systems. An example of "AA" would be *Hellblade: Senua's sacrifice* (Ninja Theory, 2017.)

"AAA" Games: Characterised by huge development and marketing budgets, longer development times, and large teams, often with joint development across multiple studios. They are expected to have high production values and aim to appeal to the widest possible audience with a view to recouping costs. An example would be *Marvel's Spider-Man 2* (Insomniac Games, 2023.)

As a rule, these terms or "tiers" are usually utilised as a guide for budgets and team sizes (that affect development time) for the "money men" – the publishers and producers who must budget and/or schedule the game production. There is as much discussion about the origin of these terms as there is irritation among developers when their games are branded with them,[8] particularly in the case of "triple A" due to the enormous pressure on the team to deliver a hit, usually due to the astronomical budgets that the company must recoup to stay afloat.

Not that we saw much of this in the nascent days of "AAA," on the original *Tomb Raider* series. Without the ridiculously comprehensive minutiae of planning, tracking, and Sprint "ownership" processes involved in current game development, if, during crunch, it looked like we wouldn't make the allocated deadline date for the design/art/puzzles for our levels, a quick design team huddle would usually conclude in plans for some hasty and extensive level "pruning."

For a more up-to-date (and sensible) reflection on these processes, see *"Blood, Sweat, and Pixels: The Triumphant, Turbulent Stories Behind How Video Games Are Made"* by Jason Schreier.

NOTE: It should also be noted, at the time of writing, that the term "**Triple I**" (for triple indie) is currently being touted, particularly with the release of promotional materials from the indie super team behind the "Triple I Initiative" (2024).

SECTION 4.3: GAME MECHANIC TAXONOMIES 1

Lecture reference: slides 30–31

"INDIE"
Signature feature: One USP mechanic (usually quirky) as the core concept
From a mechanics perspective, usually, if you have an indie game, in many cases I'd suggest there will be one unique selling point (USP) mechanic as the core concept. Let's look at some examples:

Example 1: Donut County (Esposito, 2018)

Lecture reference: slide 32

EXAMPLE 1 VIDEO LINK

https://bit.ly/EX4_1_DONUT

FIGURE 4.15   Illustration by Jack Hollick.

The core mechanic of *Donut County* is an ever-increasing hole that you feed items, and eventually the environment, into – increasing in size with everything that you feed in. It's a very clear and quirky mechanic that can be explained in a sentence, or even a single image – fantastic from the perspective of immediately understanding what the game is about. There have been some comments regarding this effectively being an "inverse *Katamari Damacy.*" *Katamari Damacy* (Namco, 2004) being the relatively unhinged game (if there was a USP for control schemes, this would certainly take a prize) where you roll a ball around collecting more and more debris and detritus, the ball getting bigger and bigger with each new item collected, until you end up absorbing planets and galaxies.[9]

I would suggest that flipping mechanics like this is a perfectly valid way of designing core or secondary mechanics into your game. I would suggest, as Derek Thompson argues in his book *Hit Makers: The Science of Popularity in an Age of Distraction* (2017), that this element of familiarity mixed with the new makes this more acceptable from a gamer perspective. Thompson argues that the most successful products and ideas are those that are balanced between "newness" and familiarity, adding just enough "novelty" to be interesting without straying too far from what people already know and like (Thompson, 2017).

Example 2: *Monument Valley* (Ustwo Games, 2014)

Lecture reference: slide 33

EXAMPLE 2 VIDEO LINK

https://bit.ly/EX4_2_MONU

FIGURE 4.16   Illustration by Jack Hollick.

In the example of *Monument Valley*, I would suggest the core mechanic is the way the player character interacts with the unnatural architecture that doesn't adhere to the normal laws of reality. This is carefully managed from a puzzle mechanic perspective with an isometric view and a camera that allows only for a 90-degree rotation as the character moves around the environment. Perhaps this is not a unique selling point (USP) mechanic, as it is similar to the mechanics of another early title, *Echochrome* (SCE, 2008), both of which, I would suggest, are heavily influenced by the artwork of the surrealist artist Escher. This also highlights that if you're able to "borrow" or create a unique art style as a hook, this will only help your chances of attracting players (or indeed publishers).[10]

Let's move on to an exercise:

IN CLASS EXERCISE 4.8: "INDIE" MECHANICS

Game Video Discussion: Game Mechanics
Question
What do you think is the "one simple, quirky indie mechanic" in the following clips?
(**Discuss**)

EXERCISE 4.8 EXAMPLE 1

The Swapper (Facepalm games, 2013)

Lecture reference: slide 34

FIGURE 4.17 The Swapper – by Olli Harjola, Otto Hantula, Tom Jubert & Carlo Castellano – http://theswappergame.com/, CC BY-SA 3.0 (The Swapper – by Olli Harjola, Otto Hantula, Tom Jubert & Carlo Castellano – http://theswappergame.com/, CC BY-SA 3.0 <https://creativecommons.org/licenses/by-sa/3.0>, via Wikimedia Commons).

EXERCISE 4.8 EXAMPLE 1 ANSWER

The answer here is the mechanic that you are able to replicate yourself to perform tasks – is it time travel? We may never know – but it's certainly a quirky selling point for the game, and facilitates complex puzzles where you must, quite literally, be in two places at the same time. I say "selling point" as opposed to "Unique selling point," as, for other good indie examples of similar mechanics, see *Braid* (Number None, 2008), and *The Misadventures of P.B. Winterbottom* (The Odd Gentlemen, 2010).

EXERCISE 4.8 EXAMPLE 2

Echo (Ultra Ultra, 2017)

Lecture reference: slide 35

FIGURE 4.18   Illustration by Shutterstock/Gorodenkoff.

EXAMPLE 2 VIDEO LINK

https://bit.ly/EX4_9_ECHO

EXERCISE 4.8 EXAMPLE 2 ANSWER

This is a fascinating concept and USP (and in this case, I believe the "U" in "USP" really *is* unique), and I think they've explained this unique mechanic very clearly in the trailer. The interesting and unique twist here is that instead of the replicating mechanic supporting the player and their progression, the replication becomes the challenge in the gameplay loop. The replicated version of the player learns their bad habits and violent nature (if that's the way the player chooses to play) and replicates them, so you are effectively fighting against yourself. Another intriguing question might be, "How did such a small team create such a polished-looking game?". This is essentially an indie game (or what might now be called "Triple I") – and other than the fact that the small team previously worked at IO Interactive and had a lot of experience developing games, I'd suggest the other hugely important element here to get this game shipped with such a small team is some very clever level design. (See Box 4.6 "The Cube Effect")

The main play area is effectively a (very Kubrick-esque, "*2001*" looking) maze, and there's a reason for it being so deliberately repetitive. That's because it's been designed as a modular environment. With a modular environment where you have repeating, snappable elements of geometry. From a level design perspective, if the artist has created these elements during pre-production (e.g., wall section, pillar section, plinth, door section), the designer has everything they need to create very large chunks of level design in a very short amount of time. In this case, the level designer basically has a snappable palace at their fingertips. One of the only downsides to this is that if you're not careful, the repetition means it may be much more confusing for the player to orient themselves. A solution here is to place unique visual orientation points at regular intervals, or perhaps to have a clear directional guidance mechanic (see *Dead Space*). Although the game does actively corral you in the correct direction, despite being hugely impressed by it, I do remember while playing *Echo* that I was never quite sure where I was going.

Box 4.6   The Cube Effect

Back in the B.I. Period (Before Indie) in games, there was a highly excitable period within the film industry where the low price and accessibility of cameras allowed what were effectively guerrilla filmmakers to break through into the mainstream. Some prominent examples of this were the filmmaker Stephen Soderbergh using low-cost domestic video cameras to create the hit *Sex, Lies, and Videotape* (Soderbergh, 1989), and around the same time Robert Rodriguez, bursting out of the confines of indie film constraints with the hit film *El Mariachi* (1992 – later remade), the making of which is described in detail in his book *Rebel without a crew* (1996). One of the core elements of this type of filmmaking was cost – some filmmakers started to realise that creating a script around one location or set was a key aspect of getting a film made. One of the key proponents of this theory was the film *Cube* (Natali, 1997), a genre-defining moment for sci-fi horror. A group of unsuspecting victims finds themselves sealed in a mysterious set of linked cubic "cells," their eventual objective to work out why they are there, with the micro-objective of trying to escape the traps in each of these rooms, one at a time. Sounds like a game, right? The genius here is that from a set design (hence budget) perspective, all the cells look the same. Adjust the cell number decals and the colour of the lighting, and bingo! You've suddenly got a vast set, hundreds of cells, all for the price of one. Transposing this into game development this modular approach and reuse of limited assets around a core concept or mechanic can allow solo developers or small teams to create games that would normally require much larger teams. A couple of notable examples of this development technique are the original *Portal* (Valve Corporation, 2007) perhaps the definitive example of single room design based around a small set of complex but clearly explained core mechanics, developed with a team of "less than a dozen people" (Reeves, 2010). In a later variant on the single room/core mechanics, the technically accomplished game *Q.U.B.E* (Toxic Games, 2011) was developed by a core team of three.

As a side note, from my own experience in teaching, what I felt was once a relatively sensible suggestion to direct students/indie developers toward more "single room" mechanic-focused games, where one simple set of assets could be reused to minimise art and level design necessities, the current proliferation of free online assets now has changed the playing field towards "managing expectations." Just because you're able to download a procedural map the size of *Skyrim* with associated shiny atmospheric effects – unfortunately doesn't mean that for a one-person 12-week assignment, you're actually going to be able to make the game *Skyrim*. (although many of my students have tried!)

EXERCISE 4.8 EXAMPLE 3

Fru (Through Games, 2016)

Lecture reference: slide 36

FIGURE 4.19   Illustration by Shutterstock/Zyabich family.

EXAMPLE 3 VIDEO LINK

https://bit.ly/EX4_83_FRU

EXERCISE 4.8 EXAMPLE 3 ANSWER

This game, created by some of our ex-students at IGAD/University of Breda,[11] was designed specifically for the Xbox Kinect. The Kinect device, although released in 2013 at the launch of the Xbox One, had yet to really find its "killer app." *Fru* to some degree, scratched that itch. It has a super simple mechanic, which you can immediately understand from just a screenshot, a quirky title, looks like a great party game, and most importantly – lag, the biggest problem cited by the games press around the Kinect, wouldn't impact the gameplay, which revolved around physically moving to reveal the play area. The unfortunate downside is that by the time the game was released, general gamer backlash against the Kinect had removed it as a mandatory element of the Xbox bundle and begun to reduce it to what was seen as somewhat of an embarrassing misstep in the history of the Xbox console.

Just to note, the game *Fru* actually came out of an internal gamejam at the university and was spotted and picked up by Microsoft at that event. This is a simple example of the power of the clarity of a simple, playable, unique mechanic.

EXERCISE 4.8 EXAMPLE 4

Black Planet (Alex Camilleri, 2012)

Lecture reference: slide 37

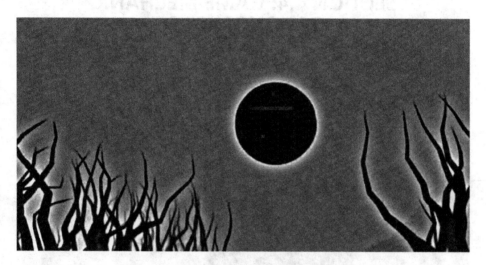

FIGURE 4.20   "Black Planet" gameplay and graphics by Alex Camilleri.

EXAMPLE 4 VIDEO LINK

https://bit.ly/EX4_8_BLAK

EXERCISE 4.8 EXAMPLE 4 ANSWER

Alex Camilleri, another of our ex-IGAD/University of Breda Game Design students, currently Lead Game Designer at Embark Studio, after graduating with flying colours moved on to working as Level Designer, System Designer, and Gameplay Programmer on Amnesia: Rebirth (Frictional Games, 2020) – and you can see why he was a good fit if we look at this mechanic from one of Alex's first-year game assignments at IGAD, with Alex's explanation. Another very clear mechanic and art style, both of which I'd argue are USPs. Basically, if you're outside and exposed, the black planet increases in size. If you're inside and hidden, the black planet starts to shrink down again; otherwise, it envelops the entire world, which is something you probably don't want to happen. This is a clear horror mechanic that also has the "curiosity" hook of wanting to play it – what happens when the black planet envelops the environment? A title that has recently utilised a similar mechanic is *The Eternal Cylinder* (ACE Team, 2020), in which a vast cylinder gradually envelops an entire alien world, destroying everything on it. Probably not one to play if you need cheering up after a bad day.

SECTION 4.4: GAME MECHANIC TAXONOMIES 2

"A" to "TRIPLE A"

Lecture reference: slides 38–39
We've had a look at how indie game designers can use mechanics as a core pillar, USP, or "hook" to support their game. Now let's have a look at how bigger games incorporate their mechanics.

FIGURE 4.21   Illustration by Shutterstock/camilkuo.

A to Triple A (AAA) licenses invariably provide designers with a set of pre-formed player mechanics. So, if you land a job at Ubisoft, Guerrilla, or another big Triple A studio, or even any of the slightly larger studios that work in the A to AA space (a company such as, at time of writing, Ninja Theory), and you're moving onto an existing franchise or a game in progress, they'll almost certainly give you a set of preformed mechanics. Let's look a brief example – the double assassination in the *Assassin's Creed* games, part of the combat system, more specifically Melee combat. The parkour and combat in *Assassin's Creed* are two of the core game systems (see Box 4.7),[12] as well as systems such as stealth and exploration, involving mechanics such as the classic Ubisoft synchronisation points which unlock P.O.I. on the map.

Box 4.7   Game Systems

Game "systems" really define the "possibility space" (Salen & Zimmerman, 2004), agency, and affordances within a specific part of your game. The rules, mechanics, and dynamics (how the mechanic reacts to player input at runtime) of a particular system define how it fits into the game and how it interacts with other systems or mechanics, again, referencing the MDA approach, (Hunicke, LeBlanc & Zubek, 2004). Let's look at an example system – the stealth system in *Assassin's Creed 2*. This system contains a wide subset of rules, mechanics, and dynamics. Let's have a closer look.

SYSTEM RULE – LINE OF SIGHT:

If an enemy spots you, it will usually trigger the various mechanics of a "search" state. The dynamics of the outcome of this situation depend on whether the player can break the line of sight by dodging, hiding, or even killing the enemy (which would involve engaging the combat system).

SYSTEM MECHANIC – BLEND IN:

This is a more specific way of avoiding detection. Moving into groups or crowds (that litter the streets) or sitting on a bench between NPCs will allow you to become less noticeable. From a dynamics perspective, you may have to carefully follow or move with the group to stay unnoticed.

SYSTEM MECHANIC – CROUCHING/WALKING:

Slowing your speed of movement also reduces noise. From a runtime/dynamics perspective, you must manage your distances – get too close and you will be heard, which will activate either line of sight or combat systems.

SYSTEM MECHANIC – DISTRACTION:

In some of the *Assassin's Creed* games, players are able to pick up and throw objects to distract enemies. Again, runtime dynamics here are based around how many throwable items you have, and areas you want to distract the enemy to – divert them to the wrong area and they may move to a search state, or you may simply run out of items.

It should be noted, if this all seems a little too close to triggering a cerebral aneurysm, that the complex game systems described above developed over a long period of time and were tweaked over the series, with elements being added, removed, or adjusted, depending not only on designer input, but (I assume) QA and player feedback. As a designer within a team on a larger game, you will rarely be tasked with an entire game system – the "micro" elements or mechanics contained within (or a subset of) the "macro" game systems are what you would usually be working with on a day-to-day basis as a designer within these franchises.

Mechanics: A to Triple A — Iteration, Iteration, Iteration!

Iterating on provided mechanics is essentially the day-to-day job of a designer on a franchise title. There are usually a huge number of interrelated systems and mechanics in triple-A franchises, and you'll need to iterate around them. For example, in something like the traversal system in a game like the original *Tomb Raider* series (yes, a six-to-eight-person core team making a game in a year was once perceived as "AAA"), you'll be working with very specific distances and metrics that are generally locked down from early prototypes – or in our case, the first *Tomb Raider* game. From an iteration perspective, from *Tomb Raider 2* (Core Design, 1997) onwards, we added to the moveset (crouch, monkey bars, etc.), but as the entire game environment was built around a grid-based metric system of blocks that the game logic and animations were fixed to, our metric system was set in stone. However, this lockdown on metrics doesn't always happen. In the GDC presentation "The Tao of Level Design: A Study of 3 AAA Games" (Alphonso, Lehtinen & Silli, 2010), level designer Elisabetta Silli discusses the development of *Mirror's Edge* (DICE, 2008), specifically addressing issues with the analogue nature of the main character, Faith's movement, causing different jump distances at different speeds –i.e., the faster she was moving, the further she jumped. This led to a rethink and some level redesign at a relatively late stage in the development, which, from a time and money perspective, is going to hurt.

Let's move on to an exercise:

IN CLASS EXERCISE 4.9: A – AAA MECHANICS

Lecture reference: slide 40–43
Game Video Discussion: Iterating around provided mechanics
Question

Which TWO CORE mechanics is the following game sequence iterating/ improving/adjusting? And (for extra points) which games were the original mechanics from?

EXERCISE 4.9 EXAMPLE 1

Dead Space (EA Redwood Shores, 2008)

FIGURE 4.22 Dead Space mechanics. Illustration by Jack Hollick.

EXAMPLE 4.9 VIDEO LINK

https://bit.ly/EX4_9_DEAD

EXERCISE 4.9 EXAMPLE 1 ANSWER

"Kinesis" is one of the mechanics here, or at least that's what they're calling it in *Dead Space*, and "Stasis" is another. These are actually quite common mechanics across games, so can we think of the original games these mechanics come from?

FIGURE 4.23   The Gravity gun. Illustration by Jack Hollick.

Mechanic 1: "Kinesis"

"Kinesis" is basically the *Half Life 2* gravity gun. The gravity gun is a device that can pick up objects in the environment and fling them around or manipulate them. Gravity guns, or physics guns, were the flavour of the month for a while, with hundreds of games attempting to shoehorn in this quite unique physics-based weapon.

FIGURE 4.24   The Mechanics Game component. Illustration by Jack Hollick.

Mechanic 2: "Stasis"

"Stasis" involves slowing time down – one of the original examples of that being the early *Max Payne* (Remedy Entertainment, 2001) games, the "bullet time" inspired by Hong Kong action films (Hilliard, 2016), allowing time to be slowed down within combat sequences ideally inspiring "balletic movement" (not that I ever managed that while playing it) while wiping out rooms of enemies John Woo/Matrix style with your double pistol loadout. For another example of balletic slomo, see *Stranglehold* (Midway Games, 2007) a licensed attempt at a direct translation of the John Woo films into a video game. Interestingly, as a side note, John Woo films such as *The Killer* (Woo, 1989) also inspired Toby (Gard) to equip Lara with the iconic dual pistol loadout in the original *Tomb Raider*, with that game being mentioned as an influence on *Max Payne*. Recycle, adjust and adapt, the cycle of creativity!

Mechanics: Less is More!

Lecture reference: slide 44

As we've discussed, showering the player relentlessly with mechanics does not a great game make. Many of the most successful A-AAA games gradually introduce a small but powerful set of mechanics (see Chapter 2: Teaching) – instead of constantly adding them, which can risk overwhelming or demotivating the player. In many cases, this core set can then be combined in a variety of ways to create more complex, deeper gameplay opportunities and player agency. As a general design rule of thumb, I'd suggest attempting to introduce interactions between your existing mechanics before introducing more. A good way of looking at it is that:

A good game should be able to exist on a few clear, basic mechanics, introduced gradually.

Let's look at an example from the classic game *Deux Ex* (Ion Storm, 2000). In the postmortem of the game from the same year, the producer and game director Warren Spector describes his design philosophy:

"Give players a rich but limited tool set that can be used in a variety of ways, not a bunch of individual, unpredictable solutions to every problem."

"Less is more" doesn't mean *don't* add tools and mechanics. It means many of the best games do work around a limited set of tools and mechanics– if you don't need to add more, try to work with what you have – the player will thank you for it.

As an example exercise, let's have a look at some mechanics introduced in the introductory section of *Portal 2*:

IN CLASS EXERCISE 4.10: MECHANICS – "LESS IS MORE"

Lecture reference: slide 45
Game Video Discussion:
Question
 Name the core mechanics featured in the following video clip:

EXERCISE 4.10 EXAMPLE 1

Portal 2 (Valve Corporation, 2011)

FIGURE 4.25   Illustration by Andrew Thornton.

EXAMPLE 4.10 VIDEO LINK

https://bit.ly/EX4_10_PORT

EXERCISE 4.10 EXAMPLE 1 ANSWER

Answer:
So, what's happening in that *Portal 2* example is that they are corralling the player and gating them so that they don't get access to the portal gun immediately. The player is pressing buttons to open the portals, and they have to clearly understand exactly what the portal does before they can exit the room. They have to get the cube and use it on the pressure plate, so when the player exits that room, the designer *knows exactly* what the player has learned: The pressure plate, the button, and in a very basic way, the beginnings of the portal mechanic. A clear example of "less is more" the original *Portal* relies on some very clear mechanics, and its sequel carefully scaffolds these. The portal mechanic is complex, but they're not overburdening the player by adding a new mechanic every level. *Portal 2* does add specific paint mechanics in the second half of the game, like the speed paint and the bounce paint, but again, it's very carefully layered into the game in such a way that the player can scaffold their knowledge gradually.

Mechanics: "Giving Producers Nightmares since 1996"

Speaking of adding mechanics, let's take a look at some mechanic-related buzzwords that producers (see Box 4.8) don't want to hear: "special case," "bespoke," and "feature creep." These three phrases are commonly used in development, and it's really the producer's job to keep on top of these and reign the designers or developers in if they suddenly start inventing new mechanics. These are what, in Kickstarter parlance, are known as "stretch goals." They are usually put onto a thing called a Wishlist, and if the developers have time at the end of development, resources will be allocated to start developing these mechanics. Designers will always come up with lots of new ideas and mechanics, and that's part of the fun of the job – keeping them on a big list (usually hidden from producers, as to not invoke hernia) and then trying to prototype them out when you have a bit of spare time.

Let's have a look at an example of a "Bespoke" mechanic/system.

IN CLASS EXERCISE 4.11: MECHANICS – "BESPOKE"

Lecture reference: slide 47
Game Video Discussion:
Question
  Why would the following sequence be described as "bespoke"?

EXERCISE 4.11 EXAMPLE 1

Grand Theft Auto IV (Rockstar North, 2008)

FIGURE 4.26 Nico Bellic. Illustration by Jack Hollick.

EXAMPLE 4.11 VIDEO LINK

https://bit.ly/EX4_11_GTA4

EXERCISE 4.11 EXAMPLE 1 ANSWER

A hiccup in the game difficulty curve of *GTA 4*, this was an entirely bespoke sequence – and to some degree, they invented an entirely new control system. I've got a feeling (and I can say this because I feel fairly safe Rockstar won't go out of their way to comment) that there were a couple of designers and programmers who had finished a task in the corner of the office, and for a week, they had nothing to do and just kind of prototyped this sequence. They took a small area of the game, independent of the main build, and just fiddled about, trying out mechanics, then took it to the producer, and said, "Can we use this 'rolling about on top of a van' sequence?" It's gone up the chain to one of the Houser's sitting by their pool drinking Pina Coladas, and they've grunted "yes." So, it's gone into the game. I should point out, it's rarer to see this sort of thing in the triple-A's these days due to the gruelling schedules required on these titles.

Box 4.8   Game Producers

Just a nod here to the somewhat misunderstood and unsung (at least outside of the industry) heroes of game development – the producers. These come in many flavours, executive, associate, junior, etc. and are (dependent on role) the people who manage the schedule of the project, making sure the team is aware of what they need to do, and when they need to do it. They deal with the outward-facing side, the clients, publishers, or investors (often a bit of a nightmare), and manage the money, finding and negotiating for more if necessary. They facilitate and often translate communication between the creative and technical departments, who often speak in completely different terminology, very much as if a cat were attempting to converse with a tree.[13] They will manage Quality Assurance and how information such as bugs and improvements are fed back to the team. All this, and much, much more. I've had some amazing ones (you know who you are) and some *really awful* ones (you probably don't know who you are, as you weren't listening) – but any studio-based game development wouldn't exist without them. All Hail the producers!

SECTION 4.5: FLIPPING THE GAME

Subverting existing mechanics:

Lecture reference: slide 48

> **sub·vert**
> [su*h*b-**vurt**] To undermine the principles of; corrupt.

Let's look at subverting existing game mechanics, in this case, using mechanics for purposes other than those for which they were created. This is a great way of thinking up unique mechanics. If we consider our previous example of *Donut County*, that's a good example of flipping a mechanic. Instead of absorbing objects onto your avatar as in *Katamari Damacy*, you're getting rid of objects to make a hole bigger. Flipping existing mechanics or systems can be an interesting idea of brainstorming new ones. Let's have a look at a couple of examples:

Subverting Mechanics: Out of the Shadows

It's always good if you're able to identify a clear mechanic in games and then think about other ways you could use it. In this example, the mechanic is *Light*. This is a commonly used mechanic within video games, e.g. day and night cycles within the game Dying Light (Techland, 2015) where night is dangerous, and encourages the player to change their playstyle entirely. Many games focus on the use of directing light as a core mechanic to illuminate the dark and banish shadows. In the *Luigi's mansion* series, the game mechanics focus on using light to reveal and fight ghosts, which hide in the dark and become vulnerable in the light. Similarly in *Alan Wake*, flashlights, flares, and other light sources are used to drive away and destroy the dark and shadowy enemies.

Let's have a look at some examples of how *light* has been "flipped" in games.

Subverting the Light Mechanic Example 1

Lost in Shadow (Hudson Soft, 2010)

Lecture reference: slide 49

FIGURE 4.27   Subverting the light mechanic. Illustration by Andrew Thornton.

In the game *Lost in Shadow*, the subversion or "flip" is that rather than driving the shadows away, the player must manipulate the light sources in the game to create a path across traversable shadows, solving puzzles and avoiding creatures while navigating across a platform game style environment. In this game, contrary to the dark representing danger, shadows mean safety.

Subverting the Light Mechanic Example 2

Helsing's Fire (Ratloop games, 2010)

Lecture reference: slide 50

FIGURE 4.28   Subverting the light mechanic. Illustration by Andrew Thornton.

Similarly, in the smartphone title *Helsing's fire*, the common game mechanic of light banishing or destroying enemies is subverted into a puzzle game format where in a top-down view, the player must manipulate the light source (the "fire" of the title) into the optimal position to defeat the enemies. Effectively, in this case, the light becomes the player's avatar.

Subverting the Light Mechanic Example 3

Mass Effect 2 (BioWare, 2010)

Lecture reference: slide 51

FIGURE 4.29 Subverting the light mechanic. Illustration by Shutterstock/CROCOTHERY.

In *Mass Effect 2*, during the loyalty mission for the character Tali'Zorah, Shepherd and team must visit the planet Haestrom, exposed to superheating and harmful radiation from the rapidly expanding sun. This mission is a subverted stealth level. Rather than patrolling enemies spotting the player and entering alert states, the enemy in this case is the sunlight. The player only has a limited amount of time in which they can be exposed to the sunlight (and accompanying radiation) before their shields and health rapidly deplete and they are boiled alive. From a design perspective, as the player/team must also enter combat situations with enemy soldiers whilst avoiding the sunlight, this is a clever way of layering jeopardy – using the sun as a secondary "enemy" it has effectively "doubled up" the peril, forcing a much more strategic approach more suited to the difficulty curve at this stage in the game.

Let's have a look at an exercise:

IN CLASS EXERCISE 4.12: SUBVERTING MECHANICS

Game Video Discussion:
Question

Are you able to identify which mechanics or game systems are being subverted in the following images/clips?

EXERCISE 4.12 EXAMPLE 1

The Ball (Teotl Studios, 2010)

Lecture reference: slide 52

FIGURE 4.30   Illustration by Shutterstock/Zoom Photo Graphic Stock.

EXAMPLE 4.12 VIDEO LINK

https://bit.ly/EX4_12_BALL

EXERCISE 4.12 EXAMPLE 1 ANSWER

This is a subversion of a first-person puzzle game – or even just a subversion of a first-person game. What the designer is doing here is providing a layer of abstraction between you and the puzzle. Instead of using an interaction button or a gravity gun to manipulate switches directly, you must utilise something between you and the switch to operate it. This adds another layer to the "possibility space" with regards to creating puzzles because you must initially manoeuvre the ball into the correct position. This means that instead of just grabbing a switch with your gravity gun, you must ensure you manipulate the ball into position to be able to access the switch, which then rolls onto the pressure pad. It's another clever subversion of the gravity gun mechanic, and also, from a puzzle design perspective, increases the variables required to solve a puzzle, helping to provide more options. I'd also note that it gives you a helpful flythrough (see Box 4.9) as you enter that chamber, giving you a starter for ten on the order in which you should approach the puzzles, effectively "chunking" them.

Box 4.9   Cutaways/Flythroughs

Cutaways and flythroughs are terms used when control is wrested away from the player, usually in first- or third-person game, to cut away to an independent camera. In games such as the early *Tomb Raider* series, we would use cutaways to show environmental elements that weren't directly where the player was – for example, a switch activating a door the player had seen previously in the level, that the cutaway would reveal swinging open. One issue with this is that in a level full of locked doors, you'd need to ensure that when the cutaway happened, the player knew which door they were looking at. Textures and lighting can help with this (i.e., a particularly recognisable pattern on a door). We also used flythroughs in some of the more difficult traversal areas, basically using the camera to indicate "follow this route," or "you're trying to get to this exit." This technique is also common in the early *Assassin's Creed* games in similarly complex traversal areas. Design issues here are that the player needs to memorise the route. Make it too long, and it will frustrate them. A solution here is to split them up – trigger first flythrough, back to player for them to complete complex traversal, trigger second flythrough, back to player for more complex traversal, etc. Puzzle games such as example *The Ball* will use flycams as a "preview" of the order of complex solutions – again, the player must memorise these, so they act as more than a simple solution. Finally, both cutaways and flythroughs can be used cinematically, for example, cutting to a fixed cam long shot of Nathan Drake clinging to the edge of a vast cliff face to show his vulnerability, or alternatively, simply as a way of showing off the game in an "attract mode" looping behind the main menu (as per *Tomb Raider 4*). Cutaways and Flythroughs are versatile tools that often help the player, perhaps consider them in more complex areas of your game.

EXERCISE 4.12 EXAMPLE 2

Siren: Blood Curse (SCE Japan Studio, 2008)

Lecture reference: slide 53

FIGURE 4.31   Illustration by Jack Hollick.

EXAMPLE 4.12 VIDEO LINK

https://bit.ly/EX4_12_BLOOD

EXERCISE 4.12 EXAMPLE 2 ANSWER

This example shows us a subversion of stealth and patrol routes. This is one of my favourite subversions of mechanics that I haven't really seen used outside of this game. The reason this may not have been used widely is that it's a very difficult mechanic to explain to the player. When you watch the video, without actually playing the game, it is quite confusing. In fact, even if you play the game, it's relatively confusing and takes a little while to figure out, as evidenced by a number of confused "let's play" videos online.[14] What's actually happening, if you haven't figured it out, is that you can "sightjack." This essentially involves taking over the view of the cursed enemies, akin to a "Monster cam," and utilising that information to avoid them. Instead of the usual patrol route observation point that, in stealth games, you usually need to have before you enter the scenario to see what the patrol routes of the enemies are – in this case, in a fascinating subversion of stealth mechanics, you're uniquely watching the patrol route through the eyes of your enemy. Clever Design! More common methods of patrol route observation are seeing through walls, being at a physically higher observation point, or in the case of *Horizon: Zero Dawn*, (Guerrilla Games, 2017) actually seeing the patrol route in the environment. From a design perspective, the player needs to be able to actually see or memorise these patrol routes; otherwise, it becomes frustrating as it's trial and error where the enemies may be. You might walk around a corner, right into a patrol. I would suggest designing some type of observation point in stealth games before a patrol route scenario, although I would note, *Dishonored* (Arkane Studios, 2012) and other more recent immersive sims are quite happy ignoring this rule and seem to be doing quite well for themselves, so I'd suggest, as ever, it's down to your own choices.

EXERCISE 4.12 EXAMPLE 3

Dear Esther (The Chinese Room, 2012)

Lecture reference: slide 54

FIGURE 4.32   "Dear Esther" illustration by Jack Hollick.

EXERCISE 4.12 EXAMPLE 3 ANSWER

Dear Esther is from The Chinese Room,[15] founded by Dan Pinchbeck, and effectively subverts the entire FPS genre. The original (before being remastered) was essentially his PhD project at the University of Portsmouth, exploring what constitutes an FPS. Pinchbeck removed all the elements typically associated with FPS games to see if it would still qualify as one – so he removed jumping, shooting, items like torches, and the manipulation of objects, and without these, it effectively became an exploration and narrative-based experience. It was hugely popular and, as many have suggested, invented a new genre, which is somewhat insultingly referred to as a "walking simulator." Again, you can see that subversion doesn't necessarily require adding elements; removing them can also be impactful. This just shows that even the simplest game mechanics can engage and provoke deep emotional responses.

And on that note, let's conclude!

CONCLUSION

Lecture reference: 55

In this lecture, we've delved into game mechanics, the core of game design that shapes player interaction and determines many outcomes for the player. We explored various definitions and academic taxonomies like the MDA system, and compared mechanics across indie and AAA games, emphasising the importance of iteration. We concluded with techniques for prompting new mechanic concepts by the innovative subversion of traditional mechanics, all of which aim to guide you towards understanding what mechanics are, where to use them, and how to make them unique, emphasising their importance in creating engaging and dynamic gaming experiences.

LECTURE FOUR "GAME MECHANICS": RESOURCE MATERIALS:

Lecture Four in PowerPoint Format:
Lecture Four Working Class:
    Edit and upload to a shared drive of your choice!
(These included instructor resources can all be downloaded from the **Instructor Hub**. For further information, please see the chapter "How to Use This Book.")

NOTES

1   Obviously, I'd note that the student who created the slide in question will know the answer, so, ideally, I'd avoid allowing answers from them.
2   Schell (2018).
3   *R/patientgamers on reddit: Assassin's creed unity [pc] - frustrating and boring.* Available at: https://www.reddit.com/r/patientgamers/comments/j32h77/assassins_creed_unity_pc_frustrating_and_boring/.
4   For further reading, see Pearce (2013).
5   During the later twenty-tens, the industry saw a significant push towards the bigger publishers creating games with larger, more expansive worlds and ongoing content updates. The philosophy was that a game with more content offered better value for money, increased player engagement, and extended the game's lifecycle through DLC and expansions, keeping the players loyal and moving into the "games as a service" model.
6   For further reading, see: *The last of Us's gay love story breaks new ground for an entire genre* (2023) *The Independent.* Available at: https://www.independent.co.uk/arts-entertainment/tv/features/frank-bill-the-last-of-us-story-b2272625.html.
7   Abeele, Spiel, Nacke, Johnson and Gerling (2020).
8   So apologies for the examples I've just branded with them.
9   Unfortunately, if you want a clearer explanation than that, I concede. You'll just have to play it.
10   I'd note a good homework exercise here is to task the students with visiting the (either university or their own local) library before the following weeks lesson, look in the "art" section, and try to find a unique art style. List the book title, author and artist, and sketch or create a sample game screen mock-up in that style (in a genre of their choice). If they are unable to find a unique style, they should find a style already used in games, and list which titles it has been used in.
11   School of international game architecture and design at The University of Breda (Previously NHTV School of Applied Sciences.)
12   More specifically in the original titles, as opposed to the later, more RPG-based entries in the series.
13   Designers are, of course, the "cat" in this analogy.
14   PewDiePie (2012).
15   https://www.thechineseroom.co.uk/

REFERENCES

Abeele, V.V., Spiel, K., Nacke, L., Johnson, D. and Gerling, K. (2020). Development and validation of the player experience inventory: A scale to measure player experiences at the level of functional and psychosocial consequences. *International Journal of Human-Computer Studies*, 135, p. 102370.

Anderson, C.A. and Dill, K.E. (2000). Video games and aggressive thoughts, feelings, and behavior in the laboratory and in life. *Journal of Personality and Social Psychology*, 78(4), pp. 772–790.

Arkane Studios. (2012). *Dishonored.* [Video game]. Lyon: Bethesda Softworks.

Atari. (1972). *Pong*. [Video game]. USA: Atari, Inc.

Ayers, N. (2023) The Definitive Guide to OG and rare fortnite skins: Rarity, value, and iconic early releases like Skull Trooper, *33rd Square*. Available at: https://www.33rdsquare.com/og-skins/

Bethesda Game Studios. (2011). *The Elder Scrolls V: Skyrim*. [Video game]. Rockville: Bethesda Softworks.

Blizzard Entertainment. (2016). *Overwatch*. [Video game]. Irvine, CA: Blizzard Entertainment.

Blow, J. (2008). *Braid*. [Video game]. Number None, Inc.

Bogost, I. (2010). *Cow Clicker*. [Video game]. Osaka: Capcom.

Capcom. (2005). *Resident Evil 4*. [Video game]. Osaka: Capcom.

Core Design. (1997). *Tomb Raider II*. [Video game]. Derby: Eidos Interactive.

Core Design. (1999). *Tomb Raider: The Last Revelation*. [Video game]. Derby: Eidos Interactive.

Council, B.D. (2005). The Design Process: The 'double diamond'design process model. Available at: https://www.designcouncil.org.uk/our-resources/the-double-diamond/

Csikszentmihalyi, M. (1990). *Flow: The Psychology of Optimal Experience*. New York: Harper & Row.

Dev, I.G. (2023) The flourishing skin market in video games, *Gaming Debugged | Gaming Site Covering Xbox, Indies, News, Features and Gaming Tech*. Available at: https://www.gamingdebugged.com/2023/08/10/the-flourishing-skin-market-in-video-games/

DICE. (2008). *Mirror's Edge*. [Video game]. Stockholm: Electronic Arts.

EA Redwood Shores. (2008). *Dead Space*. [Video game]. Redwood City, CA: Electronic Arts.

Epic Games. (2017). *Fortnite*. [Video game]. Cary, NC: Epic Games.

Facepalm Games. (2013). *The Swapper*. [Game]. [s.l.]: Curve Digital.

Frictional Games. (2020). *Amnesia: Rebirth*. [Video game]. Sweden: Frictional Games.

Guerrilla Games. (2017). *Horizon Zero Dawn*. [Video game]. Amsterdam: Sony Interactive Entertainment.

Hazelight Studios. (2018). *A Way Out*. [video game]. Redwood City, CA: Electronic Arts.

Hazelight Studios. (2021). *It Takes Two*. [Video game]. Stockholm: Electronic Arts.

Hilliard, K. (2016) Making Max Payne – how hong kong kung fu and family photo shoots built a noir thriller, *Game Informer*. Available at: https://www.gameinformer.com/b/features/archive/2016/03/27/making-max-payne-how-hong-kong-kung-fu-and-family-photo-shoots-built-a-noir-thriller.aspx (link no longer functioning, from the sadly now defunct game informer website)

Hunicke, R., LeBlanc, M. and Zubek, R. (2004). MDA: A formal approach to game design and game research. In *Proceedings of the AAAI Workshop on Challenges in Game AI* (Vol. 4, No. 1, p. 1722).

Hudson Soft. (2010). *Lost in Shadow*. [Video game]. Tokyo: Hudson Soft.

id Software. (1996–2000). *Quake, Quake II, Quake III Arena*. [Video games]. Mesquite, TX: id Software.

Infinity Ward. (2019). *Call of Duty: Modern Warfare*. [Video game]. Santa Monica, CA: Activision.

Insomniac Games. (2023). *Marvel's Spider-Man 2*. [Video game]. Burbank, CA: Sony Interactive Entertainment.

Ion Storm. (2000). *Deus Ex*. Austin, TX: Eidos Interactive.

Mazin, C. and Druckmann, N. (2023). *The Last of Us*. [TV series] New York: HBO.

McGonigal, J. (2011). *Reality Is Broken: Why Games Make Us Better and How They Can Change the World*. New York: Penguin Press.

Mobius Digital. (2019). *Outer Wilds*. [Video game]. West Hollywood, CA: Annapurna Interactive.

Natali, V. (1997). *Cube*. [Film]. Toronto: Trimark Pictures.

Naughty Dog. (2013). *The Last of Us*. [Video game]. Santa Monica: Sony Computer Entertainment.

Naughty Dog. (2016). *Uncharted 4: A Thief's End*. [Video game]. Santa Monica: Sony Computer Entertainment.

Nature, P. (2022). 10 video game characters with the best drip, *PlayerNature*. Available at: https://www.playernature.com/2022/03/video-game-fashion.html

Pearce, S. (2013). *On Collecting: An Investigation into Collecting in the European Tradition*. London: Routledge.

PewDiePie (2012). Siren: Blood curse - part 1- lets play siren gameplay [walkthrough play-through], *YouTube*. Available at: https://youtu.be/FpUKQ9m7Cqc?t=290

Playdead. (2010). *Limbo*. [Video game]. Copenhagen: Playdead.

Remedy Entertainment. (2001). *Max Payne*. [Video game]. Espoo: Gathering of Developers.

Riot Games. (2009). *League of Legends*. [Video game]. Los Angeles, CA: Riot Games.

Roediger III, H.L. and Karpicke, J.D. (2006). Test-enhanced learning: Taking memory tests improves long-term retention. Psychological Science, 17(3), pp. 249–255.

Salen, K. and Zimmerman, E. (2004). *Rules of Play: Game Design Fundamentals*. Cambridge, MA: MIT Press.

Schell, J. (2018). When games invade real life, YouTube. Available at: https://youtu.be/BPRjEuLCej4?t=1235

Schreier, J. (2017). *Blood, Sweat, and Pixels: The Triumphant, Turbulent Stories Behind How Video Games are Made*. New York: Harper.

Sicart, M. (2008). Game studies, Game Studies - Defining Game Mechanics. Available at: https://gamestudies.org/0802/articles/sicart

Team Meat. (2010). *Super Meat Boy*. [Video game]. Austin, TX: Team Meat.

Thompson, D. (2017). *Hit Makers: The Science of Popularity in an Age of Distraction*. New York: Penguin Press.

Turkle, S. (1984). *The Second Self: Computers and the Human Spirit*. Cambridge, MA: MIT Press.

Ubisoft. (2014). *Assassin's Creed Unity*. [Video game]. Montreuil: Ubisoft.

Ubisoft. (2018). *Assassin's Creed Odyssey*. [Video game]. Montreuil: Ubisoft.

Valve Corporation. (2007). *Portal*. [Video game]. Bellevue, WA: Valve Corporation.

Valve Corporation. (2007). *Team Fortress 2*. [Video game]. Bellevue, WA: Valve Corporation.

Vlambeer. (2018). *Minit*. [Video game]. Austin, TX: Devolver Digital.

Genres and Game Analysis

5

LECTURE OVERVIEW

We're going to break away from core components this week and do something a little different – we're going to look at another hugely important element of being a game designer, and that's the technique of analysing and deconstructing the design of other people's games.

CORE TECHNIQUE: ANALYSING AND DOCUMENTING

Lecture reference: slide 2

Analysing and documenting games is a hugely important part of game development. You need to be playing games regularly (believe me, it still surprises me how many

DOI: 10.1201/9781032644721-5

game developers or students don't do this). Usually, while playing a game, I'll sit with a pad or phone next to me, and make notes, or save interesting video clips of elements that interest me – also with numbering notation and notes – you'd be amazed at how quickly you forget exactly why it was you recorded a particular clip. You need to start analysing the genre pillars, mechanics, systems, and the pacing structure of the games you're playing, which, in addition, will help you to formulate ideas for new games and mechanics. It will also allow you to adjust and adapt ideas for your own games – for instance, finding mechanics you're able to "flip," as described in Chapter 4, "Mechanics."

"GAME, RUINED"

You'll find as you start to analyse the games you're playing, and working out elements like where critical paths are, how enemy encounters are paced, why you went back on yourself to look for a health pack, why you can't get to that monster closet, and why that key mechanic is flawed, etc. may spoil your game. Here's the thing: It does. But don't worry – this doesn't last long. At a particular point, other than the occasional key pillar or element of interest that pulls you out of the game momentarily, after a while, recognising all these elements becomes second nature. You start to automatically digest game components and mentally filter the ones that interest or impress you through your new game design attuned brain. Stuck when designing? Pop into the brain, unleash your toolbox, have a dig around, and bingo! You'll have something to help you move forward. Although I should point out that's not an excuse to stop making notes!

Before we look at analysis in more detail, let's recap last week's lecture.

Last Week Recap!: Mechanics

Notes for Educator:
    As described in the previous chapter, this is an example Recap exercise, the content provided from last week's student exercise. I'd suggest four or five/slides or taught examples to remind the students of last week's content, before moving on to the student examples. As previously pointed out, sometimes it's also useful to redact the titles of the mechanics and let the students attempt to remember/guess the specified mechanics, useful at the start of a lecture to trigger engagement with the class.

Recap: Mechanics – New Examples

Lecture reference: slides 4–10

Recap discussion: Mechanics
Let's have a quick look at some (self-explanatory) example Mechanic Gamecards to give you an idea of the variety of Mechanics that are available within games:

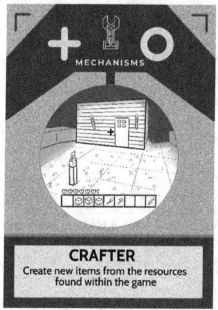

FIGURE 5.1 Example Mechanic gamecards, Card design by Andrew Thornton and illustrations by Andrew Thornton and Shutterstock/Karlovserg.

Recap: Mechanics – Student Examples

Now let's drill down, examine and discuss some of your own example mechanics from last week's exercise.

 (**Please note**, in the absence of actual student examples from last week's working class, illustrations representing games/techniques have been used instead)

IN CLASS EXERCISE 5.1

Lecture reference: slide 11
Recap discussion: Mechanics
Question:
 Are you able to identify the Mechanic in the following example?
(**Discuss**)

Example 1: *Terraria* (Re-Logic, 2011)

FIGURE 5.2 Illustration by Andrew Thornton.

Exercise 5.1 Answer

"Crafter"

Terraria has a vast array of crafting tools and resources available to the player.

IN CLASS EXERCISE 5.2

Lecture reference: slide 12
Recap discussion: Mechanics
Question:
   Are you able to identify the Mechanic in the following example?
(Discuss)

Example 2: *Genshin Impact* (miHoYo, 2020)

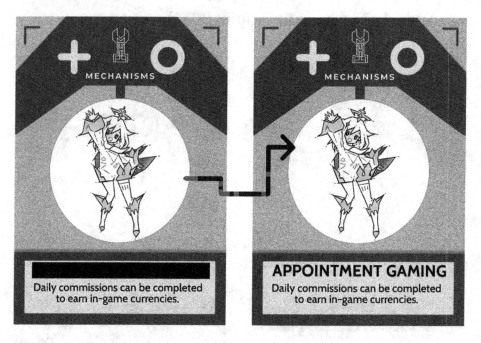

FIGURE 5.3   Illustration by Andrew Thornton.

Exercise 5.2 Answer

"Appointment Gaming"

Now let's move over to our regular fixture, USP corner!

IN CLASS EXERCISE 5.3: USP CORNER!

Lecture reference: slide 13
Game Video Discussion: Unique Selling points
Question:

Try to identify one (or more) unique selling points in the following video clips. Imagine you are pitching them to a publisher and need a hook to reel them in!

EXERCISE 5.3 VIDEO LINK

Example 1: Bad North (Plausible Concept, 2018).
  https://bit.ly/EX5_3_NORTH

FIGURE 5.4   Illustration by Andrew Thornton.

Example 5.3: Clue!

Lecture reference: slide 14

I'd suggest there is more than one USP in *Bad North*. If you have a look at the following image, perhaps this will give you some ideas:

FIGURE 5.5   "Dark Oberon" Image by Michael Reschke (Uploader), GPL (http://www.gnu.org/licenses/gpl.html, via Wikimedia Commons).

Exercise 5.3 Example Answer

One of the USP's of *Bad North* is the unique art style – an "isometric" view (see Box 5.1), although I'd argue that this takes this particular game viewpoint one step further stylistically, creating a carefully framed "diorama" (designed to look like a miniature model) which the player rotates to defend against the attacking Norsemen. This, and the "watercolour" painterly graphics, give it a unique aesthetic, which passes the "Magazine test"[1] – basically, if you saw a screenshot of this game in media, would you immediately be able to recognise which game it was? This sort of immediate visual signature USP is a useful tool in getting immediate interest from publishers, or, if in a portfolio for a job, securing an interview. Another element that shouldn't be understated is the name. *Bad North* is unique and memorable. What does it mean? This intriguing question helps it to stick in your head (see Box 5.2 "What's in a name?"). If you have a really clear graphical style and a clear name, you've "branded" your game, which will help enormously with initial recognition. The other, unfortunately much harder part is making it a really engaging and playable game. But remember, "harder" does not mean "impossible."

Box 5.1   Isometric ("ISO") Projection in Games

One of my first jobs in the industry was with the legendary games company "Bullfrog," in the not-so-legendary role of junior artist. I was tasked with converting the complex, isometric tiles of the game *Powermonger* (Bullfrog Productions, 1990) into dithered, black-and-white versions for the popular Macintosh computer range from Apple, a company that, at the time, didn't really "do" games. Converting these tiles was particularly confusing for me, a junior artist, as I hadn't really seen "isometric" games since playing *Knight Lore* (Ultimate Play The Game, 1984) on the ZX Spectrum while back in short trousers, and not only did *Powermonger* not have anything that looked like a Werewolf in it, more importantly, I had not the slightest knowledge of how to adapt game tilesets. I wondered what I had gotten myself into. What I *had* gotten into was a company run (alongside Les Edgar) by the game developer Peter Molyneux, who at that time was primarily known as the creator of the game *Populous* (Bullfrog Productions, 1989) and with it, the "God game" genre, where players are Gods that look down upon the landscape, shaping it and influencing tiny worshippers/followers. Its spiritual successor, *Powermonger*, brought the isometric viewpoint back into vogue, which became prominent in strategy and simulation games across the 1990s in titles such as *SimCity 2000* (Maxis, 1993). and *Diablo* (Blizzard Entertainment, 1996). In the early days, (and getting to the point of this boxout) the "iso" view had significant advantages from a developer and gameplay perspective – the player was able to register depth and height in a mock 3D environment, adding to the complexity and readability of the game (as opposed to the top-down view of the original *Populous*), without the extensive processing power required for actual "true" 3D graphics. The locked orthographic viewpoint allowed for the benefits (memory-wise, although perhaps not junior artist-wise) of a snappable, fixed, finite tileset. "Iso" is still popular in games, but more so from a stylistic (USP) viewpoint (see *Bad North*), or in games such as *Monument Valley* (ustwo Games, 2014) and *Echochrome* (Sony Computer Entertainment, 2008) as an element of puzzle game mechanics, where certain options are hidden until the player spins the environment in 90-degree increments (keeping the "iso" viewpoint) to uncover solutions. For a perfect example of "flipping" the expected behaviour of a camera system/fixed viewpoint, I would recommend the game *Fez*. (Polytron Corporation, 2012). And check out that retro pixelated tileset!

EXERCISE 5.3 (USP CORNER!) VIDEO LINK 2

Lecture reference: slide 15
   Example 2: Carrion (Phobia Game Studio, 2020)
   https://bit.ly/EX5_3_CARR

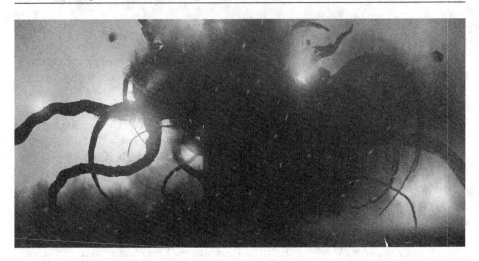

FIGURE 5.6   Illustration by Shutterstock/Tithi Luadthong.

Exercise 5.3 Example 2 Answer

Carrion states the USP within the trailer – it's a reverse horror experience where you're playing the enemy or the monster. This isn't a new approach; for example, 1997's *Dungeon Keeper* from Bullfrog Productions (them again!) cast you in a management simulation where you ran the dungeon, attempting to trap and destroy the 'good guys' – in this game, being bad is fun. Another more recent example is *Marvel's Spider-Man 2* (Insomniac Games, 2023) where, for part of the game, you take control of Venom, the alien symbiote and nemesis of Peter Parker (who is, spoiler, actually Spider man, if you didn't know). As Venom, you rampage through a lab, tossing aside armed combat units as if they were ragdolls, while tapping once more into that hugely underrated design element "Badassery"[2] Other game developers seem to have started cottoning on to how much fun playing a baddie is, as noted by the Steam Tag 'Villain Protagonist.'

SECTION 5.1: USP CATEGORIES

Lecture reference: slide 16

You'll note when discussing Unique Selling points, we will usually describe either an art style or a particular mechanic – see examples below inspired by *Superhot* (SUPERHOT Team, 2016), its unique artwork and name a classic example of an "Magazine test" success – i.e., as soon as you see it, you recognise the game.

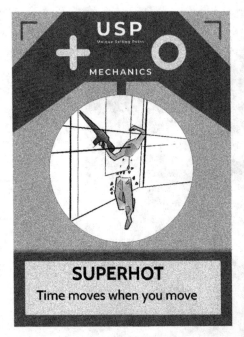

FIGURE 5.7 Illustration by Andrew Thornton.

With the "Villain Protagonist" USP, and other Unique elements such as a striking name not fitting either of these categories, it becomes apparent there are some elements that make games unique that are just as viable in catching the attention as art or mechanics – so, using the example of *Carrion*, let's create a third USP category, called "OTHER":

FIGURE 5.8 Card Design by Andrew Thornton/Illustration by Shutterstock/Tithi Luadthong.

USP Categories Defined: "Art," "Mechanic," and "Other"

Lecture reference: slide 16

We now have three new USP category GameCards, as per Figure 5.9, which is handy – as we'll be using them shortly in an exercise:

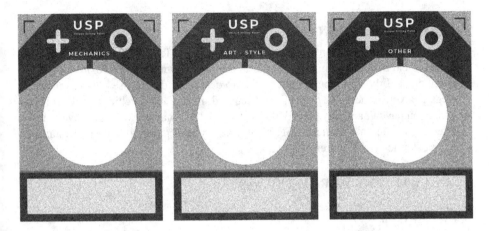

FIGURE 5.9   Illustration by Andrew Thornton.

A Note on Unique Selling Points

Before we begin the exercise, just a note of caution. One of the most common issues with trying to create, locate or isolate USP's is understanding that a USP is a *UNIQUE* selling point – *UNIQUE* being the key word. If you've seen the art style or the mechanic before, it's not a USP. This is why it is so difficult to find unique elements – but as I tell my students, each of us has something unique and original to contribute to the field of game design. The more you understand yourself and your design preferences, the better you can access your deeper creative muse. Finding and showcasing that unique element will help you get noticed in the industry.

USP exercise: lecturer notes

Before starting this team-based exercise unusually early in the lecture, an explanation: If there are two distinct areas of a subject that need to be taught within the same lesson, I find it useful to separate them with a team-based exercise around "Section one" (in this case, USP's), followed by a short break before "Section two" (in this case more general game analysis). Combining related topics within a lecture without clearly delineating them leads to (in my experience) neither of the subjects being sufficiently assimilated by the students.

EXERCISE 5.4: USP CATEGORIES TEAM EXERCISE, PART 1

Lecture reference: slides 17–21
Estimated time: 30 minutes

CLASS INSTRUCTIONS

In your teams, use the provided template to create at least **SIX example cards** (**two for each USP**) with both images and text (maximum 25 words) outlining the game and the USP you are attempting to describe. Ideally, use video analysis of games you've actually played. As discussed, if you are watching a video of a game you haven't actually played, the "art style" USP may be valid, but if you are referring to the "mechanics" USP, it's unlikely you're going to truly understand the mechanics you'll be referencing.

SEE CHAPTER 5 WORKING CLASS 1

Exercise Help

If you find yourself stuck at the outset, I include a simple exercise[3] as a quick way of identifying any possible USP's in recently played games:

Think of a game that you've enjoyed playing recently.
1. Write down the name of the game.
2. Write down an experience you had with that game which *you couldn't find anywhere else.*
3. From that experience, summarise in less than 25 words, what you believe is the unique element of that gameplay.

LECTURE FIVE WORKING CLASS 1: USP'S

Link/Notes for Educator:
    These included instructor resources can all be downloaded from the **Instructor Hub**.
    Edit and upload to a shared drive of your choice!
    (For further information, please see the chapter "How to Use This Book.")

Exercise 5.3 Answer

Recap discussion: USP's
Estimated time: 15 minutes
Lecturer Notes:
Bring up the team-based student exercise from the shared drive on the main screen and discuss prominent examples with the class.

Box 5.2   "What's in a Name?"

It seems unique and unconventional game names may influence consumer behaviour by increasing memorability and curiosity. Hunt (1995) highlights the Von

Restorff effect, where distinctive names like *Katamari Damacy* (Bandai Namco Games, 2004) improve recall of the name and therefore word-of-mouth promotion. *Don't Starve* (Klei Entertainment, 2013) lends itself to curiosity, leading to a higher possibility of seeking the game out. Stoner et al. (2018) show that names like *Hollow Knight* (Team Cherry, 2017) promote psychological ownership by evoking themes of nobility and adventure, creating a motivation to play a game that may foster these narrative elements and emotions. Schmeltz and Kjeldsen (2016) emphasise that names like *Dark Souls* (FromSoftware, 2011) convey themes of challenge, difficulty, and depth that also lead to a recognisable brand identity, attracting a dedicated, hardcore audience and continuing to reinforce the game's reputation through the series for providing a tough but rewarding experience. Strategically chosen names can enhance memorability, spark curiosity, and improve brand perception. Yes, it seems someone may actually have deliberately chosen the name *Bravely Default* (Square Enix, 2012). Think carefully about what's in a name!

(With thanks to Richard Chalmers for research assistance.)

SECTION 5.2: CORE TECHNIQUES: GAME ANALYSIS

Lecture reference: slide 22

As I've said, as Game Designers you need to be looking under the bonnet of every game you play, and the analysis does tend to start spoiling games a little bit, but it also empowers you to start understanding and dismantling the design process of games as you play them. Think of yourself as being tasked with creating the "Design" chapter[4] of a "Haynes manual"[5] for the game you are playing.

FIGURE 5.10 A current, updated example of a Haynes manual – Photograph credit osde8info licensed under CC BY-SA 2.0.

Ultimately, Play the Game!

Lecture reference: slide 23

I'll keep repeating this: As a Game Designer, you absolutely must play these games yourself. This is part of your job, although I should point out, probably not during your actual office hours (unless it's lunchtime, or you enjoy being told off by the boss). Watching a video or a live stream can give you an overview of a game, but you must play them to understand how the game works – the mechanics, the camera, the controls, the character (see Box 5.3) and the elusive "Gamefeel" (see Box 5.4).

FIGURE 5.11   Play games! – Photograph by Shutterstock/Maksym93.

You want to understand emotionally how you feel when you're playing the game and to understand exactly how the structure and systems within the game are working. Something may look fine on screen in a video, but when you're playing it, perhaps you'll realise from your perspective that it frustrates, is confusing, or simply doesn't feel right. Note this is your own *subjective* perspective, i.e. influenced by your own history of playing similar games (e.g. warm fuzzy nostalgia at a Pixel Art game) or emotions triggered by your own personal circumstances (e.g. "I've played too many games with RPG elements this month"). The difficult part is attempting to look past these subjective viewpoints and look at the game with impartiality and neutrality, i.e. an *objective* viewpoint. In hindsight I'll correct my previous statement. This objectivity is the *most* difficult part of playing and analysing games, particularly in genres you're historically not fond of. But as I say to my students: play games, keep playing them, and play as *many different types of games and genres as you possibly can.*

Box 5.3   The "Three Cs"

The three Cs are usually recognised as the holy triumvirate of Game Design – Character, Camera and control, which, when functioning together seamlessly should create "Gameplay synergy" leading towards the enlightened path of true ludic karma. It's often a difficult balancing act, and as ever, requires much iteration and "tweaking." Let's look at an example of the interplay between these systems. At the outset of your design, a different camera view will immediately adjust how you approach your character and controller. If a first-person camera, how does the player "relate" to their character? Do you see them in cutscenes to add personality, such as *Skyrim*? Or does the character become a blank shell, as per "Gordon Freeman," in the *Half Life* series (Valve Corporation, 1998–present), which theoretically allows the player to transpose their own emotions onto the blank slate? Looking at your initial design from another perspective, let's imagine you are tasked with creating a full traversable 3D cityscape to parkour through. In which case, should your character be in third person as per the *Tomb Raider* series, allowing for more precise manipulation through the environment, but requiring much more work from an art and animation perspective? Or do you feel the best route forward is to use a first-person camera as per, for example, *Mirrors Edge* – in which case you lose some of the feeling of precision, i.e., the sense of "not know-ing where your feet are" when performing complex moves. In which case, can you "zoom" your first-person view to check positioning or possible routes, as per *Portal*? or should you lock this first-person movement to metrics as per the early *Tomb Raider* games, so the character is "snapped" to a grid-based environment? how would this feel in a first-person game? And if it is a first-person game, let's say you need a sprint – do you follow the accepted current norm (on controllers at least) and click the thumbstick to sprint? Or do you already need that part of your con-troller (the stick) to shift between first- and third-person view? As you can see, one option quickly branches out into many. Although the "three Cs" probably requires an entire chapter to itself rather than my limited first/third person examples, as a "starter for ten" tip, I'd suggest in the initial stages of your design, character and controls will usually follow camera. But as ever in Game Design, this is not a hard and fast rule, and iteration is usually the key. Try, test, and try again!

(For a more in-depth overview, see Dominic Butlers Ubisoft post here: https://twitter.com/LifeatUbisoft/status/1382359744703238144)

Let's have a look at the "Three Cs" in the following clip and see if we feel they improve upon the original game concept from which the sequence has been "borrowed."

IN CLASS EXERCISE 5.5: GAME ANALYSIS

Lecture reference: slide 24
Game Video Discussion:
Question
   Identify the game this sequence imitates, and note any gameplay positives or negatives in the change of camera, character or controller from the original game on which it was based (assume regular "Call of Duty" console controller mapping.)

Exercise 5.5 Example 1

Call of Duty: Advanced Warfare (Activision, 2014)

FIGURE 5.12   Image by Shutterstock/breakermaximus.

EXAMPLE 1 VIDEO LINK

https://bit.ly/EX5_5_CODA

Exercise 5.5 Example 1 Answer

Lecture reference: slide 25

FIGURE 5.13   Illustration by Jack Hollick.

This is the "traffic" mission from *Call of Duty: Advanced Warfare*, and as I think you might have guessed, it really was me playing that, as evidenced by the rather abrupt conclusion. The answer here is that they've taken *Frogger,* a game released in 1981, and translated it into a modern game engine with flashy graphics, sound effects, a first-person controller, and some enemies shooting at you. However, the gameplay is essentially the same, with "sprinting" replacing "jumping." The only real flaw here, I would suggest, is that without the top-down view, you're unable to judge what's coming and the speed at which it's coming. Hypothetically, if an otherwise excellent player misjudged the timing, they may get hit by a car. From a "Three Cs" perspective, we can now see there was a gameplay-driven purpose for the top-down camera in *Frogger.*

Game Analysis Case Study: Tomb Raider

The "THREE Cs" in *Tomb Raider*

Lecture reference: slide 26

FIGURE 5.14   Illustration by Jack Hollick.

Another really important tip is to play the games as designed on the source machines. As if by magic, original design choices will suddenly become apparent. If it was originally a handheld game, play it on a handheld, if it's a smartphone game play it on the phone, if it's on the Wii, play it on the Wii, and if it was made for the PSVITA, play it on the PSVITA. The design choices in something like the game *Tearaway* (Media Molecule, 2013) can only be fully understood if you're playing it with the cornucopia of features that little handheld device had, the camera, the rear touch pad, the microphone, etc. This is obviously slightly more difficult than going onto a retro game site and down-loading the updated bells and whistles version, but you'll find there *are* ways to play these games on the original machines, or at least to understand the original controller inputs these games were designed around. Not only are there many retro game hobbyist festivals where these machines and games are for sale, not to mention a certain online auction site, but many computer museums[6] will allow you playable access to a variety of these classic machines.

FIGURE 5.15   PlayStation with controller. Image by Evan-Amos.

To illustrate the importance of playing on original hardware, having recently pro-cured a shiny, old, original Playstation, we set it up in the Game Design class for some playthroughs of the original *Tomb Raider* games. To my surprise, I realised I had actu-ally forgotten that when we were developing, (although originally developed for PC and SEGA SATURN) much of the traversal design was based around the default PS1 D-PAD controller[7] (see Figures 5.14 and 5.15). This is fascinating from a design analysis perspective, as it allows us to look into the original synergy between the "Three Cs." When you are using the tank controls in the original game, rotating using the left and right D-pad controls and then moving forward, it's not using modern analogue move-ment where the extent of movement on the thumbstick influences the speed of the ava-tar, adjusting movement incrementally (as previously discussed, see [8]) – the D-pad uses binary movement. It's either "on" or "off."

With binary, there is no variation to jump distances influenced by variation in speed. Push forward to move, and you move a set, finite distance each time. And this binary nature is reflected in the design of the original *Tomb Raider* editor (see Box 5.4) in which we built the games. It uses a grid-based system with a series of fixed metrics, allowing movement and animation around these metrics, in turn influencing the design of the control system. Failsafes such as Lara stopping when the finite binary move dis-tance would take her over an edge (to possible death) are also reflected in the tank-based controls. With tank-based controls, you rotate on the spot before choosing to turn in one of eight directions, (0°, 45°, 90°, 135°, 180°, 225°, 270°, and 315°) reflecting the precise nature of the metric traversal. The environments in the original *Tomb Raider* became a puzzle through the careful player manipulation and positioning of Lara and were always designed as such. These metrics constrained the player to a particular route through the environment, you would step forward and you would step back and she would lock to the metrics – and this made the whole thing into kind of like a massive grid-based game of chess. Following this ethos, the camera was not only placed in third person to reflect the super cool character, but also to show exactly how she was interacting with the environment. If you consider adjusting a "shimmy," where Lara hangs from a ledge pressed against a wall, from a third person into a first-person camera, you get the picture (and that picture would primarily be a very, very close view of a wall.)

FIGURE 5.16   Illustration by Shutterstock/lzf.

Box 5.4   Editors & Engines: Welcome to the Asylum

It amuses my students greatly to learn that during Game Development in the early noughties, in a company such as "Core Design" (where I was previously employed) we would normally have three or four game projects in development at any one time, each with a team of roughly between 5 and 20 developers. Teams were split with three of four programmers (now, mysteriously, known as "Engineers" or "Technicians"), on whom most of the fate of the game balanced. Then five or six artists, ideally with a rare as hens teeth Animator/Artist on board (no mocap[9] in those days). Around this time, the art team also had a subset of artists who worked specifically (in our case, in a separate room) on rendering the FMV (full motion video) required for the games. These sequences were "rendered" as they used much higher resolution bespoke versions of the in-game characters, models that would stop a PC dead in its tracks at runtime, but were fine if rendered one frame at a time, in a similar fashion to the processor intensive frame by frame rendering of an animation movie today. Around this time, the term "Game designers" began to be recognised, although, quite frankly, it was still a free for all in that department, with programmers and artists designing a lot of the output for the company. So far, not so amusing. The amusing part (at least, according to my students) is that during the development on the aforementioned three or four games, each would use its *own, bespoke engine.* The first few months of each of these projects would be spent in game Limbo, with design documents being drawn up and art assets being stockpiled, as the programmers *created the game engine that would power the game.* No Unreal Engine, Unity, Godot or GameMaker studio. Although, in a twisted nod to these current game engines, these overworked programmers would also be required to create editors that would allow designers and artists to enter assets, animations, and in the case of our *Tomb Raider* editor, build environments and levels (with textures and lighting), place enemies, set triggers and implement a myriad of other elements of game logic. I hear you say, "But at least you shared the editors and codebase between games in the same company, right?". Wrong. For the most part, programmers and teams would jealously guard their code and editors, especially if they had a hit on their hands, and wanted a sequel without it being sullied by some other internal project that might come out beforehand and dampen the enthusiasm for their title. "Insanity!" I hear you cry. "Yes," I answer, while ruminating to myself that in hindsight, I begin to wonder how we managed to ship any games at all.

In the recent *Tomb Raider* series reboots, (Crystal Dynamics & Eidos-Montréal, 2006) you're not locked into metrics and the games use analogue movements that allow variations in Lara's movement speed, changing the game dynamics. By metrics, I mean specific distances, jump heights, jump lengths, and run speeds, which used to all be quite commonly "set in stone" in games. However, things like climbing walls in *Assassin's Creed*, i.e., how high you can jump, etc. now tend to vary according to speed and other variables – i.e. there is no "set" jump distance. Without understanding set metrics and becoming accustomed to them, the gameplay becomes less proscribed, but I would argue, also impacts the "readability" of certain traversal elements. In metric-based games, learning these metrics is part of the reward cycle. You can judge a jump and make it. However, without clear metrics, it's a little more ambiguous.

For example, in a popular, later, non *Tomb Raider* traversal and adventure-based game series, jump distances tend to vary contextually, making it difficult to judge available routes. I found myself "trapped" in a small environmental area within one of these titles, returning to the edge of a precipice which was clearly too far to jump to with the metrics I had spent many hours learning, so I didn't bother trying. Eventually, with nowhere else to go, I returned to the edge of the precipice and jumped, expecting to plummet to my death, whereupon it switched into a cutscene where the character suddenly, cinematically propelled himself the extra few feet required to cover the gap. In common parlance, I'd refer to that as "changing the rules," taking control out of the players hands and changing the distances that I can jump. I'd suggest if you *are* going to change these, make it clear it's a boost or tool within the characters loadout.[10]

It was quite a unique piece of design at the time for Lara Croft to be able to step back, step forward, and gradually edge towards the edge of a precipice. She would stand right on the edge of a block so you knew exactly what jump distance you were going to make, adding again to the feel of it being a puzzle traversal game. I suspect this slower, more thoughtful traversal design will begin to make a comeback. It may be a niche, but a sustainable niche.

SECTION 5.3: GAME ANALYSIS – GENRES & THEIR CONVENTIONS (WITH HELPFUL DESIGN TIPS!)

Lecture reference: slide 27

Let's have a look at how genres work, and an intro to the psychology of genres:

FIGURE 5.17   Example Game Genres. Illustration by Shutterstock/Skellen.

Genres are very helpful for recognising the types of games we like. Some of us enjoy RTS games, some of you (and I would hazard a guess, most of you) enjoy RPGs such as *Skyrim*, some prefer first-person shooters, some enjoy third-person action adventures, and so on. This helps us make informed choices about what we want to invest our valuable time and money in and play, and it's even more significant when you're looking at it from the perspective of designing and creating your own games. While it may happen in the real world that you end up working in the industry as a designer on game genres that don't particularly interest you, as a student, if you're designing games that you don't want to play, something's gone awry. Genres have adapted from the early days of game development, and larger games could now safely be said to straddle several genres. With that in mind, there will always be some disagreement about which genre particular games fit into – e.g. is *Hades*, (Supergiant Games, 2020) an Action, a Roguelike or an RTS? Or a mix of all three? Is an action just a "shooter," or does it cover a broader range? As games become more complex, there will always be arguments around genre, but in the examples, I'll try to use games that best exemplify the core, undiluted conventions, or *original* pillars of that genre. Understanding these should help when we begin to mix and match in our own game designs.

Let's have a look at an example to introduce us:

Genre 1: Action Games

Lecture reference: slide 28

FIGURE 5.18   Illustration by Jack Hollick.

A clear example of the "action" game genre is the popular *Halo* series – with the original game inventing, or at least standardising some of the core conventions or pillars of the genre, such as rechargeable shields, iconic Multiplayer maps, dual stick FPS control schemes and aim assist.[11] We'll look at these in more detail shortly – in the meantime, let's have an exercise:

IN CLASS EXERCISE 5.6 PART 1

Lecture reference: slide 29
Discussion: Action games
Question:
    Other than the provided example, are we able to think of any more examples of **action games**, and are they only first person? Or can they also be third person?

Exercise 5.6 Part 1 Example Answers

First Person Action (FPS) games:
   Doom (id Software, 1993)
   Goldeneye (Rare, 1997)
   Call of Duty: Modern *Warfare* (Infinity Ward, 2007)
Third Person Action Games:
   Devil May *Cry* (Capcom, 2001)
   Control (Remedy Entertainment, 2019)

IN CLASS EXERCISE 5.6 PART 2

Lecture reference: slide 30
Discussion: Action game tropes
Question:
   Are we able to think of any examples of action game **conventions, tropes, or pillars**?

FIGURE 5.19   Illustration by Jack Hollick.

Exercise 5.6 Part 2 Example Answers

Lecture reference: slide 31

Action: Some Genre Conventions/Tropes

- *1st or (more rarely)3rd person*
- *Twitch gaming – down to reactions/quick judgements*
- *Rechargeable shields/cover a common mechanic*
- *Weapon variety/playstyles important*
- *Competitive Avatar improvement*
- *MP – playing against others a huge element*
- *Level design/balanced maps for MP important*
- *Cinematic – big SPECTACLE events!*
- *Storyline often secondary*

Let's look at some of these in more detail:

Action trope 1: multiplayer – competitive avatar improvement

Playing against others has become a huge part of action FPS games. As we've looked at previously, one of the elements driving this is "peer-review" – you get better gear, which is mostly cosmetic, to show off in Multiplayer matches. This is usually cosmetic simply because multiplayer in games like *Call of Duty* is incredibly fine-tuned; even a slightly overpowered weapon can upset the balance (or "Meta"[12]), as games like *Overwatch* (Blizzard Entertainment, 2016). Have discovered when introducing new characters such as the overpowered "Brigitte," which led to several patches and rebalances to reduce and balance various abilities until the community deemed it fixed (see "Gamespot" article addressing updates here[13]).

FIGURE 5.20   Image by Shutterstock/breakermaximus.

Action trope 2: campaign mode and spectacle

Although campaign mode has now taken a backseat to multiplayer in many action-shoot-ers, massive set pieces and spectacle remain common in action games. This is important in games like *Call of Duty*, creating anticipation and excitement with huge production values, never-before-seen effects, and playable real-time cinematic sequences, mirror-ing the film industry's desired "tentpole"[14] effect of summer blockbusters. This spec-tacle used to be crucial for selling *Call of Duty* games. For instance, in the original *Call of Duty: Modern Warfare* (since remade and rebooted), the first mission features a ship sinking and turning on its side, effectively changing the level layout as you backtrack. It's a beautiful piece of level design, with the spectacle built into the gameplay, creat-ing a huge sense of jeopardy, even though much of it is smoke and mirrors ("shock and awe" as Captain Price might growl). It should also be noted that as production values increased, and cinematics or scripted events increased, critics[15] and the community began to kick back, complaining that the campaigns often prioritised the narrative and visuals to the point where the players felt more like observers that players. In "tentpole" titles, it's often a difficult balance – the expected big-budget spectacle can sometimes get in the way of the game.

Action trope 3: control scheme – the "new norm"

People used to laugh at the idea of an FPS on a console due to the precision of PC aim-ing systems. The lack of precision with console sticks compared to a mouse made it seem impossible, but the first *Halo* game, flew in the face of accepted wisdom and rede-signed the FPS (as the "tentpole" title) for the original XBOX console. The dual-ana-logue stick setup was used for separate movement and aiming, a control scheme which gave PC users, who argued that nothing would beat the precision of a mouse for Action shooters, a run for their money. The introduction of cross-platform play has meant that many of the console features (controller support, aim assist) have now been adopted across all platforms to create a level playing field. For a more in-depth overview of how this original control scheme and original *Halo* game was created, (as well as the birth of the XBOX itself) I'd recommend the excellent documentary "Power On: The Story of Xbox."[16]

Action trope 4: rechargeable shields/cover

After being introduced in *Halo*, rechargeable shields became de-rigueur in action games, (as opposed to health pickups) and this promoted more strategic level design based around using the environment for cover. Bleeding out? Hide behind a rock for 30 seconds – you'll be fine!

Action trope 5: weapon variety

Again, it was *Halo* that prompted some innovation in action FPS's here, by implement-ing a two-weapon limit that forced players to make strategic decisions about their load-outs. This ignored the earlier FPS philosophy where capacity didn't matter, but weapon variety did (see *Doom*, where your loadout could include pistol, shotgun, chaingun, rocket launcher, plasma gun, and the BFG 9000, all at once). Some FPS games will still allow the player to load up on a huge variety of guns, but again, this is a difficult balancing act, certainly if you are improving the weapon as you progress through the game, or get used to a the playstyle of a particular weapon, you'll find, unless there are significant and obvious benefits, it's very difficult to get the player to swap them out.

Action: Some Design Tips

Lecture reference: slide 32

Action design tip 1: follow standardised control schemes

Regarding action FPS games, there is usually a recognised control system across both console and PC. I'd suggest following this norm and avoid trying to break it, or at least until you've made a game *with* the commonly recognised control scheme, so you'll understand elements you may want to change in future. Some games have ignored this, remapping certain key elements of control schemes such as *Killzone: Shadow Fall* (Guerrilla Games, 2013), which faced criticism[17] for its unconventional button mapping, with actions like aiming down sights and sprinting mapped to unusual buttons. These adjustments frustrated players who were used to the more standardised layouts of FPS action games such as *Call of Duty* and *Battlefield*. Unless there is a specific, and good reason for adjustment due to gameplay purposes, I'd suggest going with what the player knows.

Action design tip 2: build in XP and tiers

As discussed in previous lectures, we now see RPG elements incorporated into a huge number of games, including action titles, which illustrates how most game genres are becoming diluted and mixed. In many FPS's this allows players to build XP points which allows them access to new tiers of gameplay.

Action design tip 3: consider level design

As discussed, conventions such as rechargeable shields force specific cover-based level design in campaign. In Action FPS Multiplayer, this is quite a different beast from single-player level design. It needs such core elements such as orientation points to quickly reposition yourself on a respawn, and if you've got a team deathmatch you need to make sure the level is balanced on either side, you can't have camping points you can't have overpowered vantage points – you've got to be really careful with how you design that level. Multiplayer level design is a very specific area of level design and even when shipped, once "out in the wild" will usually require huge amounts of QA and player feedback to start to iron out any imbalances. Once again, these designs are very much based around ongoing iteration.

Action design tip 4: limit UI on the screen for clarity and immersion

In many modern FPS action games, developers are simplifying the on-screen display by removing everything except the player's weapon and the bullet count, often shown directly on the weapon. This minimalist approach focuses on immersing players in the action without cluttering the screen with HUD elements creating a more "cinematic" experience.

Genre 2: Action-Adventure

Lecture reference: slide 33

FIGURE 5.21　Image by Shutterstock/Fotiev.

Some examples of games in this genre are the *Tomb Raider, Uncharted* (Naughty Dog, 2007–present) and *Assassin's Creed* (Ubisoft, 2007–present) series of games. All feature core pillars of exploration, traversal, and a strong narrative element. Let's have a look at an exercise with some more examples.

IN CLASS EXERCISE 5.7 PART 1

Lecture reference: slide 34
Discussion: Action-Adventure games
Question:
Other than the provided example, are we able to think of any more examples of **Action-Adventure games**? Are they only third person? Or can they also be first?

Exercise 5.7 Part 1 Example Answers

The Legend of Zelda: Ocarina of Time (Nintendo, 1998)
The Legend of Zelda: Tears of the Kingdom (Nintendo, 2023)
Spider-man 2 (Insomniac Games, 2023)
Batman: Arkham city (Rocksteady Studios, 2011)
Grand Theft Auto V (Rockstar North, 2013)

IN CLASS EXERCISE 5.7 PART 2

Lecture reference: slide 35
Discussion: Action-Adventure games
Question:
Are we able to think of any examples of **action-adventure game** conventions, tropes or pillars?

FIGURE 5.22 Image by Jack Hollick.

Example 5.7 Part 2 Answers

Lecture reference: slide 36

Action-Adventure: Some Genre Conventions/Tropes

Action-adventure trope 1: third person

In third-person games, you primarily have a third-person view, though you can sometimes shift to first person. (see *GTA V*).

Action-adventure trope 2: exploration

A hugely important aspect. This genre of games usually gates exploration as reward (i.e., travelling to a new location or biome).

Action-adventure trope 3: puzzles

Are usually a part of the design, and frequently environment based (re-routing water, illuminating areas, etc.).

Action-adventure trope 4: cinematics and plot

Narrative is usually very important in these games and often relies on a well-characterised player avatar to drive the plot forward.

Action-adventure trope 5: A.I., NPC's and enemies

A.I. is important in how enemies react, especially in terms of their attack methods and behaviours on the levels, such as patrolling, sniping, and tank style characters as "sub bosses." Bosses are also frequently used to gate-level progression. In some cases there will also be player "companions" who are required to guide or accompany the player.

Action-adventure trope 6: combat

Combat is frequently either hand-to-hand or weapon based. In early *Assassin's Creed*, combat would be simple rock-paper-scissors manoeuvres where you timed a parry and pressed a button to counter, like early *Uncharted* and *Batman* titles. Other variations include upgrading to more weapons with ranged attacks as you progress. Some players prefer the option of ranged attacks because you don't have to get too close, allowing you to kite enemies and avoid damage, which, not mentioning names, is preferable for those gamers of a certain age who have reflexes like treacle.

Action/Adventure: Some Design Tips

Lecture reference: slide 37

Action-adventure design tip 1: have a strong character to empathise with

Core Design hit gold dust with Lara for a variety of reasons at that particular time in the history of the Universe, which we won't go into here, but a strong character builds its own reward system as you want to see their journey through the narrative. In more complex narrative-based games (which you could count on the fingers of one hand), they will "arc," which we'll talk about in the later narrative lecture.

Action-adventure design tip 2: traversal design is (may be?) very important

I'm not sure this is true for all action-adventures, but it's certainly an important and common convention or trope. The 2014 reboot of *Thief*, for example, is effectively an action-adventure in first person. *Mirror's Edge*, more of a traversal game in first person, highlights that first-person traversal games are rare because as discussed, it can be hard to know where your feet are during complex jumps and parkour. It's obviously easier if you can see the character in a 3D space, or in a platform game where specific metrics are visible in the level design. And talking of metrics:

Action-adventure design tip 3: metrics

As discussed, these were once crucial at the outset of action-adventure titles. Nowadays, characters and the player often snap to the environment. In *Assassin's Creed*, for example, you can now pretty much climb anything.[18] Designers used to have "Environment hooks" where level designers could design the player route through the environment carefully, adding affordances that would tell the engine where the player could grab, switching the camera and control mode, and playing the correct animation. Not anymore – algorithms now let players snap onto anything within reason, adding to player agency but perhaps removing some of the more directed "environment as a puzzle" level design.

Genre 3: RPG/MMORPG/JRPG (etc.)

Lecture reference: slide 38

FIGURE 5.23   Illustration by Shutterstock/Warm_Tail.

Some variants in this wide-ranging field, and their definitions are below:

RPG: Role-Playing Game

MMORPG: Massively Multiplayer Online Role-Playing Game

JRPG: Japanese Role-Playing Game

Well-known examples in this genre would be *World of Warcraft* (MMORPG), origi-nally released in 2004, and *Final Fantasy VII* (JRPG), released in 1997, and rebooted due to popular demand in 2024. Although both these games are from separate time periods and variations within the RPG genre, some common conventions here are:

- A focus on character development (both games feature character progression through experience points (XP) and levelling up),
- Quests and missions (specifically with side quests),
- A heavy focus on exploration, and also team dynamics – *FFVII* focusing on an A.I. roster, whereas in *World of Warcraft*, players form groups or raids with other players, in both cases combining their strengths to tackle difficult challenges.

Let's have a look at an exercise with some more examples.

IN CLASS EXERCISE 5.8 PART 1

Lecture reference: slide 39
Discussion: Action-Adventure games
Question:
    Other than the provided examples, are we able to think of any more examples of **RPG/MMORPG/JRPG** games?

Exercise 5.8 Part 1 Example Answers

RPG

The Elder Scrolls V: Skyrim (Bethesda Game Studios, 2011)
> *Open world exploration, extensive character customisation, and extensive lore.*

JRPG

Persona 5 (Atlus, 2016.)
> *Social simulation elements and turn-based combat in a modern Japanese setting.*

Pokémon Red and Blue (Game Freak, 1996)
> *Turn-based combat, character levelling, and extensive exploration.*

MMORPG

EverQuest (Verant Interactive, 1999)
> *One of the MMORPG grandaddies. Large-scale world, extensive lore, and cooperative gameplay.*

Final Fantasy XIV (Square Enix, 2010)
> *Deep storylines, class-based system, and frequent content updates.*

IN CLASS EXERCISE 5.8 PART 2

Lecture reference: slide 40
Discussion: Action-Adventure games
Question:
Are we able to think of any examples of **RPG/MMORPG/JRPG** conventions, tropes or pillars?

FIGURE 5.24   Illustration by Shutterstock/Terkell.

Exercise 5.8 Part 2 Example Answers

RPG/MMORPG/JRPG: some genre conventions

Lecture reference: slide 41

RPG/MMORPG/JRPG trope 1: "role playing"

Lest we forget the core pillar of these games, RPG systems are now commonplace across many genres, resulting in much bloat across titles, e.g. gigantic RPG fests in your action/adventure games, where you end up perpetually fiddling with skill trees and upgrading and repairing items, when all this player really wants to do is run around on rooftops, jump between large buildings, and assassinate major historical figures. (No game names mentioned to protect the innocent.)

RPG/MMORPG/JRPG trope 2: avatar improvement vital

Character improvement is built into any good RPG system and provides constant feedback and rewards. In games like *Fallout* or *Skyrim*, you want to ensure you're strengthening your character to match the game difficulty curve and allow access to progress. If you're like me, you'll spend quite a lot of time thinking about the power armour, a power fantasy that *Fallout 4* cleverly provides at the outset, dangling a massive carrot in the form of "this is what you'll eventually get after 60 hours of play."

RPG/MMORPG/JRPG trope 3: levelling up, XP points and "perks"

Fallout and the Bethesda games do this perfectly by combing XP with perks, so the deeper into the game you get, the more personalised your character is, leading to "ownership" and empathising more with your character. This is one of many re-engagement systems that make the player want to get back in and hunt that next XP hit.

RPG/MMORPG/JRPG trope 4: characters with different skills to be utilised

In a lot of these games, building a team is very much like building the perfect loadout. Level up your team by adjusting a series of intricate variables that reflect your own playstyle to better face the challenges ahead.

RPG/MMORPG/JRPG trope 5: collecting & personalisation

Getting pets and mounts, and so on, adds an element of peer review and personal ownership, allowing you to make your in-game character an extension of your own real-life choices and desires. (i.e. the desire to commute to work on a giant Tiger)

RPG/MMORPG/JRPG trope 6: grinding

To increase your XP from the bottom level, grinding remains a common mechanic. This frequently supports its sister mechanic, often referred to as "pay to win" or "cash rich, time poor." A mechanic system we've looked at earlier in the lecture series.

RPG/JRPG/MMORPG: some design tips

Lecture reference: slide 42

RPG/MMORPG/JRPG design tip 1: allow for full customisation

Allow extensive personalisation of the player avatar. You're not forced into specific classes anymore and can create a character that mixes different class traits without needing to specialise in one, or even shift your build and character class entirely during the playthrough.

RPG/MMORPG/JRPG design tip 2: interface design important

In games like *World of Warcraft*, the screen can become cluttered with UI information, and on PC, this sometimes requires downloading plugins to manage various elements. Try to design sub-menus to chunk the information and avoid overloading the player.

RPG/MMORPG/JRPG design tip 3: shops & trading

In *Fallout*, for example, traders are useful for offloading the 7000 tons of tin cans you've collected of after scavenging abandoned buildings, bins, and broken drawers for umpteen hours. Certain shops or traders will also often provide certain rare items, prioritising exploration.

FIGURE 5.25   Illustration by Jack Hollick.

RPG/MMORPG/JRPG design tip 3: outcome of choices is frequently probability based

It's all down to probabilities. In games like *World of Warcraft*, it's akin to playing *Dungeons & Dragons* with your multi-sided dice, although we don't see those dice rolls – they're calculated instantaneously. In games like *Fallout* or *Baldur's Gate 3*, some of the inner or "under the bonnet" workings are cleverly shown to the player. I'd argue one of the most addictive elements in *Fallout* is achieving the percentage chances of hitting enemies – there's certainly a slightly guilty dopamine rush at blasting a super mutant's head off its body when you only had a 15% chance of success.

IN CLASS EXERCISE 5.9:

Lecture reference: slide 43
Discussion: genres
Question:

Can you think of any games where there is one, clear, primary genre, or cases where games actually invented a genre?

Exercise 5.8 Example Answers

Single genre/genre source games

Lecturer Notes:
With exercise 5.8 and 5.9 I've provided a (non-exhaustive) list of core genre examples. For the exercise I would suggest canvassing a few game examples from the class and then focusing on/discussing three to five of the clearest until you feel they've understood the concept before moving on.

Platform:
   Super Mario Bros. (Nintendo. 1985).
Dota/MOBA:
   League of Legends (Riot Games, 2009).
Action-Adventure:
   The Legend of Zelda: Ocarina of Time (Nintendo, 1998).
Stealth:
   Metal Gear Solid (Konami, 1998).

FIGURE 5.26   Illustration by Shutterstock/Roberto Marantan.

Simulation:
> **The Sims** (Maxis, 2000).

Casual/Social:
> **Animal Crossing** (Nintendo, 2001).

Puzzle:
> **Tetris** (Pajitnov, 1984) *(I would clarify this as "2D puzzler")*

God Games:
> **Black & White** (Lionhead Studios, 2001).

FIGURE 5.27   Illustration by Jack Hollick.

Sandbox:
> **Minecraft** (Mojang, 2011).

Music:
> **Beat Saber** (Beat Games, 2018).

Survival Horror:
> **Resident Evil** (Capcom, 1996).

Tower Defense:
> **Plants versus Zombies** (PopCap Games, 2009).

RogueLike:
> **Spelunky** (Mossmouth, 2008).

FIGURE 5.28   Image by Shutterstock/Costertoast.

Combining genres:

As we've seen, with so many genres now combined and with the increasing complexity of modern games it's sometimes hard to separate them out to a single specific genre. And the rise in popularity of a specific genre (e.g., Roguelike) will skew combinations in that direction for a period. Let's have a think about games that combine genres.

IN CLASS EXERCISE 5.10

Lecture reference: slide 44
Discussion: genres
Question:
Can you think of any games where there are two, clear, genres combined?

Exercise 5.10 Example Answers

Combination genre games:
Portal (Valve Corporation, 2007)

Genres: *Puzzle, First-Person Shooter (FPS)*
Rocket League (Psyonix, 2015)
Genres: *Sports, Racing*
Faster Than Light (FTL) (Subset Games, 2012)
Genres: *Roguelike, Real-Time Strategy*

FIGURE 5.29 *Niddhogg*, by Messhof (*Nidhogg* creator), Copyrighted free use, via Wikimedia Commons.

Niddhogg (Messhof, 2014)
Genres: *Fighting, Platformer*
Kerbal Space Program (Squad, 2011)
Genres: *Simulation, Sandbox*

Genre conclusion. New genres

New, popular and unique games that have caught the players imaginations and filled a gap in the market, such as *Demons Souls* and *Dark Souls* have gradually introduced the "Soulslike" genre, of which the market is now flooded with clones. Some games such as DOTA and MOBA are combinations and adjustments around other games and genres that then create their own genre. Learning genres and their conventions is enormously useful from the perspective of mixing them up and creating your own USP's and even, in some cases, a new genre. It's not as rare as you think. Find two genres that you've never seen together before and brainstorm mechanics – you never know what will come up!

SECTION 5.4: GAME ANALYSIS: "THE 10-STEP PLAN"

Lecture reference: slide 45

Now let's move our focus back to Game Analysis, with a simple checklist which will help you to identify core gameplay elements, some of which re-iterate components and techniques we have already learned, and some which we'll look at as we progress further into our learning. This checklist will allow you to identify some common design techniques in the games you will be analysing, but there will always be more to find, so keep your eyes peeled! Without further ado, let's look at the checklist.

Lecturer Notes: Questing without a Map

Exercises that include elements not yet taught (e.g., "level types") help introduce new concepts and let students attempt to figure them out on their own without worrying about making mistakes. They are introduced (in this example) to some analysis and game design techniques before being formally taught them, encouraging them to make predictions based on what they already know about Game Design. This encourages them to think critically about how to approach further analysis, activates their prior knowledge, fires up their curiosity, and allows them to take "ownership" of their learning and develop their unique interpretations, or "take," on new concepts when they are formally introduced. As per the prominent educational theorist John Dewey's concept of "learning by doing" (Dewey, 1986), the emphasis on these introductory exercises is that learning should be active, where students build on prior knowledge while the educator introduces new concepts through exploratory exercises in an interactive learning environment (e.g. class discussions or team exercises) helping build a solid foundation for their own, personal, deeper understanding of the subject.

Analysis: 10 Common Techniques

Lecture reference: slides 46–47

1. **Onboarding and Gating/Gradual Mechanics Introduction**
   *Look for safe zones for experimentation at the start or when introducing new mechanics. Are mechanics gradually introduced to prevent overwhelming players? Is **Gating** (e.g., skill or gear) used to pace the introduction of new elements?*
2. **Clear Objectives with Feedback and Rewards**
   Assess how games use signposting (lights, corralling, big signs) to guide players and other breadcrumbing techniques, or direction markers required

in more complex maps. Does the variety and effectiveness of rewards used keep players engaged and motivated? Or is it the same thing repeated over and over?

3. **Affordances and Readability**

    How do games ensure players understand what they can interact with? Look at consistent visual (or sometimes auditory) game language that improves "readability" and player understanding.

4. **Player Agency and "Badassery"**

    Does the player have a wide range of tools and skills available to interact with the game world? Is the player overpowered, underpowered or "just right"? Look at design techniques used to make the player feel the way they do.

5. **Progression and Escalation**

    How does the game maintain flow by balancing skill and difficulty? Look at how difficulty increases as player skill improves and how this is handled (i.e., mini boss, environmental hazards?)

6. **Level Type/Layout**

    Try to recognise different level types (linear, sandbox, Arena) within the game, and their purpose and effectiveness. Look at the inclusion of orientation and planning points, especially in multiplayer games, and their role in guiding players.

7. **Level Design Methodology**

    Look at the use of critical paths, risk-reward setups, and environmental storytelling in the design of the game or level. Look at how environments reinforce genre-specific systems (e.g., tight corridors for limited reaction time/tension in horror games, open spaces for sniping in shooters).

8. **Paced Encounters or Events**

    Look at NPC behaviour (attack types, alert states) and the use of "monster closets." Assess the impact of encounters – is it the same encounter repeated or different every time? – and the necessity of downtime for pacing. Do elements such as traversal sections or puzzles slow the player down?

9. **Foreshadowing, Telegraphing, and Tells**

    Investigate how games use enemies, landmarks, and other cues to guide players. Evaluate types of foreshadowing (i.e., seeing part of the next level) and tells (seeing an enemy in combat before facing it yourself) in allowing players to plan and strategise.

10. **Spectacle, "WOW" Factor, and Hooks**

    Does the game have memorable setpieces and "water cooler" moments? Does the game have a positive hook or element that would inspire players to talk about it to their friends?

Now let's attempt to use these techniques in our final, in-depth analysis exercise:

IN CLASS EXERCISE 5.11: GAME ANALYSIS

Lecture reference: slide 48
Game Video Discussion:
Question
   Note down the genre, and any design conventions from the following game clip. Use both the game analysis checklist, and your own design intuition!

EXERCISE 5.11 VIDEO LINK
THIEF (Eidos-Montréal, 2014)
   https://bit.ly/EX5_11_THIEF

FIGURE 5.30 Illustration by Jack Hollick.

Exercise 5.11 Answers

Exercise 5.11 General Analysis
   There were quite a lot of mechanics introduced in that first small section. Elements such as the rope arrow were effectively gated, as introducing traversal mechanics like grappling hooks into games is quite difficult. Players will try to grapple everywhere, and as a designer, you can't let them do that, otherwise, they'll climb up and out of your map, which you, and more specifically, your creative director, doesn't want to happen. To prevent this, we have specific readability, such as the white marker on the post that you can fire the rope arrow onto. These are exactly the types of design elements you should be analysing. Let's look at some more types of design elements that you should start thinking about when playing sequences like that. As I said, if you can't play it, watching it is always going to be the second-best option because if you're not playing it,

you're not getting the direct feedback, which is what you need to analyse these mechanics in the precise detail required as a designer.

Let's have a look at some answers that correspond with our checklist:

Exercise 5.11 Checklist Analysis

FIGURE 5.31   Illustration by Jack Hollick.

Clear objectives with feedback and rewards

You start in a room with only one way out. The micro-objective here is learning how to steal (re-enforced by the rewards, both monetary and animation wise), and the macro is leaving the room, guided by the light of the window. Once you're out of the window, you're locked onto a critical path which is designed to teach in this first section of the game.

Onboarding and gating/gradual mechanics introduction

There are a lot of mechanics in that initial sequence. You saw some traversal mechanics, such as climbing out the window (a contextual button press/canned animation), and the skill wheel. Additionally, there were mechanics where you should walk to avoid alerting the birds, although this is "perceived jeopardy" rather than there being any actual danger of being exposed, although the sound of the birds warns the player. It's an area for safe experimentation. Likewise, it's hard to fail at the lockpicking mechanics. There's gear gating here with regards you can't get up to the next level or set of platforms without the rope arrow. From a game design perspective, it's difficult to stress urgency here, as the savvy player will know the game will effectively wait until they are done working out how to use the rope arrow. "readability" is a core element of where you're able to fire the rope arrow – directing the player visually to the solution.

Player agency and "badassery"

Did you feel in control? You should have – This initial section is designed as a power fantasy – unseen by the general populace, plying your trade, invisible to the proles below – only interrupted by a former colleague with the same skillset to put you back in your place (while teaching you basic traversal). Later in this initial tutorial sequence, you are awarded various tools and skills, like climbing and lockpicking, which also increase empowerment.

Affordances and readability

Consistent visual cues (like the lighted window) guide player actions, as well as specific objects that trigger particular mechanics or systems, such as the paintings.

Progression and escalation

This is basically a tutorial area, so no real evidence of this.

Level design methodology

Again, as a tutorial area, the critical path is obvious, with limited risk/reward. The environment supports the genre's mechanics.

Level type/layout

The critical path is fairly obvious in this example as you can't really diverge from the set route. Risk/reward and backtracking – it's a tutorial level, so not much evidence of these here, but we'll look at further examples in later chapters, although I think we can specify the level type is linear – it's a linear tutorial section where the player is gated into a small and corralled area, guided by the NPC Erin.

Paced encounters or events

The sequence includes safe experimentation with mechanics and minimal encounters, pacing the tutorial well. As a stealth game, the player will usually be directed towards avoiding direct encounters – but must have the tools available for combat if this does happen, neither of which scenarios are apparent in this training section. The NPC guiding A.I. is apparent here with Erin, although as you're unable to catch her, this is basically just a canned animation with triggered voice delivery. As a tutorial area, no "monster closets." Monster closets are the level design term for where you hide and spawn your enemies, the areas that feasibly the player can't get into. Unless you, hypothetically, find yourself working on a particular, unnamed game in which case you *can* get into the monster closets and then get stuck in them, necessitating a visit to the lead programmer to ask why the monster closet didn't have any monsters in it, stayed open, and then closed on you and locked you inside it.

Foreshadowing, telegraphing, and tells

Visual and auditory cues, like birds, provide feedback and foreshadow challenges for future encounters, where the jeopardy will become more prominent.

Spectacle, "WOW" factor, and hooks

We did have a spectacle event in this, and I would suggest it was the coming out onto the balcony and looking out over the river and a version of Olde Worlde faux London. Spectacle and set pieces are hugely important in level design and again this is something we'll look at in more detail in the specific lecture. I should note that the initial sequence is a cutscene (or cinematic) and other than introducing narrative or plot elements, these don't really qualify as "game design" as there is no interaction or player agency (other than the player usually clicking the "skip" button as quickly as possible, which I write, as a game scriptwriter, with some exhausted melancholy).

And on that note, let's conclude!

CONCLUSION

Lecture reference: slide 49

Analysing and deconstructing game designs is a vital skill for game designers. Regularly playing and critically examining games, noting genre pillars, mechanics, systems, and pacing, can inspire new ideas and refine your own game development skills. Knowledge of unique selling point categories, the three Cs – Character, Camera, and Control, and genre types and tropes will enhance your analysis. Practical application of these techniques, such as analysing game clips with the provided ten-step plan, will help further solidify understanding and help you understand and adapt these game elements into to your projects. The practice of playing and analysing games not only informs new game ideas but will also inspire innovation. Never stop playing![19]

LECTURE FIVE "GAME ANALYSIS": RESOURCE MATERIALS:

Lecture Five in PowerPoint Format:
Lecture Five Working Class 1 – USP's:
Lecture Five Working Class 2 – Ten Step Plan:
    Edit and upload to a shared drive of your choice!
(These included instructor resources can all be downloaded from the Instructor Hub. For further information, please see the chapter "How to Use This Book.")

NOTES

1 "Online test" might be a better name for students under 50.

2 See Chapter 3, Box 3.3.

3 As created and used by Jack Venegas my previous producer at Stainless Games, and former lecturer colleague at the University of Breda.

4 The other chapters obviously being Art, Programming, Production and Q&A.

5 The Haynes series of manuals, although recently updated for a modern audience, will mostly remind readers of a certain age of digging about in the engine of their broken car with the relevant, oil covered Haynes manual for that vehicle.

6 For some fantastic examples of video game-based museums in the UK, see "National Videogame Museum (NVM)" in Sheffield, the "The Centre for Computing History" in Cambridge, and a good selection of playable cabinets and consoles at the "National Science and Media Museum" in Bradford.

7 PS1 Dualstick controllers *were* available at this time – we didn't develop on them because no-one used them.

8 See chapter "Mechanics," specifically level designer Elisabetta Silli discussing issues with the analogue nature of the main character, Faith's movement, causing different jump distances at different speeds (DICE, 2008.)

9 "Motion capture," or the art of managing to act a scripted role proficiently while wearing a wetsuit with ping-pong balls on.

10 See Chapter 2 "Teaching," Skill/Gear Gating case study, *Assassin's Creed 2* and the infamous "climbing glove" of Leonardo Da Vinci.

11 Staff (2016, November 4). How bungie pioneered the modern console shooter – with a strategy game built for PC. gamesradar. https://www.gamesradar.com/how-bungie-pioneered-the-modern-console-shooter-with-a-strategy-game-built-for-pc/

12 Short for "metagame," refers to the prevailing strategies, tactics, character selections, and playstyles.

13 Janca (2023, May 9). *Overwatch 2 update adds Star Wars-inspired event, balance changes, and hero-specific settings.* GameSpot. https://www.gamespot.com/articles/overwatch-2-update-adds-star-wars-inspired-event-balance-changes-and-hero-specific-settings/1100–6513961/

14 "Tentpole" referring to movies or games designed to support the finances of the studio or developers' yearly earnings.

15 Wilde (2014, November 8). *Call of duty: Advanced warfare review.* pcgamer. https://www.pcgamer.com/call-of-duty-advanced-warfare-review/

16 Microsoft (2021) Power On: The Story of Xbox [TV series]. Redmond, WA: Microsoft. Available at: https://www.xbox.com/en-US/power-on – On an unrelated note, make sure to look out for the unexpected cameo!

17 Michalik (2013, November 19). Review: Killzone: Shadow fall (PlayStation 4). Push Square. https://www.pushsquare.com/reviews/ps4/killzone_shadow_fall

18 As a case in point, I never imagined running up the side of the great pyramid of Giza would be quite so effortlessly uninteresting.

19 (Unless it's during a lecture, obviously.)

REFERENCES

Activision. (2014). *Call of Duty: Advanced Warfare*. [Video game]. Santa Monica, CA: Activision.

Atlus. (2016). *Persona 5*. [Video game]. Tokyo: Atlus.

Bandai Namco Games. (2004). *Katamari Damacy*. [Video game]. Tokyo, Japan: Bandai Namco Games.

Beat Games. (2018). *Beat Saber*. [Video game]. Prague: Beat Games.

Bethesda Game Studios. (2011). *The Elder Scrolls V: Skyrim*. [Video game]. Rockville, MD: Bethesda Softworks.

Bethesda Game Studios. (2015). *Fallout 4*. [Video game]. Rockville, MD: Bethesda Softworks.

Blizzard Entertainment. (1996). *Diablo*. [Video game]. Irvine, CA: Blizzard Entertainment.

Blizzard Entertainment. (2004). *World of Warcraft*. [Video game]. Irvine, CA: Blizzard Entertainment.

Blizzard Entertainment. (2016). *Overwatch*. [Video game]. Irvine, CA: Blizzard Entertainment.

Bullfrog Productions. (1990). *Powermonger*. [Video game]. United Kingdom: Electronic Arts.

Bullfrog Productions. (1997). *Dungeon Keeper*. [Video game]. Guildford, UK: Electronic Arts.

Capcom. (1996). *Resident Evil*. [Video game]. Osaka: Capcom.

Capcom. (2001). *Devil May Cry*. [Video game]. Osaka: Capcom.

Core Design and Crystal Dynamics. (1996–present). *Tomb Raider series*. [Video games]. Derby: Eidos Interactive; Redwood City, CA: Square Enix.

Crystal Dynamics and Eidos-Montréal. (2006–present). *Tomb Raider Series*. [Video games]. Redwood City, CA: Square Enix.

Dewey, J. (1986, September). Experience and education. The Educational Forum, 50(3), pp. 241–252.

DICE. (2008). *Mirror's Edge*. [Video game]. Stockholm: Electronic Arts.

Eidos-Montréal. (2014). *Thief*. [Video game]. London: Square Enix.

Eidos-Montréal. (2014). *Thief*. [Video game]. Montréal: Square Enix.

FromSoftware. (2011). *Dark Souls*. [Video game]. Tokyo, Japan: FromSoftware.

Game Freak. (1996). *Pokémon Red and Blue*. [Video game]. Kyoto: Nintendo.

Guerrilla Games. (2013). *Killzone: Shadow Fall*. [Video game]. Amsterdam: Sony Computer Entertainment.

Hunt, R.R. (1995). The subtlety of distinctiveness: What von Restorff really did. *Psychonomic Bulletin & Review*, 2(1), pp.105–112.

id Software. (1993). *Doom*. [Video game]. Richardson, TX: id Software.

Infinity Ward. (2007). *Call of Duty 4: Modern Warfare*. [Video game]. Santa Monica, CA: Activision.

Infinity Ward. (2019). *Call of Duty: Modern Warfare*. [Video game]. Santa Monica, CA: Activision.

Insomniac Games. (2023). *Spider-Man 2*. [Video game]. Burbank, CA: Sony Interactive Entertainment.

Klei Entertainment. (2013). *Don't Starve*. [Video game]. Vancouver, Canada: Klei Entertainment.

Konami. (1981). *Frogger*. [Video game]. Konami.

Konami. (1998). *Metal Gear Solid*. [Video game]. Tokyo: Konami.

Larian Studios. (2023). *Baldur's Gate 3*. [Video game]. Ghent: Larian Studios.

Lionhead Studios (2001). *Black & White*. [Video game]. Guildford: Electronic Arts.

Maxis. (1993). SimCity 2000. [Video game]. Redwood City, CA: Electronic Arts.

Maxis. (2000). *The Sims*. [Video game]. Redwood City, CA: Electronic Arts.

Media Molecule. (2013). *Tearaway*. [Video game]. Sony Computer Entertainment.

Messhof. (2014). *Nidhogg*. [Video game]. Los Angeles, CA: Messhof.

miHoYo. (2020). *Genshin Impact*. [Video game]. China: miHoYo.

Microsoft. (2021). *Power On: The Story of Xbox.* [TV series]. Redmond, WA: Microsoft. Available at: https://www.xbox.com/en-US/power-on

Mojang. (2011). *Minecraft.* [Video game]. Stockholm: Mojang.

Mossmouth. (2008). *Spelunky.* [Video game]. Seattle, WA: Mossmouth.

Naughty Dog. (2007–present). *Uncharted Series.* [Video games]. Santa Monica, CA: Sony Computer Entertainment.

Nintendo. (1985). *Super Mario Bros.* [Video game]. Kyoto: Nintendo.

Nintendo. (1998). *The Legend of Zelda: Ocarina of Time.* [Video game]. Kyoto: Nintendo.

Nintendo. (2001). *Animal Crossing.* [Video game]. Kyoto: Nintendo.

Nintendo. (2023). *The Legend of Zelda: Tears of the Kingdom.* [Video game]. Kyoto: Nintendo.

Pajitnov, A. (1984). *Tetris.* [Video game]. Moscow: Academy of Sciences of the Soviet Union.

Phobia Game Studio. (2020). *Carrion.* [Video game]. Austin, TX: Devolver Digital.

Plausible Concept. (2018). *Bad North.* [Video game]. Sweden: Raw Fury.

Polytron Corporation. (2012). *Fez.* [Video game]. Canada: Polytron Corporation.

PopCap Games. (2009). *Plants versus Zombies.* [Video game]. Seattle, WA: PopCap Games.

Psyonix. (2015). *Rocket League.* [Video game]. San Diego, CA: Psyonix.

Rare. (1997). *GoldenEye 007.* [Video game]. Twycross: Nintendo.

Re-Logic. (2011). *Terraria.* [Video game]. Massachusetts: 505 Games.

Remedy Entertainment. (2019). *Control.* [Video game]. Espoo: 505 Games.

Riot Games. (2009). *League of Legends.* [Video game]. Los Angeles, CA: Riot Games.

Rockstar North. (2013). *Grand Theft Auto V.* [Video game]. Edinburgh: Rockstar Games.

Rocksteady Studios. (2011). *Batman: Arkham City.* [Video game]. Burbank, CA: Warner Bros. Interactive Entertainment.

Schmeltz, L. & Kjeldsen, J.I. (2016). Naming as strategic communication: *Corporate names in play. Corporate Communications: An International Journal,* 21(2), pp.196–210.

Sony Computer Entertainment. (2008). *Echochrome.* [Video game]. Japan: Sony Computer Entertainment.

Square Enix. (1997). *Final Fantasy VII.* [Video game]. Tokyo: Square Enix.

Square Enix. (2010). *Final Fantasy XIV.* [Video game]. Tokyo: Square Enix.

Square Enix. (2012). *Bravely Default.* [Video game]. Tokyo, Japan: Square Enix.

Squad. (2011). *Kerbal Space Program.* [Video game]. Mexico City: Squad.

Stoner, J.L., Loken, B. and Stadler Blank, A. (2018). The name game: How naming products increases psychological ownership and subsequent consumer evaluations. *Journal of Consumer Psychology,* 28(1), pp.130–137.

Subset Games. (2012). *Faster Than Light.* [Video game]. London: Subset Games.

SUPERHOT Team. (2016). *Superhot.* [Video game]. Poland: SUPERHOT Team.

Team Cherry. (2017). *Hollow Knight.* [Video game]. Adelaide, Australia: Team Cherry.

Ubisoft. (2007–present). *Assassin's Creed Series.* [Video games]. Montreuil: Ubisoft.

Ubisoft. (2021). Character camera controls Dominic Butler, projects director in our editorial technology team, breaks down the 3 cs... a fundamental aspect of game design pic.twitter.com/iocnoh9rjc, *Twitter.* Available at: https://twitter.com/LifeatUbisoft/status/1382359744703238144

Valve Corporation. (1998–present). *Half-Life Series.* [Video games]. Bellevue, WA: Valve Corporation.

Valve Corporation. (2007). *Portal.* [Video game]. Bellevue, WA: Valve Corporation.

Core Techniques
Challenge

6

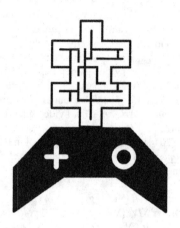

LECTURE OVERVIEW

Lecture reference: slides 1–2

In this lecture, we'll be looking at Game Challenge. This is a core element of the Objective/Challenge/Reward gameplay loop and a hugely important aspect of what creates "Game."

 DOI: 10.1201/9781032644721-6

GAME COMPONENTS

FIGURE 6.1   Game Components. Illustration by Andrew Thornton.

Challenge is a core element not only of our gameplay loops, but also of our **Game Component** list. Try to refer to this list to ensure you are aware of which element of the game design you are focusing on. Challenges cover a huge range of game elements, which we'll look at these in more detail shortly, but in the meantime let's get the ball rolling with our recap.

RECAP OF LAST WEEK'S TOPIC: ANALYSIS

Lecture reference: slide 5

Notes for Educator

Last week's analysis exercises were primarily video based, so these recap exercises will also focus on video clips. Note that if you'd like to start with student Gamecard slide examples, the USP exercise from last week is a good bet!

ANALYSIS – NEW EXAMPLE

IN CLASS EXERCISE 6.1

Lecture reference: slides 6–7
Recap discussion: Mechanics
Question:
   Look at the following student example from last week's Game analysis exercise, and mark down any design elements you spot from the "ten-step plan" (listed below)

   1. Onboarding and Gating/Gradual Mechanics Introduction
   2. Clear Objectives with Feedback and Rewards
   3. Affordances and Readability
   4. Player Agency and "Badassery"
   5. Progression and Escalation
   6. Level Type/Layout
   7. Level Design Methodology
   8. Paced Encounters or Events
   9. Foreshadowing, Telegraphing, and Tells
   10. Spectacle, "WOW" Factor, and Hooks

EXERCISE 6.1 VIDEO LINK

Lecture reference: slide 8
   Example 1: Skyrim (Bethesda Game Studios, 2011)
   https://bit.ly/EX6_1_SKYR

Exercise 6.1 Example Answer

"Affordances and readability"

FIGURE 6.2   Illustration by Shutterstock/Lukianenko Igor.

Although not *the* most recognisable barrel type in video games, that award goes to the classic exploding red barrel depicted in Figure 6.2. If you're not familiar with this design icon, I'd suggest the clue is in the name. Regarding our example video clip, the player is quickly able to recognise which of the barrel types can be interacted with via subtle visual design to inform the player which are "interactable" (when, in this case, searching for items) saving much unnecessary trial and error. The RPG game systems are working around the risk (time) versus reward (resources) of carefully sifting through the environment for these resources.

Recap: Analysis – Student Examples

Lecture reference: slide 9

Notes for Educator

Begin with the slides of the ten-step analysis plan. Then, choose an example from last week's exercise (or ideally, to avoid students knowing the answers, once you have started to accumulate examples, simply use the previous year's). Run the video clip as included by the student for class viewing. Next, use the students' PowerPoint analysis with the analysis elements blacked out (see Figure 6.3, Example, "Affordances and Readability"), which can be run as a Q&A or in-class recap quiz.

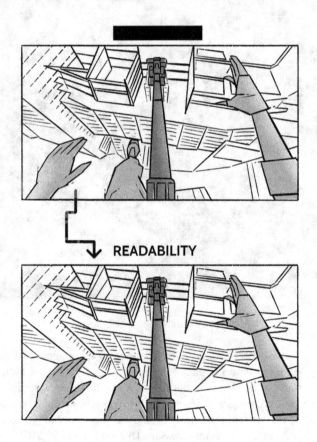

READABILITY

FIGURE 6.3   Readability in "Mirrors Edge." Illustration by Andrew Thornton.

Let's move on to USP corner!

Exercise 6.2 Answer

USP: A turn-based FPS!

Now back to the main event!

SECTION 6.1: CORE TECHNIQUES: GAME CHALLENGE

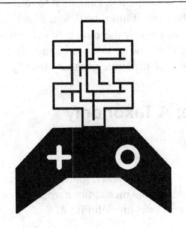

FIGURE 6.4   Illustration by Andrew Thornton.

Game Challenge – An Overview

Lecture reference: slide 12
Challenge is obviously a core feature of the Objective/Challenge/Reward loop, but the question really is: What defines challenge? I would suggest that the core element of the challenge is that it makes "*Gameplay*." Let's look at a previous example in more detail:

Imagine you are in a room. Your objective is to reach the door or exit. If you are simply able to walk to the door, open it, and leave the room, thus achieving your objective, I would argue this does not represent the conditions of a "game."

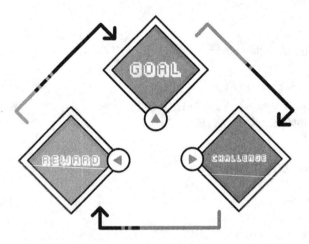

FIGURE 6.5   The objective challenge reward cycle. Illustration by Andrew Thornton.

On the other hand, if you had a large red turtle patrolling between you and the door, there are now strategies you must consider. Jump over it? Let's say you attempt to jump over it, and accidentally jump *on* it, causing it to retreat into its shell. Good news, right? But then you kick the shell, it hits a wall, and flies back towards you, hitting you and causing you to die. Wow. Luckily these sorts of incidents don't normally happen in reality – but in the game world, you've lost a life, and must restart from a checkpoint. I'd argue these **challenges** force the strategies that make "game."

Game Challenge: A Taxonomy

Lecture reference: slide 13

As we discussed at the start of the chapter, game challenges encompass a wide range of gameplay functions, systems, and mechanics across various genres, but now let's try and pin this down to a general working definition:

"A Game Challenge is a designed but surmountable obstacle that delays or prevents the player from reaching their objective in the objective/challenge/reward cycle."

We'll discuss "delay" and "prevent" in the context of challenge as we progress into the lecture. In the meantime, to introduce and provide context on the diverse and varied challenge systems within a single game series, let's focus on what I believe we would all agree is recognised as a particularly challenging series (and now genre): "Soulslikes."

Game Challenges – Examples

Dark Souls 1–3 (FromSoftware, 2011–2016)
The Soulslike genre features a comprehensive set of challenging game systems and mechanics. Let's review some examples from those titles and then use an exercise to cast the net for broader examples.

Challenge Example 1: "Mob Rule"

Lecture reference: slide 14

FIGURE 6.6   Card Design by Andrew Thornton. Illustration by Jack Hollick.

Let's start with a Soulslike mainstay – being overwhelmed by large numbers of ene-mies at one time – indeed, from a personal perspective I still have reoccurring night-mares about the "rat vanguard" in *Dark Souls 2*. The challenge of large numbers of enemies in Soulslikes is frequently designed around using the environment to "pull mobs" – keeping the group at a safe distance while attracting the attention of one or two enemies to draw them away and fight them in more manageable numbers. This is a design choice – certain games will design in this manageability, "feeding" the player enemies one at time while the rest of the group "waits" for combat. (See early *Assassins Creed* games). In Soulslikes, no one waits politely in turn to try to kill you, unless their collision box has got stuck on the environment, they will come "en masse."

IN CLASS EXERCISE 6.3: GAME CHALLENGES

Lecture reference: slide 15
  Game Challenge Discussion:
  Question:
  Are you able to think of any more examples of the "Mob Rule" challenge in games?

Exercise 6.3 Example Answer

Dead Rising 3 (Capcom Vancouver, 2013).
In the game *Dead Rising 3*, if the player is not careful, the high density of zombies (often hundreds on screen at once) can limit escape routes. This creates the challenge of either fighting them or strategic route planning (i.e., divert zombies).

Challenge Example 2: "Roaming"

Lecture reference: slide 16

ROAMING!
Allowing the player access to areas with
challenges outside of the regular difficulty
curve - allowing for bonuses - or death!

FIGURE 6.7   Card Design by Andrew Thornton. Illustration by Shutterstock/Warm_Tail.

Although not specifically part of the *Dark Souls* series, but (obviously) within the Soulslike genre, I'd suggest *Elden Ring* (Bandai Namco Entertainment, 2022) offers one of the clearest examples of this "risk/reward" challenge. Go for bigger enemies, gain more souls, better weapons, and allow access to game areas outside of the balanced difficulty curve, which then allows the player to repeat the cycle, leapfrogging some of the "grind." The only issue here is that without any real clear signposting, part of the challenge is frequently the trial and error of roaming far and wide across the landscape to construct your own manageable difficulty curve.

IN CLASS EXERCISE 6.4: GAME CHALLENGES

Lecture reference: slide 17
Game Challenge Discussion:
Question:
    Are you able to think of any more examples of the "Roaming" challenge in games?

Exercise 6.4 Example Answer

World of Warcraft series (Blizzard Entertainment, 2004–present)
Although there have been many balancing and design adjustments since *World of Warcraft* first launched in 2004, once you progress beyond the initial areas, the game generally allows free roaming regardless of level. The challenge here, like *Elden Ring*, involves risk-reward dynamics and the potential to leapfrog some extensive "grinding." Unfortunately, if a low-level player ventures into high-level areas and gets killed, there is the potential for a lengthy "corpse run," where the player must drift vacuously back across the landscape, in floaty unkillable spirit form, to where you were unceremoniously murdered. From a game design perspective, the negative reinforcement here is the potential time wasted, while the positive is getting all your gear back. Upon reaching your corpse, you must then resurrect, and then swiftly run away in your old, now once more disappointingly killable body, from the nearby enemies that did you over in the first place. "Challenging", right?

Example 4: "Loadout"

Lecture reference: slide 18

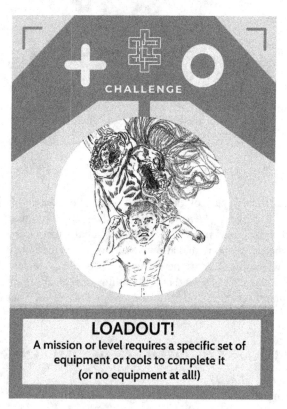

FIGURE 6.8   Card Design by Andrew Thornton. Illustration by Jack Hollick.

Although "Loadout" more specifically describes the equipment you prepare for your avatar before entering a level, this challenge example also represents the difficulty of choosing the correct tool or weapon for the correct job within the level - and, in many cases, the challenge of finding the correct tool or weapon in the first place. The trend in "naked" (or "fist only") runs across the Soulslike series highlights a community challenge where, although players are allowed consumables (i.e., Estus flasks), they must rely on their bare hands and, without any other gear, utilise precise dodging, rolling, and parrying to avoid damage and exploit enemy weaknesses to complete the game. As you can imagine, successfully completing these insane challenges earns players significant respect and admiration from their Soulslike peers. This trend also highlights a common issue from the game designer perspective: you may design your game in a specific way, but it's the players who choose how they play it!

IN CLASS EXERCISE 6.5: GAME CHALLENGES

Lecture reference: slide 19
Game Challenge Discussion:
Question:
    Are you able to think of any more examples of the "Loadout" challenge in games?

Exercise 6.5 Example Answers

Call of Duty series (Infinity Ward and Treyarch, 2009–present)
    In the *Call of Duty* series, (Mostly MP but relevant for SP) the challenge for players is customising their loadouts with specific weapons, attachments, perks, and equipment. Having the right combination tailored to playstyle and the requirements of the level or match (i.e., sniper campaign mission, team deathmatch) is vital for success. It should be noted that in Multiplayer modes access to these weapons and perks must be strictly balanced to avoid "overpowered" (OP) players disrupting the match, as an overpowered item or tactic can make it very difficult for players using standard loadouts to compete fairly. These are usually quickly jumped on by the community, prompting the devs to address overpowered items through patches and updates (in most cases) to "rebalance" the game.

Now we've looked at some examples across not only Soulslikes, but various genres, let's again choose a specific genre with a view to more of a deep dive into its challenge conditions:

SECTION 6.2: GAME CHALLENGE FOCUS – "PUZZLERS"

Lecture reference: slide 20

In last week's lecture, we considered Exploration, environmental hazards, and puzzles as key tropes in the action-adventure genre. Let's consider one element of these, puzzles, from the perspective of the **challenge** in our gameplay loop. We see that puzzle challenges are now widespread in various games. In *Call of Duty: Black Ops Cold War* (Activision, 2020) players solve a puzzle to find a safe combination from a calendar on the wall to unlock a shiny new gun (see boxout here[1]) while in *Marvel's Spider-Man 2* (Insomniac Games, 2023) players find themselves jumping desperately from wall to wall to connect electricity nodes and recharge a generator. This increasing proliferation of puzzles has a design purpose, which we will explore shortly, but in the meantime, let's clarify: for our focus on challenges, let's concentrate on an introduction to *puzzles* as the challenge component, with an overview of how to integrate them into first and third person games, drawing from my own experience creating them to deconstruct some industry examples. So, without further ado, let's get cracking!

Defining Puzzles: 2D versus 3D

Lecture reference: slide 21

I should note that for the purposes of this lecture we're not talking about 2D puzzle games, match-threes, *Tetris*, or *Boulder Dash*, genres and games which all have their own very specific challenge conditions, pillars, rules, and systems. Puzzles in "flat" 2D games tend (although not exclusively) to focus on direct interaction with abstract mechanics in playing areas and with a fixed top-down view. First- and third-person puzzles, which we'll be looking at, emphasise direct player character control, narrative integration, and environmental interaction from a dynamic viewpoint. This can be a side-scrolling perspective such as *Limbo* (Playdead, 2010) or *Inside* (Playdead, 2016) or alternately first-person or over-the-shoulder third-person perspective such as *Tomb Raider* (Core Design, 1996), allowing them to move through and interact with a 2.5D (see Box 6.1) or three-dimensional space, and will usually feature environmental puzzles as a core element of their challenges. This direct character control also covers specifically puzzle-based first-person titles such as *Portal* (Valve Corporation, 2007), *Q.U.B.E* (Toxic Games, 2011), and the *Talos Principle* (Croteam, 2014.)

FIGURE 6.9   "Inside." Illustration by Jack Hollick.

Box 6.1: 2.5D

What is a 2.5D game? If you ask the class what a 2.5D game is, there will usually be one or two students smiling back at you blankly. It's really simple, and once explained, you'll spot it immediately. It's similar to an isometric game, where the camera is set to a specific fixed (in that case, orthographic) viewpoint, but in a 2.5D game, you have a parallax effect, meaning you play on a fixed plane in the foreground, while the background is utilised as scenery. This used to frustrate me as a player, because I wanted to get to the juicy stuff in the background, but you can't because you're locked to the foreground plane. Some games, like *LittleBigPlanet* (Media Molecule, 2008) and *Little Nightmares* (Tarsier Studios, 2017) have multiple planes, allowing you to move back and forth slightly into the screen, so theoretically you are allowed to interact with more game elements as you have not only left and right movement, but "in and out" as your other axis. This can sometimes cause issues in that because of the locked front-facing camera position, it makes it difficult to determine your position on the screen. You'll make a jump, and the platform you're jumping to is slightly closer to the camera than the platform you're jumping from, and has a gap behind it, and you jump, and then you fall down the gap, and then you'll die. So, if you are designing around this extra axis in your 2.5 game, please make sure the holes behind these hypothetical platforms are obvious to cater for players (or possibly unnamed lecturers) with slightly less aptitude. And that's 2.5D.

Defining Puzzles: First- and Third-Person "Pillars"

Lecture reference: slide 22

Furthermore, let's tie down some pillars or common tropes in specifically first or third-person puzzle games:

Environmental challenges

Players must usually interact with the environment to solve puzzles. This can involve manipulating objects, finding hidden items or codes in the environment, or "traversal puzzles" (finding the route through the environment.)

Logical challenges

These puzzles will often require logical thinking and problem-solving skills. Players might need to figure out patterns, sequences (e.g., a code to open a safe), or the correct order of actions to progress, i.e., pulling levers or pressing buttons in a specific sequence.

Mechanics challenge

Core puzzle-specific mechanics integrated into the puzzle, like moving objects with a gravity gun in *Half-Life 2* or using portals in *Portal*.

Object-based challenges

Specific objects are required to progress, i.e., missing cogs to drive a mechanism. More complex examples of this will involve combining objects.

Feedback

Clear feedback needs to be given when a puzzle is solved correctly. This can be visual, auditory, haptic, or a combination of all. This will re-enforce the "Eureka!" moment of solving the puzzle, as well as the reward of recognising progress in the game.

SECTION 6.3: CHALLENGE: DESIGNING PUZZLES IN A-AAA TITLES

Lecture reference: slide 23

Designing puzzles is complex and requires consideration of specific elements unique to this field. In his book *The Art of Game Design: A Book of Lenses*, Jesse Schell highlights one of the core issues with puzzle design: *"The thing that really seems to bother people about calling puzzles games is that they are not replayable. Once you figure out the best strategy, you can solve the puzzle every time, and it is no longer fun."* (Schell, 2008).

So how do we build the fun back in? Is it possible to create puzzles with multiple solutions? What if there can only be one solution, described by Bob Bates as "binary" in his 2001 book *"The game design: The art and business of creating games"*? Does that automatically negate all fun? It certainly doesn't help, and we'll examine (and hopefully "solve") an industry example of that in this lecture.

NOTE: Although we'll introduce some aspects of the complexities of puzzle design in this lecture, there will be a puzzle-specific set of lectures to dive deeper into these topics later in the lecture series.

So, without further ado, let's start by looking at a puzzle in a AAA third-person title – in this case a mechanic we've seen previously, but this time, as an exercise we'll be deconstructing it from a puzzle perspective.

> **IN CLASS EXERCISE 6.6: CHALLENGES – PUZZLES**
>
> *Lecture reference: slide 24*
> *Game Video Discussion:*
> *Question:*
>   Do you notice anything about the design of the puzzle challenge in the following clip?

Exercise 6.6 Example 1

Dead Space (EA Redwood Shores, 2008)

FIGURE 6.10   Illustration by Jack Hollick.

EXAMPLE 1 VIDEO LINK:

https://bit.ly/EX6_6_DEAD

Exercise 6.6 Example 1 Answer

Lecture reference: slide 25

The core takeaway for creating a puzzle in A-AAA is that in these titles the puzzle challenges are *usually constructed around a few simple key mechanics*. For example, there are a lot of puzzles in *Dead Space* where the mechanics are introduced gradually and become more complex, often by combining these mechanics. As we see, the first time we use stasis in *Dead Space*, it is in isolation; you use it to slow down a malfunctioning door, that in true *Dead Space* style, cuts you in half if you get it wrong (effectively gating the player until they've learnt it). In *Dead Space*, you really have three core or "key" puzzle mechanics:

- Stasis module.
- Gravity gun.
- Zero-gravity environments.

The gravity gun, as discussed, used frequently since *Half-Life 2*, is a core element of many physics-based puzzles. Nowadays, we have very robust physics systems provided within our "off the shelf" game engines for us, whereas back in the day programmers were actually coding physics systems into their own engines (see link to previous boxout on this here[2]) with resultant nervous breakdowns aplenty. Physics systems are enormously complex, and to some degree it's a double-edged sword being provided with these so readily in modern game engines. It is quite common for students to sit down and attempt to make a physics-based puzzler because they've simply been given the engine that contains a physics system in it, and then start to find that creating a game that is entirely reliant on physics means that some of the systems they have designed may have suddenly become more unpredictable and slightly more, let's say, "fluid."

The upside of creating physics-based challenges or puzzles is that we don't need to explain the rules to the player – they mimic reality. For example, we understand that an apple falling from a tree will drop on our head due to gravity – or to use a *Dead Space* style analogy, when a piece of malfunctioning heavy machinery falls on our head, we understand it's going to shear it off.

Lecture reference: slide 26

"A to AAA puzzles are usually constructed around a few simple key mechanics"

So, to recap – In *Dead Space*, the "few simple key mechanics" the puzzles are built around that stasis modules slowing things down, and the gravity gun moves them. If we were also to include the zero-gravity systems into future puzzles, we see that by gradually scaffolding and combining these mechanics, the designer is able to create more complex and engaging puzzles and challenges. Let's look at another example of this:

> **IN CLASS EXERCISE 6.6: CHALLENGES – PUZZLES PART 2**
>
> *Lecture reference: slide 27*
> *Game Video Discussion:*
> *Question*
>   Try to note all the mechanics or systems utilised in the following clip (from a puzzle-based challenge perspective.)

Exercise 6.6 Example 2

Portal 2 (Valve Corporation, 2011)

> **EXAMPLE 2 VIDEO LINK:**
>
> https://bit.ly/EX6_6_PORT

FIGURE 6.11   Illustration by Shutterstock/irin-k.

Exercise 6.6 Example 2 Answer

Lecture reference: slide 28
Overlooking the minor mishap at the end of the video (>ahem<), let's list the mechanics and systems utilised in the design of that sequence:

- Portal gun
- Orange paint (speed)
- Blue paint (bounce)
- Button/switch
- Fizzler (Material Emancipation Grid)
- Platforming/Flinging

As we can see, there's a huge number of mechanics in that sequence, and you can't introduce all of them at once, or the player will become enormously confused. The portal itself is a complex enough mechanic for the player to learn, introduced at the start of *Portal 2* in such a way that Valve makes sure you know how to operate the "in" portal before allowing you access to the "out" portal later in the game. Also, a note on the "fizzler" as an important design feature: This prevents you from taking objects through it, and helps the player understand the limitations of the puzzle. It also prevents game-breaking issues, such as spawning 7000 cubes in one room and potentially overwhelming the GPU. Additionally, there's jumping and traversal, as well as flinging, which involves momentum as a variable in the puzzle design. These are the main puzzle/challenge mechanics, and as you can see, to reach this point, as a designer, you've got a lot of player training to organise and facilitate.

Puzzle challenges in AAA titles

Lecture reference: slide 29

Certainly if we are looking at A-AAA games that aren't specifically marketed as "puzzle" or "puzzle platformers," it should be noted they don't sell themselves on their puzzles. I would suggest you wouldn't purchase a *Tomb Raider*, *Uncharted*, or particularly a *Dead Space* game specifically for the puzzles, but the puzzles are an important element of these games, and from a design point of view, often for a specific reason:

Returning to the book *The Art of Game Design: A Book of Lenses*, Jesse Schell describes "what all puzzles have in common is that they make the player *stop and think.*"

Echoing this sentiment specifically from a game developer perspective, in many cases, I would suggest puzzles are included to extend playtime and ensure players feel they get value for the money they've spent. If we look at website "HowLongToBeat"[3] we see some evidence players expect considerable gameplay hours from high-cost games. For example, a main story playthrough of *Elden Ring* averages around 60 hours, while if completing all additional content the game can take up to 132 hours. These figures reflect those games in the highest bracket price range have expectations to deliver large amounts of content, certainly in amount of hours of play time. When asked, students will often respond that they are willing to pay higher prices for multiplayer elements that can extend playtimes exponentially. The codstats/time-playedtotal[4] site suggests that on average, players tend to invest substantial time, often exceeding 200 hours annually, on Call of Duty games. So if you're designing a mid-priced A-AAA without Multiplayer, and want to give value for money from a time-played perspective (without creating a world that is the developer breakdown invoking size of *Elden Ring*) I would refer you back to Jesse Schell:

"What all puzzles have in common is that they make the player *stop and think.*"

Stopping, or at least slowing down the player can be important. Sounds cynical? Not so – in the case of puzzles, these can be hugely rewarding for the player. If a complex and well-designed puzzle slows the player's progress while they enjoy solving it, and this in turn eliminates the need for the developer to build and light ten more rooms and decorate them with spanking new textures and low-poly models, saving a week of crunch on a game such as, plucking a name out of the air, the original *Tomb Raider* series, then this would surely be a win-win for both player *and* developer, right?

Indie puzzle mechanics: opening the VALVE

Lecture reference: slide 30

FIGURE 6.12   In the style of "Tag: the power of paint." Illustration by Andrew Thornton.

Regarding Student/Indie games, as discussed in Chapter 4 (Mechanics), without the vast production budgets of A-AAA titles, puzzle-specific indie games need to focus on one core USP with one or two clear mechanics for their puzzles. And if these mechanics are unique and playable enough, a triple-A company like Valve might notice them and incorporate them into their current game, as happened with the propulsion and repulsion gels originally featured in student indie title *Tag: The Power of Paint*[5], the mechanics further repurposed in *Portal 2*, with the original team hired by Valve to develop these systems further.[6]

Let's have a look at another (DigiPen) student indie puzzle title to remind (and inspire) ourselves:

IN CLASS EXERCISE 6.6: PART 2, CHALLENGES – INDIE PUZZLERS

Lecture reference: slide 31
Game Video Discussion:
Question
    Can you identify the unique mechanics that form the puzzle challenge in the following clip?

Exercise 1.2 Example 3

Perspective (Boxerman et al., 2012*)*

FIGURE 6.13   In the style of "Perspective." Illustration by Andrew Thornton.

EXAMPLE 3 VIDEO LINK:

https://bit.ly/EX6_2_PERSP

Exercise 6.6 Example 3 Answer

You have a camera you can move freely and lock into position. Once locked, this allows you to control the character. The blue lines indicate where the character can walk, providing clear readability. These two simple systems or mechanics combine to create a totally unique gameplay challenge. Sounds easy? Not so, as per this insight from student producer Pohung Cheng as featured on "Geekwire"[7]: "The team members poured their heart into the game, overcoming stressful nights and times when they wondered why they picked such a "ridiculously difficult game to make," as producer Pohung Chen puts it: "Making games is hard, making great games is even harder!".

Indie to Single A Titles – Managing Content

Lecture reference: slide 33

Let's have a little look at techniques for how smaller games with smaller teams and production values are managing content, and how less can be more. If you're able to find one or two intriguing puzzle mechanics that focus your design down to smaller areas, this again re-iterates some of our discussions about reducing content "bloat" and managing your scope in smaller teams or indie game development. I'll show you an example of a very clever way that a smaller team have managed this in the game *The Room*, created by Fireproof Games (2012). They've made a number of sequels, so a successful series, and rightfully so, as they are beautifully designed – a mix of an escape room and the *Hellraiser* puzzle box, originally designed for tablets and smartphones – let's have a look and see if you're able to work out what they are doing from a design perspective.

IN CLASS EXERCISE 6.6: PART 3,
CHALLENGES – INDIE TO "A" PUZZLES

In class reference: Lecture slides?
Game Video Discussion:
Question
    List various methods the developers have used to reduce content "bloat" in the following clip:

Exercise 6.6 Example 4

The Room Series (Fireproof Games 2012–2018)

FIGURE 6.14 Illustration by Shutterstock/Alex Sind.

Exercise 6.6 Example 3 Answer

One of the genius design elements here is that they've got one very complex piece of geometry, which in this case is the safe, or puzzle box, and they've limited the assets required with this one complex piece of geometry, which allows it to run across a huge variety of (less processer intensive) platforms. Design-wise, you're basically moving through layers of the geometry – you unlock one layer and then find something else that then leads you to another part of the object, and you're spinning it, investigating this super interesting puzzle box – and the element here, that works particularly well on a tablet or smartphone, which is primarily what the original games were designed, for is that the controls for the game are utilising a particular type of challenge, and that's through the way you're navigating through and with the box, and that's particular type of control system is called **"Mimetic."**

Mimetic means you're actually moving the game object or moving the game in the way that you would actually be moving or investigating the real-world object. For instance, you're having to swivel sections, turn elements, and swipe mechanical components. It's mimetic, and it helps with the immersion of the title, and certainly, the "uniqueness." Certainly, the Wii U (Nintendo, 2012) was based a lot around mimetic control systems. A lot of the early Wii game USP's were simply based around the fact that you felt like you were moving in the same way that you would playing the game in the real world – i.e., swinging your nunchuck in the tennis racket peripheral[8] when playing digital tennis, for instance. Part of the success of this console was arguably down to the fact that you could play with family members who didn't need to learn complex controller inputs, simply grab the stick, press a button, and play – although it should be noted that accessibility isn't much of a consolation if your grandma accidentally propels the nunchuck violently out of your patio door and through the side of your neighbour's greenhouse.

Indie to Single A Titles – Managing Content Part 2: Scoping

Lecture reference: slide 34

Scope sensibly

As a student at an early stage in your game design career, it's obviously important to design around constraints. Although there is now an abundance of free resources online, from low-end pixel art to a full gamut of AAA content (i.e., the free EPIC *Paragon* assets, "built at a cost of over $17,000,000"[9]) game design at student, junior or solo level requires **scoping.**

Some elements to consider as a student or junior designer (from the perspective of our focus on puzzle games):

Scoping: narrative

Is narrative an important element? Are you able to strip it back to voiceover (i.e., "Portal")? Try to avoid costly NPCs, and if they are required, is there a way to avoid facial animations, such as lip-syncing? Are you able to infer the narrative in subtext instead of spelling it out with "on the nose" exposition?[10]

Scoping: player character

First or third person? First person removes the need for time-consuming animations but generally doesn't work well with precise interaction or combat, which third person is more suited to i.e., *Hyper Light Drifter* (Heart Machine, 2016). If you have to have third person, can you simplify the character design to fit the environment, i.e., *Journey*, or abstract it to basic humanoid shapes, i.e., Superhot (*SUPERHOT* Team, 2016)? If you're still set on a complex third-person character, remember that there are now plenty of complex models, free auto-rigging tools and vast libraries of mocap data for your character online. The only thing you need to bear in mind is that you'll need someone to code the animation (or even more complicated traversal) systems!

FIGURE 6.15   Illustration by Andrew Thornton.

Scoping: environment

Can you use the *Cube* technique (see Chapter 4, Box 4.6 "The Cube Effect") to reuse the same environment and lighting? Or is your puzzle challenge built into the environment, requiring extensive level design, i.e., the student game *Perspective*? Are you able to use a core object/mechanic that adds deep complexity and layering to a relatively simple environment, i.e., the "Memento Mortem" pocket watch in *Obra Dinn* (Pope, 2018)? If you need to build levels, try to design them as modular as possible – use tilesets or modular chunks of geometry that can be snapped together instead of creating single, bespoke levels.

Scoping: mechanics

Ideally, one clear unique mechanic is what you are looking for (i.e., "time moves when you move" from *Superhot*) but finding a USP for each project is not realistic or viable.[11] Find one core mechanic that works, ideally through prototyping, e.g., the rewind feature in *Braid* (Number None, 2008), and design your game around that. If one is not enough (test it with others, and you'll know pretty quickly!), try prototyping other mechanics that are symbiotic with your first – design around the possibility of combining these two mechanics to create puzzles. A good example of this is the different abilities of the two characters that work together in the game *Brothers: A Tale of Two Sons* (Starbreeze Studios, 2013).

Learning to scope your project within time constraints is probably one of the most important elements of time management on a game development course, and, once graduated, there are valuable lessons here that can be taken through into solo or indie game development.

Before moving on, let's look at a couple of final examples of some "indie" puzzle games that I'd suggest have managed scope in particularly clever ways.

IN CLASS EXERCISE 6.7: CHALLENGES – SCOPING

In class reference: Lecture slides?
Game Video Discussion:
Question
    Use the four scoping elements (Narrative, Character, Environment, Mechanics) to try to identify ways in which the developer(s) have limited "scope bloat" in the following titles:

Exercise 6.7 Example 1

Inscryption (Mullins, D. 2021)

Lecture reference: slide 35

FIGURE 6.16   Illustration by Jack Hollick.

EXAMPLE 6.7 VIDEO LINK:

https://bit.ly/EX6_7_INSC

Exercise 6.7 Example 1 Answer

Narrative

The storyline and lore are shown through text and simple visuals, avoiding the need for extensive cutscenes or complex animations. NPC's are represented as static or minimally animated, reducing modelling and animation costs.

Character

First person, although hands and animations are required for interactions.

Environment

The first act of the game is set in one primary location, the cabin, with variations in lighting and minor changes to create different moods.

Mechanics

The same playing card graphics and mechanics are used throughout, with new rules and abilities introduced progressively.

Exercise 6.7 Example 2

Papa Sangre (Somethin' Else, 2010)

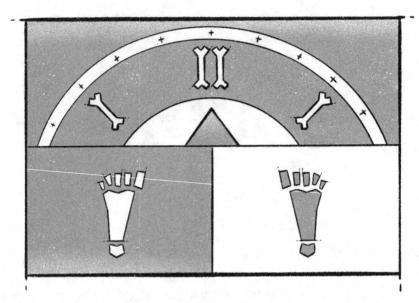

FIGURE 6.17   Illustration by Andrew Thornton.

EXAMPLE 6.7 VIDEO LINK 2:

https://bit.ly/EX6_7_PAPA

Exercise 6.7 Example 2 Answer

Narrative

The game uses narrative delivered through voiceovers, avoiding the need for complex visual storytelling and extensive animations.

Character

The game is Audio-Centric, focusing on binaural sound, which allows the player to be abstracted to a simple graphical display that allows them to move around an environment created/imagined from the sounds the player hears.

Environment

See above. It's all in the mind! Development Win!

Mechanics

Simple navigation and interaction mechanics. Players use taps and swipes to move and interact with the environment, reducing the inclusion of other costly gameplay elements.

SECTION 6.4: SCAFFOLDING CHALLENGES

Lecture reference: slide 38

Let's move back into our deep dive into focusing on challenges in puzzle design, and in this section we'll introduce "The anatomy of a challenge," a taxonomy created from analysis and application of challenge and puzzle design techniques that should supply you with a framework to begin to constructing or implementing your own.

FIGURE 6.18   Koichi Hayashida, illustration by Jack Hollick.

Let's begin by looking at a quote from Koichi Hayashida, director of *Super Mario Galaxy 2* (Nintendo, 2010) and *Super Mario 3D Land* (Nintendo, 2011), who, in an interview with Game Developer[12], reveals one of "Miyamoto's[13] secrets" for creating entertaining level design:

"First, you have to learn how to use that gameplay mechanic, and then the stage will offer you a slightly more complicated scenario in which you have to use it. And then the next step is something crazy happens that makes you think about it in a way you weren't expecting. And then you get to demonstrate, finally, what sort of mastery you've gained over it."

This is our first introduction to a tiered system of challenge design, which gradually guides the player through challenge "steps," whether this be specific elements of gameplay, or as we'll see from further examples as we progress, puzzles. As we've seen, this approach for "onboarding" the player is common in many titles, especially Nintendo series like *Zelda* and *Mario*. The tiered system is designed to gradually introduce the various mechanics or systems without overwhelming the player.

Let's have a look at further examples, this time from a valve, in a puzzle section of the seminal title *Half-life 2: Episode One* (Valve Corporation, 2006), foreshadowing the use of the light bridge puzzles in *Portal*.

Half Life 2: Episode One (Valve Corporation, 2006)

Lecture reference: slide 39

FIGURE 6.19　Image by Shutterstock/Robyn Mackenzie.

EXAMPLE 1 VIDEO LINK:

https://bit.ly/EX6_4_HALF

In the developer commentary on this clip, Scott Dalton describes the Valve design philosophy (listed in the transcript as the "three step approach"[14]):

The light bridge ball sockets are a clear example of our training approach to new gameplay elements. We train players with a leading example, confirm they understand the concept, then switch up the problem set and make them use it in a new way. The first bridge shows players the solution, the second one confirms they understand, the third, knowing they understand the gameplay mechanic, challenges them in a new way using that mechanism.

We begin to see there is a common language in how game challenges, or in this case, puzzles, are designed. Let's translate this into a simple challenge/puzzle design system:

SECTION 6.5: ANATOMY OF A CHALLENGE

Lecture reference: slides 40–41

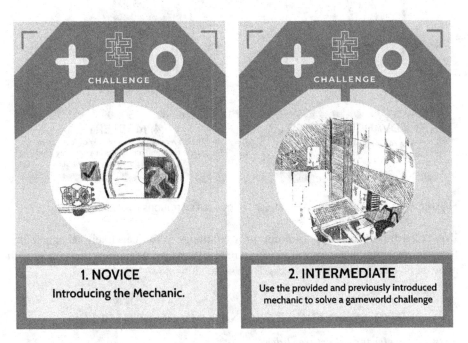

FIGURE 6.20 Card Designs by Andrew Thornton. Illustrations by Jack Hollick.

Boiling down Hayashida/Miyamoto's "Structure of fun[15]" challenge design structure with Valve's "three-step approach," we can construct a scaffold to onboard players to puzzles (or, indeed, various types of game challenges).

- **Novice:** Introduce the mechanic in a safe environment.
- **Intermediate:** Use the previously introduced mechanic(s)[16] to solve a game-world challenge.

- **Advanced/Leftfield:** The player can use the taught mechanic(s) in a different or unique way.
- **Mastery:** the player uses all prior knowledge of the mechanics and their combinations to solve the challenge

Lecture reference: slide 42

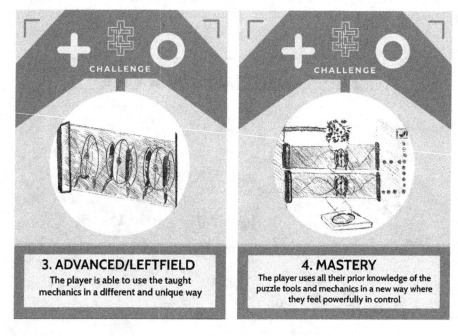

FIGURE 6.21   Card Designs by Andrew Thornton. Illustrations by Jack Hollick.

I've called this taxonomy "**Anatomy of a challenge**": You can likely recognise this four-step structure in games you've played recently, and we'll reinforce this system with more game examples as we progress. Here's one along now!

IN CLASS EXERCISE 6.8: ANATOMY OF A CHALLENGE

In class reference: Lecture slides?
Game Video Discussion:
Question
    Which of the four "Anatomy of a challenge" stages (*novice, intermediate, advanced, mastery*) do you think the following example illustrates?

Exercise 6.8 Example 1

The Witness (Thekla, Inc., 2016)

Lecture reference: slide 43

FIGURE 6.22   In the style of "The Witness." Illustration by Andrew Thornton.

EXAMPLE 1 VIDEO LINK:

https://bit.ly/EX6_8_WITN

Exercise 6.8 Example 1 Answer

Novice

Okay, so we'll note some classic onboarding here, which would point us to the "Novice" stage of the "Anatomy of a challenge" system. You start in a very clean environment with a solitary objective, which is the door at the end. It's linear. Get to that, and your mechanic is moving a dot through a fixed track or path. This is an example of "gating" – you can't leave until you understand that mechanic. Next, you move into a darker environment where the only thing illuminated is the interface – the dot and path system, with clear readability – the screen looks interactive and your cursor changes and "locks" to the interface panel making it clear you are in a different mode that requires "solving." When you come out onto the surface, the first thing you see is the panel you'll interact with, along with several cables clearly leading out of the panel. As you begin to explore more of the environment, you find more of these panels, recognisable via a visual language and set of affordances made very clear to the player, helped by amazing flat-shaded art, adhering to the design choice of keeping it simple but beautiful to not further confuse the increasing complexity of the puzzles.

Now let's have a look at one of my own industry examples of a "novice" challenge:

Industry Example: Novice

"Unpublished title"

This example is from an unpublished (or "canned" in dev parlance) A-AAA third person puzzle and exploration game. The design team was tasked with creating puzzles from pre-designed mechanics, a simple day-to-day design task (as discussed in Chapter 4, "Mechanics"). The pre-provided mechanics I chose to design this puzzle (from a larger list) were:

- Physics gun.
- Objects that could snap or lock into place (usually with the use of the Physics gun).

Let's have a look at the results:

NOTE: I've included Figure 6.22 as an example of a simple industry blockout diagram. You'll note we're not talking AAA production values here, and bear in mind that's the point – it's meant to be to a quick way of describing the core elements of a proposed puzzle to the design team. If the team is happy with it (as decided by Lead Designer, Programmer, Artist and Producer), these blockout elements from the diagram would be re-designed to fit aesthetically into the game, while retaining the game logic. (i.e., the game was never going to feature a giant standalone rabbit cage with a huge key floating in it.)[17]

IN CLASS EXERCISE 6.9: ANATOMY OF A CHALLENGE – NOVICE

Lecture reference: slide 44
Industry diagram Discussion:
Question
   Using the list of provided mechanics, are you able to explain how the following puzzle works?

Novice Example 1: "Industry Puzzle Game"

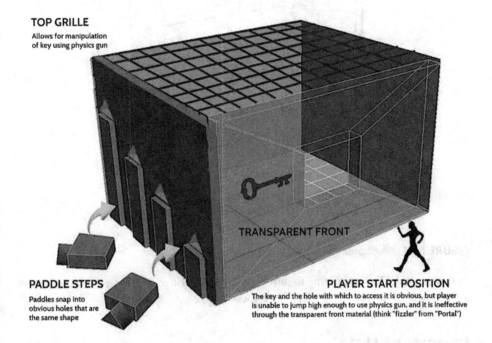

TOP GRILLE
Allows for manipulation
of key using physics gun

TRANSPARENT FRONT

PADDLE STEPS
Paddles snap into
obvious holes that are
the same shape

PLAYER START POSITION
The key and the hole with which to access it is obvious, but player
is unable to jump high enough to use physics gun, and it is ineffective
through the transparent front material (think "fizzler" from "Portal")

FIGURE 6.23   "Industry Novice puzzle." Illustration and design by the author.

Exercise 6.9 Example 1 Answer

As you arrive at the area the player should know that they are going to need a key. Whatever shape that key might actually take in the final game is down to the art department, but the key will have been set up as a player objective. The key in the hole through which to access it is obvious, but players aren't able to jump high enough to get it into range to use the gravity gun to pull it out (alternatively, you're unable to use the gravity gun if jumping, which would be a control choice). If you go around the side of this room or cage, you have two of these steps or wedges on the floor. Note that you're introducing the player to these mechanics in a safe environment. You need to get onto the top of the structure, which you can see is a grill from the glass pane at the front. The steps slot into the obvious "step shaped" gaps, the "clever"[18] bit here being that once on the first step, you have to pick up the step from the bottom, put it into the next step slot, and then reuse the bottom steps to get to the top. Then, you can grab the key and toss it out of the hole in the front pane ready for collection.

Novice Example 2

Portal 2: Perpetual testing initiative (Valve Corporation, 2011)

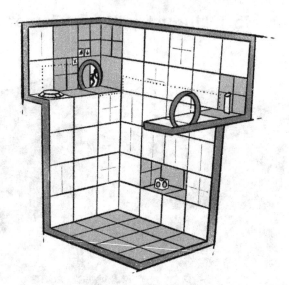

FIGURE 6.24   Illustration by Andrew Thornton.

In this example, I'm attempting to introduce the Lightbridge following the "Anatomy of a challenge" "Novice" stage – let's have a look:

Important Note!

This example has been created this example using the Perpetual Testing Initiative (PeTI) editor, available in *Portal 2*, which allows players to create their own levels.[19] *This level has NOT been created by or endorsed by Valve, other than using the software provided by Valve.*

EXAMPLE 2 VIDEO LINK:

https://bit.ly/EX6_9_PORT

Lecture reference: slide 45

The novice lightbridge

When the puzzle begins, the player can see the exit, and can also see a pressure pad on the other side of the gap. The player has their objectives clearly set out. You just need to get the cube and drop it on the pressure pad to open the door. I've put anti-portal paint on the interior of that room as an easy fix to prevent the player portalling their way out of trouble, but I imagine there are other solutions you could choose to implement here. It's all down to getting the cube, and you have the light bridge mechanic to play around with in a safe environment, and I'm also introducing the fact you can portal the light bridge. You can fire the light bridge out from various walls which is important for the solution. And that's me creating a very simple version of how I would introduce the light bridge as a "Novice" challenge element.

With this in mind, let's refer back to the *Half Life 2: Episode One* developer commentary again, this time Valve dev Matt T. Wood describing the initial rollermine challenge:

> *"Training is one of the fundamental tenets of our design philosophy. Before the player is required to utilize some new game mechanic or new weapon, or face a new monster under pressure in a dangerous situation, **we always introduce the concept in a relatively calm but ideally still entertaining way"**[20]*

And again, to repeat Scott Dalton describing the pre-portal Lightbridge:

> *"The light bridge ball sockets are a clear example of our training approach to new gameplay elements. We train players with a leading example, confirm they understand the concept, then switch up the problem set and make them use it in a new way. **The first bridge shows players the solution, the second one confirms they understand, the third, knowing they understand the gameplay mechanic, challenges them in a new way using that mechanism."***

If we note my emphasis on both quotes, we see the Valve three-step puzzle design re-enforced and mappable to "novice" through "advanced/leftfield" in our taxonomy (no Mastery yet!):

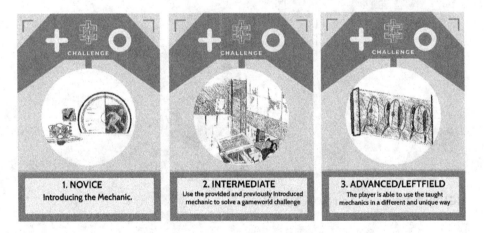

FIGURE 6.25 Card Designs by Andrew Thornton. Illustrations by Jack Hollick.

Now let's have a look at an example the actual first "Hard Light bridge" puzzle from *Portal 2*, which arrived 5 years later – and watch out for which category it falls under:

IN CLASS EXERCISE 6.10: ANATOMY OF A CHALLENGE

Lecture reference: slides 46–48
Industry diagram Discussion:
Question
    List some of the design elements in this first Lightbridge puzzle, and try to identify which one of "Anatomy of a challenge" stages (*novice, intermediate, advanced, mastery*) it illustrates.

Exercise 6.10 Example 1

"Portal 2" (Valve Corporation, 2011)

FIGURE 6.26   Illustration by Jack Hollick.

EXAMPLE 1 VIDEO LINK:

https://bit.ly/EX6_10_PORT

Exercise 6.10 Example Answer

Other than the surprise of another navigation-based fail on my part, I think the first and most striking element here is that I'd suggest we've moved straight into **intermediate**. It's still a well-designed puzzle, there is no doubt about that, but if we return to part of the Valve design edict, *"we always introduce the concept in a relatively calm but ideally still entertaining way,"* I'd suggest we have an element here of Jeopardy which counteracts that, in the water hazard at the bottom of the map that can kill the player. It's an intriguing example, and a useful one from a teaching perspective because you'll remember it – as Valve don't really "do" flawed puzzles. And indeed, in this instance I'd suggest (as is commonly mentioned in their various dev logs), I've got a funny feeling again that they've had to cut out an initial "novice" room here for some unknown purpose. Maybe, given its position in the game's difficulty curve, they didn't feel a novice puzzle was necessary and thought it would upset the game's difficulty balance. So, they've cut it. Although I should point out, that's only my two cents worth of opinion, and your mileage may vary.

Let's do a little bit of level analysis and break down some of the other design elements in that clip:

Player training

- *Different Bridge Levels (i.e. dropping)*
  This introduces the mechanic of being able to drop onto another portalled light bridge, but obviously in a non-safe environment, as we can see through player incompetence, results in death.

- *Lining up bridges (with entrances) and right-angle bridges*
  Designed to train/onboard the player in those mechanics.

Design

- Player can see the exit (their objective) clearly from the start of the level.
- The first light bridge exit goes directly past the cube dispenser, setting it up.
- Some of the switches are hidden, meaning the player must work through it in stages (they are revealed gradually through level design "chunking")
- Puzzle choices and player Agency (provided by light bridge positioning)

So, as I've said, I'd suggest this is more of an intermediate challenge, and with intermediate, there are certain problems we should be aware of:

SECTION 6.6: ANATOMY OF A CHALLENGE: INTERMEDIATE

Where Problems Can Begin!

Lecture reference: slide 52

Let's return to an example, this time intermediate, designed by Thomas White using Unreal Engine 5 (Epic Games, 2021) for clarity and speed to create simple industry whitebox puzzle diagrams. Here's a list of the available design toolset, in the style of commonly recognised *Portal* mechanics for easy notation:

- Pressure Plate
- Cube
- Cube Dispenser (in case the player somehow drops the cube in the water)
- Exit Door
- Pedestal Button (Timed Bridge Button)
- Water (Kills player and destroys cubes)

IN CLASS EXERCISE 6.11: INTERMEDIATE

Lecture reference: slides 53–61
Industry diagram Discussion:
Question

Looking through the steps in the following intermediate puzzle, what makes it intermediate? And are you able to recognise the "flaw" in the puzzle design?

Intermediate Example 1

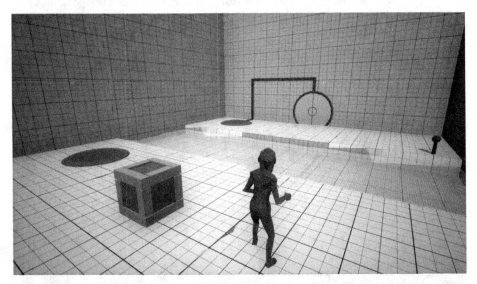

FIGURE 6.27   Image by Thomas White/ Synty Studios/Epic Games UE5.

Introductory overview

The player starts from one side of the room, (side 1) and the door is on the other side (side 2). Sides 1 and 2 are segregated by a water channel which the player cannot cross. The exit door is closed but obvious as an objective.

FIGURE 6.28   Image by Thomas White/ Synty Studios/Epic Games UE5.

STEP 1:

On side 1, put the cube onto the pressure plate. This creates a bridge between 1 and 2.

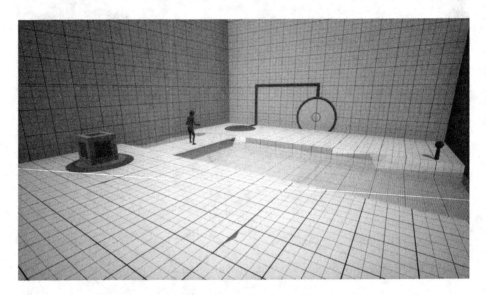

FIGURE 6.29   Image by Thomas White/ Synty Studios/Epic Games UE5.

STEP 2:

Walk across the bridge to side 2.

FIGURE 6.30   Image by Thomas White/Synty Studios.

STEP 3:

Activate the pedestal switch. This creates a second bridge, this time between side 2 and side 1.

FIGURE 6.31   Image by Thomas White/ Synty Studios/Epic Games UE5.

STEP 4:

Walk back across to side 1.

FIGURE 6.32   Image by Thomas White/ Synty Studios/Epic Games UE5.

STEP 5:
   Pick up cube.

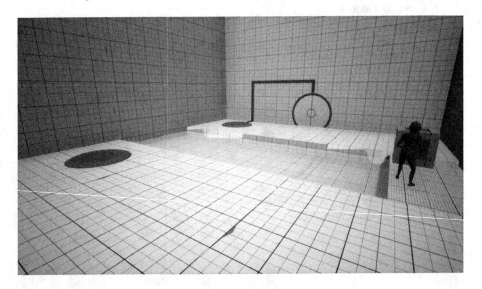

FIGURE 6.33   Image by Thomas White/Synty Studios.

STEP 6:
   Walk back across with the cube to side 2.

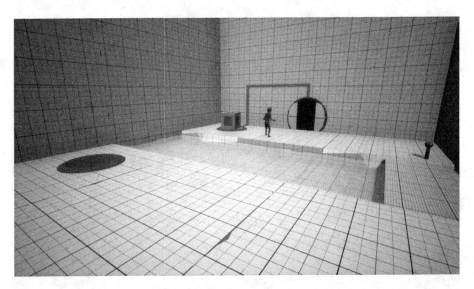

FIGURE 6.34   Image by Thomas White/ Synty Studios/Epic Games UE5.

STEP 7:
Place cube on second pressure pad to open door.

Exercise 6.11 Example 1 Answer

Intermediate

This puzzle is intermediate because it requires the player to apply previously taught mechanics in a logical manner. The player must use a cube and pressure plate to create a bridge, activate a pedestal switch to create a second bridge, collect the cube, and then place it onto the second pressure plate to open the exit door. This multistep process combines taught mechanics, moving it from "Novice" and into an "Intermediate" challenge.

The flaw

Lecture reference: slides 61–62

The flaw is quite difficult to spot unless you actually look for it, and is often contextual depending on the game/mechanics you are creating the challenge/puzzle in, but in this case the problem is:

THERE ARE NO ALTERNATIVE SOLUTIONS!

From a puzzle design perspective at the intermediate stage, this isn't a deal-breaker – but we need to be aware of it. Other than falling in/dropping the cube in the water. There are no strategies here where you can go wrong – no trial and error, moving the cube and getting it in the wrong order, no incorrect way you can activate the bridge. And as a result, no reward – you haven't fathomed out a solution, you've carried a block into a specifically corralled route to a solution. There are currently no alternative solutions or options. without variations and alternatives available so you can mess up, basically, you won't get the "Eureka!" lightbulb moment, the reward for all your hard work that, as discussed in the overview[21] section, is vital in puzzle design. (as opposed to general challenge design)

Let's specify this important part of our challenge design, so we are able to avoid it:

FIGURE 6.35   Image by Shutterstock/Berto Ordieres.

Bad Puzzle Design! No Options!

Looking at the "Eureka!" moment as an important element of puzzle design, giving the player no options or strategies massively reduces the impact for the player of working out how to solve it. Without strategies or options, you have, as Bob Bates describes in his chapter on Puzzle design[22] "*binary puzzles. These are puzzles with "yes" or "no" answers that yield instant success or failure.*" (Bates, 2001, p. 129). As a player, we want to try out different solutions, fail, and finally, after having tried what we assumed was every option suddenly, at 3 am suddenly wake up realising *why* the designer put the bicycle inner tube in the drawer.[23] This sudden epiphany that drives us back to our smartphone, computer, or console to try out this new strategy, and if successful, supplying you with the "Eureka!" moment, and the reward of all that cognitive processing providing the dopamine hit you've been yearning for. THIS is good puzzle design, it's very difficult to do, and it will always involve allowing the player options. No options means no "Eureka!" moment, so try not to design a puzzle without them![24]

Intermediate – Just Add Options!

With that in mind, let's have a look at some possible solutions to add options to our previous example:

Exercise 6.12 Example 1

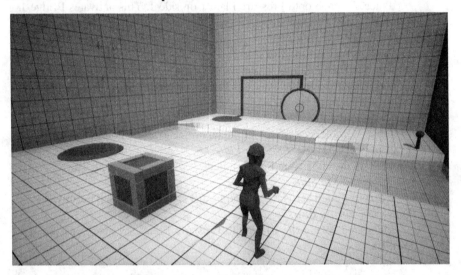

FIGURE 6.36   Image by Thomas White/ Synty Studios/Epic Games UE5.

Example answer

There are a number of possible solutions to adding options into this puzzle, but we must be careful not to overwhelm the player with these options (see "Chunking/Scaffolding" in Chapter 2, "Teaching"). Let's look at one possible option:

Initial setup
   Two additional elements:

- A Cube Dispenser that drops cubes continuously into the water, aligned with the pedestal button. (cubes that hit the water will disintegrate and respawn from dispenser)
- An adjustment to the pedestal button that creates a TIMED bridge. (timing would be tweaked at the prototype phase)

One additional rule:

- Instead of side 1, Player starts on side 2 (side with pedestal button)

Solution Steps

1. *Activate the Timed Bridge*:
   Starting on side 2, press the Pedestal Button (Timed Bridge Button).
   This activates the timed bridge, stopping the cubes from falling into the water and allowing the player to collect a cube.

2. *Collect a Cube*:
   Quickly walk across Bridge 2 to side 1 while the timed bridge is active. Pick up a cube from the timed bridge before it deactivates.

3. *Place the Cube on Pressure Plate 1*:
   Place the cube onto Pressure Plate 1 on side 1. This activates Bridge 1, connecting side 1 to side 2.

4. *Cross Bridge 1 to Side 2*:
   Walk across Bridge 1 to side 2.

5. *Activate the Timed Bridge Again*:
   On side 2, press the Pedestal Button (Timed Bridge Button) again to reactivate the timed bridge.

6. *Return to Side 1*:
   Quickly walk back across the timed bridge to side 1 before it deactivates.

7. *Retrieve the Cube from Pressure Plate 1*:
   Pick up the cube from Pressure Plate 1, deactivating Bridge 1.

8. *Carry the Cube to Side 2*:
   Carry the cube across the timed bridge to side 2 before it deactivates.

9. *Place the Cube on Pressure Plate 2*:
   On side 2, place the cube onto Pressure Plate 2. This opens the exit door. Exit.

In this redesign, we've introduced the strategies of the timed bridge and the spawning cube. The player needs to carefully time their actions to collect a cube without it falling into the water. The timed bridge mechanism adds an extra layer of challenge, ensuring the player needs to co-ordinate their timing to solve the puzzle. It's always a difficult balancing act designing challenges and puzzles in games, certainly in respect of your difficulty curves, but testing will always help with this. Hand it over to a friend, or even better, a QA department, and they'll usually have no qualms in telling you why it does or doesn't work.

SECTION 6.7: INTERMEDIATE TO ADVANCED/LEFTFIELD

Lecture reference: slides 64–65

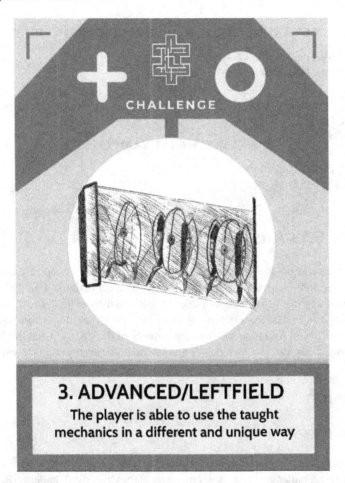

FIGURE 6.37   Card Design by Andrew Thornton. Illustration by Jack Hollick.

Let's wrap up the lecture with some examples of advanced/leftfield puzzles leading up to Mastery. We'll explore these in more detail as the culmination of a series of more specific puzzle lectures, focusing on designing puzzles from the ground up, rather than our current overview on how we introduce them to the player (the anatomy of a challenge).

Leftfield Lightbridge

We started with the Lightbridge from *Portal 2*, so it seems as good a place as any to end. Let's have a look at the following clip and think about how they are effectively subverting a taught mechanic, or as Hayashida says "challenges them in a new way using that mechanic"

IN CLASS EXERCISE 6.13: ADVANCED/LEFTFIELD

Lecture reference: slide 66
Game Video Discussion:
Question
    Which previously taught mechanic is being used here, and how is it being subverted?

EXERCISE 6.13 EXAMPLE 1

Portal 2 (Valve Corporation, 2011)
https://bit.ly/EX6_13_PORT

Exercise 6.13 Answer

In this subversion of the Lightbridge mechanic, they've flipped its purpose from something you stand on to something used as a shield. When you enter that first arena, it's impossible to miss the light bridge being used as a shield directly in front of you. You then have to use the light bridge to get past the turret as a shield, gating the player. It's an absolutely left-field use of that mechanic. And with such an elegant piece of design, we'll end this lecture, and I look forward to seeing your own novice and intermediate examples in the working class.

Conclusion

Lecture reference: slide 67

In this chapter, we've explored the essential nature of game challenges, focusing particularly on puzzles. Challenges are a core component of the Objective/Challenge/Reward loop, defining gameplay by introducing obstacles that players must overcome to achieve their goals. We defined the pillars of puzzle design in first and third-person games, emphasising how A to AAA titles construct their puzzles around a few simple key mechanics, and how even in non "puzzle-centric" games, these challenges add value to the player experience.

Lastly, we introduced the concept of "Anatomy of a challenge," providing a framework for designing puzzles that cater to different skill levels, from novice to mastery, this framework ensures that games can offer progressively complex challenges, working within the context of the difficulty curve to keep players engaged and motivated towards the dopamine hit of the "Eureka!" moment, and continued engagement with your game.

LECTURE SIX "CHALLENGE" RESOURCE MATERIALS:

Lecture Six In PowerPoint Format:
Lecture Six Working Class:
  Edit and upload to a shared drive of your choice!
(These included instructor resources can all be downloaded from the **Instructor Hub**. For further information, please see the chapter "How to Use This Book.")

NOTES

1 Chapter 2: Teaching, Box 2.8 "Blocks" (Junior Designer Tip #1).
2 See Chapter 5, "Analysis," Box 5.3 Editors & Engines: Welcome to the Asylum
3 *HowLongToBeat.com | Game Lengths, Backlogs and more!* Available at: https://how longtobeat.com/
4 *Total time played leaderboards (no date) Total Time Played Leaderboards.* Available at: https://codstats.net/leaderboards/timePlayedTotal
5 Brown, Lyons, Teitelbaum and Van Wingen (2008).
6 As previously noted, the DigiPen student game "Narbacular Drop" was adapted by the original students (hired by Valve) to become "Portal". *Narbacular drop, DigiPen.* Available at: https://www.digipen.edu/showcase/student-games/narbacular-drop.
7 Soper (2012).
8 Sold separately, I might note. Nintendo, are, after all, a business.
9 *17,000,000 of Paragon content for free - unreal engine.* Available at: https://www.unrealengine.com/en-US/paragon
10 See the game *Inside* for a masterclass on non-verbal plot exposition.
11 If you are able to do this, please contact me immediately, and mark the email "retirement fund".
12 Nutt, C. (2012) *The secret to mario level design, Game Developer.* Available at: https://www.gamedeveloper.com/design/the-secret-to-i-mario-i-level-design
13 Shigeru Miyamoto, the renowned Japanese video game designer and producer at Nintendo, often referred to as the "father of modern video gaming."
14 *Developer commentary/half-life 2: Episode One* (no date) *Developer commentary/Half-Life 2: Episode One – Combine OverWiki, the original Half-Life wiki and Portal wiki.* Available at: https://combineoverwiki.net/wiki/Developer_commentary/Half-Life_2:_Episode_One
15 As described by Nutt, C. (2012) *The secret to mario level design, Game Developer.* Available at: https://www.gamedeveloper.com/design/the-secret-to-i-mario-i-level-design
16 Note the complexity here can be introduced through the combination of two previously introduced mechanics. e.g. the water temple example from *The Legend of Zelda: Ocarina of Time*, where the player Equips the Iron Boots to sink and walk on the lakebed, allowing Link to access underwater switches and doors, and uses the Hookshot/Longshot to reach targets on the walls and pull himself to new areas that are otherwise unreachable.
17 Although I have worked on some games where that wouldn't surprise me in the slightest.
18 Please don't quote me on this puzzle being "clever." It's not.
19 A beautiful, simple example of editor design that providing a user-friendly interface for designing custom test chambers (and also share them with the community).

20 *Developer commentary/half-life 2: Episode One* (no date) *Developer commentary/Half-Life 2: Episode One – Combine OverWiki, the original Half-Life wiki and Portal wiki.* Available at: https://combineoverwiki.net/wiki/Developer_commentary/Half-Life_2:_Episode_One
21 See "Feedback" section of "Defining Puzzles: First- and Third-person 'Pillars.'
22 Bates (2001).
23 *Tomb Raider 5: Chronicles.* (Core Design, 2000). Don't ask.
24 As I've said, this is not a deal breaker – it just means that your puzzles with have less of a reward, and hence less "impact."

REFERENCES

Activision. (2020). *Call of Duty: Black Ops Cold War.* Santa Monica, CA: Activision.

Bandai Namco Entertainment. (2022). Elden Ring. Tokyo, Japan: Bandai Namco Entertainment.

Bandai Namco Games. (2014). *Dark Souls II.* Tokyo, Japan: Bandai Namco Games.

Bates, B. (2001). *Game Design: The Art and Business of Creating Games.* Roseville, CA: Prima Tech, p. 129.

Bates, B. (2001). *The Game Design: The Art and Business of Creating Games.* Portland: Premier Press.

Bethesda Game Studios. (2011). *The Elder Scrolls V: Skyrim.* [Video game]. Rockville, MD: Bethesda Softworks.

Blizzard Entertainment. (2004-present). *World of Warcraft series.* Irvine, CA: Blizzard Entertainment.

Brown, N., Lyons, G., Teitelbaum, D., and Van Wingen, J. (2008). *Tag: The Power of Paint.* DigiPen Institute of Technology. Available at: https://games.digipen.edu/games/tag-the-power-of-paint.

Core Design. (1996). *Tomb Raider.* Montreal, Canada: Eidos Interactive.

Core Design. (2000). *Tomb Raider: Chronicles.* Montreal, Canada: Eidos Interactive.

Croteam. (2014). *The Talos Principle.* Zagreb, Croatia: Croteam.

DigiPen Institute of Technology. (2012). *Perspective.* Redmond, WA: DigiPen Institute of Technology.

EA Redwood Shores. (2008). *Dead Space.* [Video Game]. Redwood City, CA: Electronic Arts.

Epic Games. (2021). *Unreal Engine 5.* Cary, NC: Epic Games.

Fireproof Games. (2012). *The Room.* Guildford, UK: Fireproof Games.

Fireproof Games. (2012–2018). *The Room Series.* [Video Games]. Guildford, UK: Fireproof Games.

FromSoftware. (2011–2016). *Dark Souls Series.* [Video games] Tokyo: FromSoftware.

Heart Machine. (2016). *Hyper Light Drifter.* Los Angeles, CA: Heart Machine.

HowLongToBeat.com | Game Lengths, Backlogs and more! Available at: https://howlongtobeat.com/.

Insomniac Games. (2023). *Spider-Man 2.* Los Angeles, CA: Sony Interactive Entertainment.

Media Molecule. (2008). *LittleBigPlanet.* Guilford, UK: Sony Computer Entertainment.

Mullins, D.. (2021). *Inscryption.* [Video Game]. Austin, TX: Devolver Digital.

Nintendo. (2010). *Super Mario Galaxy 2.* Kyoto, Japan: Nintendo.

Nintendo. (2011). *Super Mario 3D Land.* Kyoto, Japan: Nintendo.

Nintendo. (2012). *Wii U console.* Kyoto, Japan: Nintendo.

Number None. (2008). *Braid.* San Francisco, CA: Number None.

Pope, L. (2018). *Return of the Obra Dinn.* San Francisco, CA: 3909 LLC.

Ratloop Games Canada. (2021). *Lemnis Gate.* [Video game]. Canada: Frontier Foundry.

Schell, J. (2008). *The Art of Game Design: A Book of Lenses.* Boca Raton, FL: CRC Press, p. 208.

Schell, J. (2008). *The Art of Game Design: A Book of Lenses*. Boca Raton, FL: CRC Press, p. 209.

Somethin' Else. (2010). *Papa Sangre*. [Video game]. London: Somethin' Else.

Soper, T. (2012). *The Power of Perspective: Digipen Students Debut Popular Mind-Bending Game*. GeekWire. Available at: https://www.geekwire.com/2012/perspective-game-digipen-students-award-winning/.

Starbreeze Studios. (2013). *Brothers: A Tale of Two Sons*. Stockholm, Sweden: Starbreeze Studios.

SUPERHOT Team. (2016). *Superhot*. Łódź, Poland: SUPERHOT Team.

Tarsier Studios. (2017). *Little Nightmares*. Malmö, Sweden: Bandai Namco Entertainment.

Thatgamecompany. (2012). *Journey*. Santa Monica, CA: Sony Computer Entertainment.

Thekla, Inc. (2016). *The Witness*. Directed by Jonathan Blow. San Francisco, CA: Thekla, Inc.

Toxic Games. (2011). *Q.U.B.E.* London, UK: Toxic Games.

Valve Corporation. (2006). *Half-Life 2: Episode One*. Bellevue, WA: Valve Corporation.

Valve Corporation. (2007). *Portal*. Bellevue, WA: Valve Corporation.

Valve Corporation. (2011). *Portal 2*. Bellevue, WA: Valve Corporation.

Core Techniques
Win/Lose Conditions & Social Gaming

7

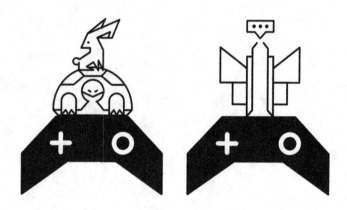

LECTURE OVERVIEW

Lecture reference: slides 1–3

Today we're going to look at the two final elements of our **Game Component** set: Win–Lose conditions and social gaming.

Win/lose conditions in video games are arguably the core rules that define victory or defeat. These rules are closely tied to player objectives and can vary drastically from game to game, also depending on whether the set objectives are micro or macro. Achieve them to win, fail to achieve them and lose, often with various intermediate states that allow branching into further player objectives.

The role of "Social" in gaming involves a connection between players, either cooperatively, competitively, or simply to share social experiences[1] such as a *Fortnite* (Epic Games, 2017) concert, or party within *World of Warcraft* (Blizzard Entertainment,

 DOI: 10.1201/9781032644721-7

2004). Social gaming allows players to team up, compete, share achievements (with the now ubiquitous integration for rapid posting across media platforms), and build friendships and communities. Multiplayer and social elements in games have gradually become invaluable as powerful tools for re-engagement, particularly from the perspective of "Games as a service" (see Box 7.1). I should note at the outset that this chapter will not specifically address multiplayer Game Design, a vast and complex aspect of Game Design covered specifically in later lectures but will instead focus on an overview of the structure and functions of social systems within games, effectively the "wrappers" around your social or Multiplayer experiences.

Now Let's get the ball rolling with an exercise **recapping** our challenge techniques from the last lesson:

RECAP OF LAST WEEK'S TOPIC: CHALLENGE

Lecture reference: slide 4

Recap discussion: Challenge
Before we start, let's have a quick look at some of the "Anatomy of a challenge" components we discussed last week to remind you of some of the possible answers:

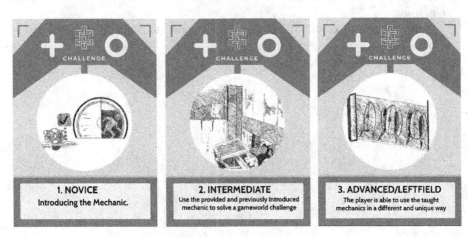

FIGURE 7.1   Card Designs by Andrew Thornton. Illustrations by Jack Hollick.

Recapping the four stages, we have:
Novice: Introduce the mechanic in a safe environment.
Intermediate: Use the previously introduced mechanic(s) to solve a gameworld challenge.
Advanced/Leftfield: The player can use the taught mechanic(s) in a different or unique way.

MASTERY

As you may have noticed, only novice, intermediate, and advanced/leftfield have been included in Figure 7.1, as "Mastery," effectively a combination of the previous three, will be taught separately in the puzzle design specific lectures.

RECAP: CHALLENGE – STUDENT EXAMPLES

Now let's drill down, examine and discuss some of your own example mechanics from last week's exercise.

(**Please note**, in the absence of actual student examples from last week's working class, illustrative examples have been used instead.)

IN CLASS EXERCISE 7.1

Lecture reference: slides 7–8
Recap discussion: Challenge
Question:
    Are you able to identify the "Anatomy of a challenge" stages in the following examples?
(**Discuss**)

EXAMPLE 1: *THE LEGEND OF ZELDA: BREATH OF THE WILD* (NINTENDO, 2017)

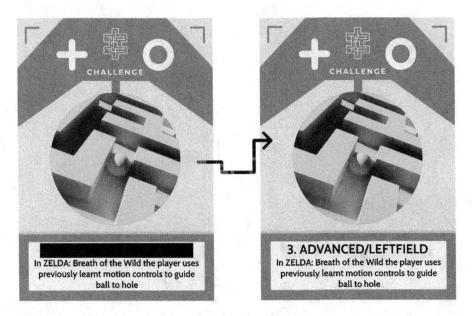

FIGURE 7.2   Card Designs by Andrew Thornton. Illustration by the Author.

EXERCISE 7.1 ANSWER

The motion control maze puzzle in *Breath of the Wild* is a unique challenge that tests the player's previous knowledge of using the joy-con controllers and motion control mechanics in a new and unique way.

EXAMPLE 2: *THE ELDER SCROLLS: SKYRIM* (BETHESDA GAME STUDIOS, 2011)

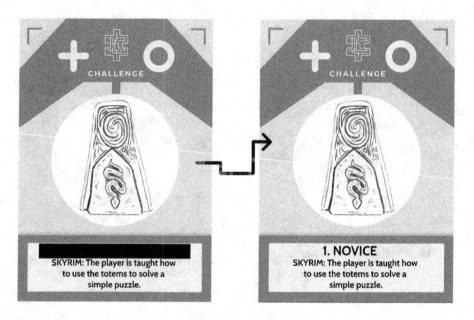

FIGURE 7.3   Card Designs by Andrew Thornton. Illustration by Jack Hollick.

EXERCISE 7.1 EXAMPLE 2 ANSWER

Lecture reference: slides 8–9

This is "Novice" and introduces the pattern/combination based "find the solution in the environment" puzzle.[2]

EXAMPLE 3: *THE ELDER SCROLLS: SKYRIM*

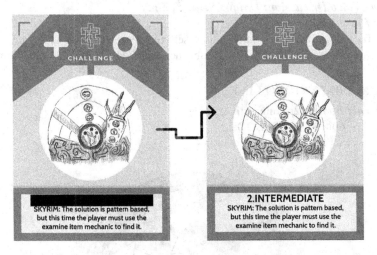

FIGURE 7.4 Card Designs by Andrew Thornton. Illustration by Jack Hollick.

EXERCISE 7.1 EXAMPLE 3 ANSWER

Lecture reference: slides 10–11

This is "Intermediate," as it utilises a combination of two previously learnt mechanics/ systems (examine item and environmental pattern recognition.)

Box 7.1 "GaaS"

Games as a Service (GaaS) is a business model where video games are continually developed and monetised post-launch. This aims to ensure sustained player engagement and steady revenue and usually includes regular content updates, such as expansions and seasonal events, and diverse (and often polarising) monetisation methods such as microtransactions and battle passes. Examples include *Call of Duty: Warzone* (Activision, 2020), *Fortnite* (Epic Games, 2017), *Destiny 2* (Bungie, 2017), and *League of Legends* (Riot Games, 2009). Benefits of GaaS include extended game lifespan, improved player retention, and consistent income for the developer (meaning continuation and improvement of favourite franchises). However, it can also present challenges such as the huge and continuous amount of updates expected from the community (see *GTA V Online* Rockstar Games, 2013), requiring publishers with big pockets. Other example issues are maintaining gameplay balance in updates, and market saturation – where one GaaS survives, many fall. And due to the often massive size of the development teams required for GaaS, many jobs will often fall with it!

IN CLASS EXERCISE 7.2: USP CORNER!

Lecture reference: slides 12–13
Game Video Discussion: Unique Selling points
Question:
   Try to identify one (or more) unique selling points in the following video clips. Imagine you are pitching them to a publisher and need a hook to reel them in!

EXERCISE 7.2 VIDEO LINK

Heavenly Bodies (2pt Interactive, 2021)
      https://bit.ly/EX7_2_BODY

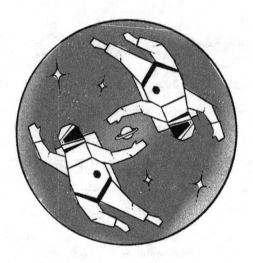

FIGURE 7.5   Illustration by Andrew Thornton.

EXERCISE 7.2 ANSWER

So that's called *Heavenly Bodies*, and in it players control cosmonauts performing tasks in zero gravity. One of the USPs here is **Couch-Co-Op** (see Box 7.2) – you're both playing at the same time in the same room, something that (after the Wii and Wiimotes were relegated to the back of the cupboard under the stairs) came back to the fore with games like *Overcooked* (Ghost Town Games, 2016) that focused on the co-op "fun factor" that comes with a shared physical space, including all the physical and verbal interactions that playing together usually entails. In addition, the players are tasked with helping one another, not helped by the physics-based controller/avatars (see boxout *here*[3]) causing, one would expect, much-frustrated hilarity.

Box 7.2   "Couch CO-OP"

The concept of playing together on the same screen in the same physical space can be traced back to *Pong* (Atari, 1972), originally in arcades and later on home consoles such as the Atari 2600. With games like *Gauntlet* (Atari Games, 1985) allowing up to four players, arcade game designers began to realise that "the more, the merrier." Nintendo embraced shared game experiences with the NES, featuring classics such as Contra (Konami, 1987), *Double Dragon II* (Technōs Japan, 1989), and the home grown *Battletoads* (1991). From UK studio RARE (see Figure 7.6). This focus on multiplayer continued with the *Nintendo 64* console (1996), which included four controller ports for games like *Mario Kart* (Nintendo, 1996), Prompting much four-player hilarity and tension relief – or at least that's my memories of my Core Design housemates playing at all hours – the game almost invariably prompting some kind of self-destructive "Stay up all night" cycle whenever there was a super important milestone deadline the next day. The "Nintendo Wii" (2006) further popularised multiplayer gaming with its easy-to-understand controls and family-friendly launch titles like *Wii Sports* (Nintendo, 2006), enabling shared experiences across generations. And we shouldn't forget games such as the "ultimate badassery" of the *Guitar Hero* series (2005–2015) (you and your friends become Rockstars in your lunch hour! Wow!) and Traveller's tales *LEGO* series (2005), where couch co-op allowed players to work together in split screen or take turns, an excellent format for families, enabling parents or grandparents to play with their kids or grandkids and act as in-game mentors while enjoying the game together. Despite many developers now favouring online multiplayer over couch co-op (possibly due to technical and design limitations), recent successful co-op games like *Wobbly Life*, (RubberBandGames, 2020) *Overcooked*, (Ghost Town Games, 2016) *It Takes Two* (Hazelight Studios, 2021), and the split-screen mode in *Minecraft* (Mojang Studios, 2011) highlight the benefits of in-person multiplayer. These games promote shared emotional experiences and direct physical interaction, which will always be an important goal to aim for in our game design. Viva couch co-op!

FILENAME: "KNOB NASH"

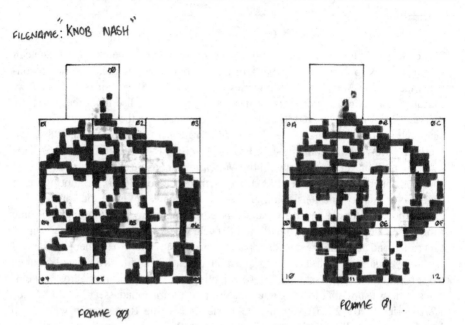

FRAME 00

FRAME 01

FIGURE 7.6 Original unused 1990's sprite designs for 8-bit NES title/UK Studio RARE. Illustration by Heather Stevens (Heather, one of the original Tomb Raider level designers, started her games career at RARE).

Now back to the main event!

CORE COMPONENTS: WIN, LOSE, AND SOCIAL

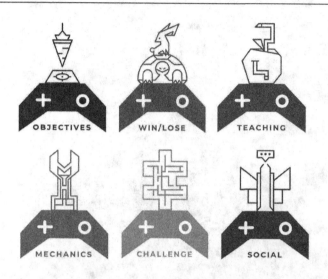

GAME COMPONENTS

FIGURE 7.7   Game Components. Illustration by Andrew Thornton.

We've covered the game design components objectives, teaching, challenge and mechanics, and now we'll conclude this first set of fundamentals with an overview of win, lose, and social conditions, starting with WIN/LOSE.

SECTION 7.1 CORE COMPONENTS: WIN–LOSE

Lecture reference: slide 14

FIGURE 7.8   The Win–Lose component. Illustration by Andrew Thornton.

Win/lose conditions are the most fundamental outcomes or rules of a game. Let's have a look at how we establish these conditions in Game Design.

FIGURE 7.9   Illustration by Shutterstock/Dod Pavlo.

Since the first sticks were thrown across a board in *Senet*[4], (most[5]) games have been designed with clear win/lose conditions. From dice-based and paper-based games to board and digital games, many include win/lose conditions, each tied to rules and variable states (e.g., losing a "piece" in chess or a "life" in a video game). These provide feedback, allowing players to adjust their strategies and work towards their objective, typically the "win condition."

Win/Lose Conditions: Rulesets

Lecture reference: slide 15

FIGURE 7.10   Illustration by Shutterstock/BillionsPhoto.

Although it could be argued that the win/lose conditions of a sport like football make it appear to be a fairly rudimentary game (objective: score goals by getting the ball into the opponent's net; the team with the most goals at the end of the match wins), analysing some of the subsets of these win/lose conditions reveals great complexity. The ruleset for football includes (for example) offside, free kicks, and throw-ins, with conditions to trigger these such as fouls, player positions, and ball positions on the pitch. These variables can influence the outcome of a game before even considering the skill set of the players and the team as a whole.

FIGURE 7.11 Illustration by Shutterstock/Morphart Creation.

Lecture reference: slide 16

Conversely, if we look at a game like chess, which is often assumed to have a complex set of rules, breaking them down reveals that the rules are relatively simple (except for perhaps the endgame). The basic objective is to checkmate the opponent's king. Beyond that, pieces have their own moveset, but once you have learnt these, it is essentially a push forward in a war of attrition, capturing pieces to strategise your position on the board to win. The enormous strategic possibilities primarily come from two players, the board size, the number of pieces, and specific movement patterns of the pieces. The ruleset is contained and hence the variables are reduced, although still astronomical, but knowing this contained ruleset allows strategies to be learnt. Chess masters are able to strategise by calculating moves many steps ahead, considering hundreds of potential moves and their variations. If we return to our football example in comparison, the rules must cover a huge number of variables, with more players, each of whom has no set or contained moveset (and their own free will to roam the "board"). This means rules must be designed to cover various in-game situations and variables, creating huge complexity, and that's before we even *start* to mention other tactics such as team strategies and substitutions. It's probably no wonder so many referees retire before their fiftieth birthday.[6]

These rules are what we need to look at from a game design perspective – without a clearly defined set that the player understands, the game (for both the player and designer) is almost lost before you begin.

FIGURE 7.12   "Conversion gel." Illustration by Jack Hollick.

"Less is More"

Lecture reference: slide 17

One of the key rules you learn as a game designer is that, as we've seen with chess, a relatively limited, coherent, and clearly articulated ruleset can allow for enormous amounts of variables and strategies for the player. As discussed in previous lectures, you don't need to overload your game with dozens of core rules, mechanics, or systems. To re-iterate, *Portal* is a clear example of this – the actual portal mechanic is relatively complex to explain to the player, but once they grasp it (through gating them until the only way out of an area is to successfully employ it), the available solutions to the puzzle chambers are only limited by the positioning of "portalable" surfaces.

Think of the black and white grid in chess, which constrains where the pieces can move – the "Portal" designers created similar rules to limit options and not overwhelm the player. Upon being introduced to the "Conversion Gel" in *Portal 2*, which allows the paint to be sprayed onto surfaces that are *not* originally portalable, making them suitable for placing portals, I feared the players available choices may cause overload, or in layman terms "mind snappage." Not so – the designers at Valve again found methods to corral the placement of this paint, making it manageable and scaffolding the mechanic from a "chunking" perspective. Although I note they didn't use it a lot across the game, likely because I'm guessing the complexity required to design those spaces and keep the player corralled into some kind of logical order, would give even the most stout-hearted game designer the heebie-jeebies.

Winning and Losing at Videogames: The Beginnings

FIGURE 7.13   Early video game. Image by Wikimedia commons/Asier03.

Lecture reference: slides 18–19

Early digital games had clear, simple win–lose conditions. With *Pong*, you have a score at the top of the screen, a ball, and two paddles. Realistically, you could look at that and understand what to do, even if you were a Neanderthal.[7]

FIGURE 7.14   Illustration by Shutterstock/Oscar Olguin.

Space Invaders (Taito, 1978) is a more complex game, but its genius lies in the strategies and the increasing tension and jeopardy (re-enforced by the auditory feedback of the sound speeding up in synch with the enemies) as the aliens gradually move down the screen. You have numerous strategies available depending on your position, where you are firing from, and where the aliens are dropping bombs from. Extra lives are also available if you hit the flying saucers. So, you have huge number of strategies all based around a simple line of aliens moving down the screen pixel by pixel (the CRT screen was only 256 lines high[8]) and some cover – Never mind showboating your "Roadie Run" between cover in your *Gears of war*, this was effectively *the* first cover-based shooter – and I still remember playing it with the ever so mild sensation of almost but not quite nail-biting tension to this day.

SECTION 7.2: GAMES EVOLVED...

Complicated Win/Lose Conditions and Emergent Gameplay

Lecture reference: slide 21

You'll find that the rules about win conditions are sometimes obfuscated, i.e., hidden and/or disguised. In a game like *Hitman*, there are several variables around how you can "win" a level, a concept sometimes known as "Swiss cheese" level design (Scott, Burgess, & Gaynor, 2012).

FIGURE 7.15   Illustration by Jack Hollick.

In "Swiss Cheese" level design, you'll have several holes or "possibility spaces" in the level design that you can navigate to reach the next sub-objective. Finding your way through any one of these holes leads to the next set of options, creating a branching set of strategies. How you start a level impacts how you end it. For instance, choosing between going in guns blazing or using stealth will significantly affect how the level plays out. You might steal a uniform from staff or guards to infiltrate a high-security area and eliminate the target in a violent grandstanding fashion, or alternately imitate a bartender, poison the target, and sneak out – both, effectively being win conditions. If you want to design a huge number of player options leading to your win condition, go for Swiss cheese level design.

FIGURE 7.16 Illustration by Shutterstock/DomCritelli.

And of course, if we are talking about complexity, I'd be in remiss if I didn't talk about the game on which I had the privilege to work on as Design Lead, *Magic: The Gathering – Duels of the Planeswalkers* 2012 for Stainless Games (2011). As Design Lead, part of my role was to simplify the essence of an enormously complex game to onboard new players more easily (see Box 7.3).

Box 7.3 "Officially the World's Most Complex Game"[9]

The core game systems and rules for *Magic: The Gathering* (MTG) were initially created by Richard Garfield (tellingly, a mathematician) in 1993 and the first *Duels of the Planeswalkers* digital spin-off version by the team at Stainless Games in 2009. I would suggest one of the main challenges (from a digital design perspective) in adapting the game for a broader audience was addressing the complexity of the game and guiding players towards quickly understanding its systems. MTG can be overwhelming to newcomers due to the vast number of variables, which for fans, is part of its appeal – the multitude of available options. Stainless's efforts with MTG were pivotal in translating complex collectible card game (CCG) mechanics into a digital format, though the game possibly remained too intricate for mass appeal, and the argument remains that simplifying some of the systems in MTG would strip away the complexity that fans love. Consequently, other designers and companies seized the opportunity to distil these core elements of CCGs. Games such as *Hearthstone* (Blizzard Entertainment, 2014) isolated and simplified core systems, making it easier for new players to start without extensive pre-knowledge. This focus on simplicity and fast-paced gameplay attracted a broader audience and contributed to the growth and boom in digital CCGs. As Dick Markinco, our hero in the not so classic "game" *Rogue Warrior* (Rebellion Developments, 2009) says, "Keep it simple, stupid." Maybe he had a point.

Sandpits or Playgrounds…

Lecture reference: slide 22

FIGURE 7.17   Illustration by Andrew Thornton.

Many games don't have win conditions, and there is frequent discussion as to whether they are games at all.[10] Perhaps this is why Mojang introduced the "Ender Dragon"[11] into *Minecraft* in 2011, introducing an achievable end objective and "win condition" that the player could aim for. Initially, *Minecraft* lacked specific win conditions, functioning primarily as a sandbox game. Interestingly, once players survive the first night, after that point, once you have shelter, you are effectively not really in danger anymore and are in a position to just continue collecting resources and building. I'd call this an "inverse difficulty curve" – you are gradually becoming more and more overpowered in the game until you are basically a god. It should be noted that now *Minecraft* has now separated these modes out, offering Creation mode, Exploration mode, and Survival mode ("the one with the Ender Dragon".)

The thing here is that if you are creating, and we've already talked about this a little regarding the psychology of gaming, ideally you need peer review as a reward for time investment. So I'd suggest the person[12] who began building Westeros in *Minecraft* in 2011, wouldn't have invested quite considerable time and effort into that without ongoing support and "cheering" from their peers – as we've discussed previously, it's what I call the "mum factor" – you want your mum to pat you on the head and say "Well done!" In this case, the support has now evolved into a vast, ongoing community project to "create one of the largest and most detailed *Minecraft* worlds ever built."[13]

It should be noted that while *Minecraft* in creation mode doesn't have set win/lose conditions, it still provides rewards through allowing creativity, social recognition and peer review, giving it intrinsic rewards (see Chapter 3, *here*[14]) that promote re-engagement. Another built-in reward system that gets players over the first bump in the road is "discovery." When people first started taking their tentative steps to play *Minecraft* back in 2009, none of us really had the slightest idea what our objectives were or how to achieve them. Discovery was a huge part of the motivation for playing it, along with creating early forums and peer groups to share discoveries and discuss what on earth we were supposed to be doing together. Exploration, discovery, and sharing, it seems, are ingrained into our DNA.

Let's have a look at an exercise:

IN CLASS EXERCISE 7.3: WIN/LOSE CONDITIONS

Lecture reference: slide 23
Game Video Discussion: Win/Lose conditions
Question
   Have a look at the following video clip and see if you're able to recognise one of the most common "Win/Lose" conditions.

EXERCISE 7.3 VIDEO LINK

Dragon's Lair (Don Bluth Studios, 1983)
   https://bit.ly/EX7_3_LAIR

FIGURE 7.18   Illustration by Shutterstock/rudall30.

Exercise 7.3 Answer

So that's *Dragon's Lair*, and many of you under a certain age might wonder why we are looking at a video of what seems like an old cartoon from the 1980s. Well, it's not actually a cartoon; it's a game created by Don Bluth Studios, a legendary animator, previously at Disney, who went on to found his own studio in 1979. *Dragons Lair* was one of the first games to run off the new LaserDisc tech introduced by MCA/Phillips in 1978, a LaserDisc basically being a Compact Disc (CD) in XL size for playing movies (and if you don't understand what a CD is, perhaps it's time to grab a shiny £1 coin, take a trip to your local charity shop and treat yourself!). Bluth introduced (or popularised) a concept or game mechanic that we still use today, which you may have recognised in the clip, and we'll look at shortly, still quite divisive among game designers to say the least. *Dragons Lair*, at the time, for a 10-year-old, was world changing. A chum and I would take the long walk down to the beach arcade,[15] four sweat soaked 50 pence pieces gripped white knuckled in our fists, ready to feed coins into this cabinet because it was, quite literally, THE MOST AMAZING THING IN THE WORLD. It was a *movie you could play*. The only downside was that it was probably the hardest game ever made, and required reaction times that would have made a fighter pilot blush. At best, I think we managed to progress to about five scenes into the game – and even to get that far probably cost us, in 50ps, over a period of about 2 years, adjusted for inflation, the price today of a modest sized Scottish castle.

But returning (finally) to the initial question, that clip demonstrates the most common lose condition in games, which has remained largely unchanged since the inception of the industry[16]: Yes – it's **DEATH.**

FIGURE 7.19   Illustration by Andrew Thornton.

SECTION 7.3: LOSE CONDITIONS

Lecture reference: slides 24–25

Death

So, starting with a focus on specific LOSE conditions, **Death** is really one of the core lose conditions of games that we want to avoid as an outcome of our choices – the death of our avatar or player character. Other than permadeath (see Box 7.4), death in games almost always results in a respawn or restart, so it's not really death per se; it's the game designer's way of penalising you for not playing well.

Box 7.4 "Permadeath"

Permadeath in games refers to a mechanic where a player's character (or characters) is permanently removed from the game upon dying. This means the player doesn't respawn or continue from a checkpoint and must start over from the beginning or a save point. This, it has been argued, adds a higher level of consequence and jeopardy to the gameplay. For a good example of this, see the *X-COM* series of games (MicroProse, 1994–2001; Firaxis Games, 2012–present).

Now let's have another look at *Dragon's Lair* and see if you're able to recognise the mechanic we mentioned earlier, and how it is designed specifically around death.

IN CLASS EXERCISE 7.4: WIN/LOSE CONDITIONS

Lecture reference: slide 26
Game Video Discussion: Mechanics
Question:
    Have a look at the following video and see if you're able to recognise which mechanic, still used today, it popularised, and why it might have been originally designed that way.

EXERCISE 7.4 VIDEO LINK

Dragon's Lair (Don Bluth Studios, 1983)
    https://bit.ly/EX7_4_LAIR

FIGURE 7.20   Quick time event. Illustration by Jack Hollick.

Exercise 7.4 Answer

Lecture reference: slide 27

If you were looking at the top, bottom and left and right sides of that video clip, you will have seen a little compass of arrow points that were mirrored in the physical control scheme on the arcade cabinet (i.e., you have a joystick for up, down, left, and right directions, and a button to press for actions). When one of the compass points is illuminated, you must quickly push the joystick in that direction. By "quickly," I mean with the reflexes of a panther trained to play video games all day. What we're talking about here, is of course, **QTEs** or **QuickTime Events** (see Box 7.5), much loved by designers, and featuring prominently in games such as the original *Resident Evil 4* (Capcom, 2005) and the output of David Cage in games such as Heavy Rain (Quantic Dream, 2010) and *Detroit: Become Human* (Quantic Dream, 2018). I would suggest these last two titles are groundbreaking, cinematically focused games but perhaps not catering to players lacking a certain "reflex focused" aptitude (no specific lecturer names mentioned) who may, hypothetically end up losing all of their major characters in the first quarter of the game (see, again, Box 7.4 "Permadeath"). With *Dragons Lair*, I'd suggest the QTE mechanic, as with the majority of arcade games of the time, was designed specifically around the balance between the "sweet spot" of the reward of the next short animated sequence before ultimately failing and pumping another 50 pence in with anticipation, or the frustration of realising that there is no chance of progressing any further, putting the 50 pence's back in your pocket, and putting on your emergency survival equipment[17] to pop down to the beach instead and watch the waves.

The jury is still out on whether QuickTime events are a nightmare mechanic or an interesting diversion within a game.

Box 7.5   "Press X, Y, B and A to LIVE"

Quick Time Events (QTEs) require the player to rapidly choose specific buttons and/ or joystick directions to perform certain actions (e.g. dodging attacks, performing complex manoeuvres) within a specified sequence (shown on screen) and a limited time frame. These events will often occur during setpieces, cinematics or scripted moments due to the limited actions available to the player (i.e. a sequence of button presses). Failure to complete a QTE correctly typically results in a negative consequence, such as taking damage, failing and repeating the sequence, character death, or even permadeath (thank you David Cage). For more details, see *here*[18].

IN CLASS EXERCISE 7.5

Lecture reference: slide 28
Discussion: OTHER Lose conditions
Question:
　　Are we able to think of any more examples of other specific "lose" conditions in games?

Exercise 7.5 Example Answer 1

Time trials

Lecture reference: slide 29

See: *Super Mario Kart* (Nintendo, 1992)

FIGURE 7.21   Illustration by Wikimedia Commons/SuperTuxKart contributors.

Losing is really a case of *not* achieving stipulated conditions or objectives, so by set-ting up player evaluation such as time trials, scores, and rankings, you're creating or setting rules that the player should be clearly aware of, and if they are "winning" or "losing" at any single moment. Think of the large "position/place" and "direction" markers displayed prominently in a race game, and the timer relentlessly ticking away. Ideally, the penalty or reward should motivate the player to strive for a win condition. In couch co-op with your friends playing the *Mario Kart* series, it's peer review and being "top dog" and having bragging rights over the others (at least until the next race). And although the *Forza Horizon* series (Playground Games, 2016–2021) provides the player with almost non-stop rewards, coming first place means a hefty chunk of extra XP and a possible chance at a "Wheelspin" that could net you a supercar. The negatives? The downside? The time sink. Running a race again in *Forza* takes time – time you'd rather spend exploring the other exciting juiciness waiting for you out in the rest of the care-fully crafted game world. XP for discovering a new road? Count me in!

Other examples of "Time Trial":

TrackMania Series (Nadeo, 2003–present):
Challenges players to complete tracks as quickly as possible, with leaderboards displaying the best times globally.

Crash Team Racing Nitro-Fuelled (Beenox, 2019):
This kart racing game includes time trials where players try to set the fastest lap times, and the inclusion of previous best "ghost drivers" allow players to compete against and learn from themselves.

Exercise 7.5 Example Answer 2

Lecture reference: slide 30

Leaderboard/Score/Ranking

See: *Cuphead* (Studio MDHR, 2017)

FIGURE 7.22   Illustration by Jack Hollick.

Cuphead is a "run-and-gun" platformer with the USPs of a 1930s cartoon art style combined with an unforgiving difficulty curve. The game ranks players at the end of each level, looking at results such as time, health, and parries, with the leaderboards allowing players to compare their scores with others. Interestingly, it's a design choice (or possibly more an aesthetic choice to not detract from the cartoon feel) that these are not shown on screen during the game. The in-game feedback itself allows you to get a feel for how well it is going, and if these roughly match the end-of-level analysis, then you're happy. If the outcome doesn't match the expectations? The player may start to distrust the game, developer and designer, not a good place to be for any add-ons or the sequel. Regarding the lose conditions, other than your own expectations, ranking, leaderboards, and competition will again drive player motivation. Other than that, the moment-to-moment "run and gun" rules are quickly established. If you don't run, dodge, or hit your target precisely enough, then it's "game over."

Other examples of "Score/Ranking/Leaderboard":
   For clear examples of these rules and conditions, we only need to look at the E-sports arena:

Counter-strike: global offensive (CS:GO)
(Valve Corporation, 2012)

Employs a skill group system that ranks range from Silver to Global Elite. Players' ranks are influenced by match outcomes, individual performance, and consistency, making the ranking system a key aspect of the game's competitive design. The game also features leaderboards that display top players and teams, particularly in professional tournaments, tracking performance metrics.

SECTION 7.4: WIN CONDITIONS

Lecture reference: slides 31–33

Some Examples

Survive, kill everything, high score, come first...

The flip side of the Lose conditions – again, a set of rules which must be quickly and clearly taught to the player. Win/Lose are almost[19] always symbiotic, although this section focuses on some clear win conditions solely for the purposes of clarity. Survival games like *The Long Dark* (Hinterland Studio, 2014) or *The Forest* (Endnight Games, 2018) specify that you've got to keep yourself warm, well-fed, hydrated and maintain your ammunition. It's about achieving the stipulated conditions, which as discussed with a game like *Hitman* are designed to allow for many strategies and playstyles, making succeeding in any of these an extremely complex task.

FIGURE 7.23   Illustration by Jack Hollick.

Let's look at *Deathloop* (Arkane Studios, 2021), an "Immersive sim" (see Box 7.6) as an example. Your objective in that game is to assassinate eight key targets, each of these "visionaries" situated in a particular place at a particular time in the game. However, there is an almost overwhelming set of rules, conditions, and variables that affect that outcome. *Almost* because the designers have an ace up their sleeve – the game is structured around a time loop, where the player relives the same day repeatedly. Each loop provides opportunities to gradually not only learn the complex rules of the game, but also the patterns of the targets (*when* they come out, *where* they are on the island) gather information and unlock new abilities, to gradually reveal the best way to complete the mission.

Box 7.6 "Immersive Sims"

An immersive sim is a video game genre that emphasises player agency and emergent[20] gameplay, where complex game systems can react in unpredictable ways allowing the player a powerful sense of agency within the game world and allowing players to approach objectives and challenges in multiple ways with choices in playstyle such as stealth, combat, or diplomacy; Common features include environmental interactivity, where players manipulate objects and elements to solve problems, and a narrative usually closely integrated with gameplay. Notable examples include *Deus Ex*, (Ion Storm, 2000), *Dishonored* (Arkane Studios, 2012), and *Prey* (Arkane Studios, 2017.)

FIGURE 7.24   Illustration by Shutterstock/Temstock.

In this case learning these rules conditions and variables through trial and error is not a bad thing. Trial and error design is, depending on the game context, usually frowned upon – as you usually have to die to work out the solution. I'd suggest the most important of the rules in *Deathloop* revolves around the Day–Night Cycle: Certain areas and pathways are accessible only during specific times of day. For instance, a building might be locked in the morning but open in the afternoon. The interesting negative re-enforcement designed into this cycle that drives the player to stay alive longer is the loss of progress or, thematically aligned with the game, *time*. Dying early in the day means loss of the opportunity to gather intel later in the day. If you die early, the day will reset in the morning, meaning starting pretty much from scratch – fine if you're aiming for a target in the morning, not so if your target comes out a night. In a further stroke of genius, this also manages the difficulty curve of the game, the final targets requiring staying alive the longest.

Game systems such as *Deathloop* and *Dishonored* support player agency and strategic options, but the challenge as a designer lies in communicating this information to the player. If you have very complex strategic systems within your levels, you need to find a way to gradually introduce these conditions to avoid overwhelming the player. This may be why *Dishonored, Deathloop* and other immersive sims can be considered by some as "Marmite" games – players either love them or hate them. Personally, Although I enjoy them, I find that the lack of signposting in immersive sims leaves me yearning for more player guidance. The vast array of options can feel overwhelming, and sometimes I prefer a bit of hand-holding with my win/lose conditions.

Let's look at an exercise:

IN CLASS EXERCISE 7.6

Lecture reference: slide 34
Discussion: Win conditions
Question:
    Are you able to think of any odd or uncommon win conditions in games?

Exercise 7.6 Example Answer 1

Win Condition: Collecting

Lecture reference: Slide 35

FIGURE 7.25   Illustration by Shutterstock/ndutfrea.

See: *Pokemon Series* (Game Freak, 1996–2023)

"Gotta catch 'em all!", capitalising on the human instinct to collect, this win condition is designed around the player capturing all available Pokémon in the game to complete the Pokédex.

Exercise 7.6 Example Answer 2

Win Condition: Zero Deaths/No Damage

Lecture reference: slide 36

See: *Dark Souls Series* (From Software, 2011–2016)

Interestingly, this is a community-developed and self-imposed player objective, the idea being to complete the game without dying or taking any damage. This has become a significant trend over the years, popularised by community forums,[21] YouTube channels, and Twitch streams, where players offer support and cheers to those who manage it, while others share their techniques on how they did it, reportedly creating a positive and encouraging environment for others to attempt the same.

FIGURE 7.26   Illustration by Shutterstock/Digital Genetics.

SECTION 7.5: WIN/LOSE CONDITIONS

Let's wrap up with some general Win/Lose condition examples. These examples are more specifically based around the Win/Lose *rules* that are set up by the designer and should be as simple as possible to quickly impart this information to the player. Think of it as a game system where players can either win or lose based on specific criteria being met, achieving certain goals to win or failing to meet them, thereby losing, as opposed to specific Win or Lose conditions.

As usual, you'll have an opportunity to create some of these yourself in the following exercises, but for now, let's look at some simple, recognisable examples.

Win Lose Example 1: Subterfuge

Lecture reference: slide 38

WIN/LOSE

SUBTERFUGE!
The player has to accomplish a certain
objective without being detected or
revealed.

FIGURE 7.27   Card Design by Andrew Thornton. Illustration by Jack Hollick.

The stealth or subterfuge genre, largely pioneered by Hideo Kojima, is a unique set of
game systems and strategic designs that essentially created a new genre. A new genre
pops up once in a blue moon in games and, as we've looked at in the Analysis lecture,
is frequently adapted out of other games or game systems (think *League of Legends*, or
the *Gears of War* cover system) I would suggest coming up with an entirely new genre
off the top of your head is quite uncommon – and I imagine that's one of the reasons
many people would cite Kojima as a genius.

IN CLASS EXERCISE 7.7: WIN/LOSE

Lecture reference: slides 39–40
Discussion: Subterfuge
Question:
      Are we able to think of another example (that hasn't already been mentioned)
of the "subterfuge" or "stealth" win/lose condition?

Exercise 7.7 Example Answer

Nothing to Hide (Next Friday Interactive, 2014)

FIGURE 7.28   Illustration by Andrew Thornton in the style of "Nothing to Hide."

As we've discussed previously, flipping mechanics and systems can be a great way to generate new game ideas, so we'll focus on flipped examples for these exercises. In the indie game *Nothing to hide* you have to actually make sure you are *seen* by cameras, rather than hiding from them, in a Big Brother-type dystopian future. In this game, you sometimes need to move cameras around to ensure you're always visible to the state; in a twist on the common stealth format if you're *not* seen by the cameras, you are terminated.

Win Lose Example 2: Time Trials

Lecture reference: slides 41–43

FIGURE 7.29 Card Design by Andrew Thornton. Images by SuperTuxKart contributors.

In the "Time Trials" example gamecard (Figure 7.29), the win/lose condition is usually based on completing a course or level within a set time limit or achieving the fastest possible time. The win condition is met by finishing within the specified time or setting a record, while the lose condition occurs if the player exceeds the time limit or fails to achieve a competitive time. This condition can be found across genres, in racing games like *Mario Kart* and platformers like *Crash Bandicoot 4: It's about time* (Toys for Bob, 2020).

IN CLASS EXERCISE 7.7: WIN/LOSE PART 2

Discussion: Time trials
Question:
    Are we able to think of another less common example (that hasn't already been mentioned) for the "Time Trials" Win/Lose condition?

Exercise 7.7 Part 2 Example Answer

Desert Bus (Sega, 1995)

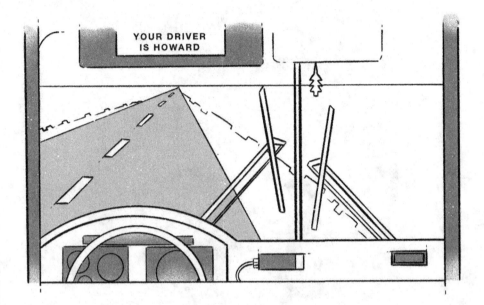

FIGURE 7.30 Illustration by Andrew Thornton.

Regarding the concept of flipping genres, although we still don't really have a specific time trials example of where "coming last wins," we have something that feels very close to it: In the 1995 game *Desert bus* (Penn & Teller, 1995), the concept of the fastest time is flipped on its head – in this game time really is the trial. Conceived by the American Magicians Penn and Teller as "a video game that could work as a satire against the anti-video-game lobby." (Parkin, 2013), the player must drive a bus from across a desert at a maximum speed of 45 mph, the objective being to continuously correct the steering to stay on the road and avoid crashing. But with no pause game available, to complete the journey and "win" the player must play (or as Teller comments "stay conscious") for 8 hours straight. Understandably unavailable for many years, determined masochists can now find it on Smartphone.[22]

Win Lose Example 3: Bodyguard

Lecture reference: slides 44–45

FIGURE 7.31   Card Design by Andrew Thornton. Illustration by Jack Hollick.

The "Bodyguard" win/lose condition involves protecting or defending an NPC character, or sometimes an object, usually with a health bar that must be maintained to avoid hitting the lose condition. This mechanic is prevalent in classic games such as Ico (SCE Japan Studio, 2001), *Resident Evil 4*, and even in some *Grand Theft Auto* missions (Rockstar Games, 1997–present). Warning! Mentioning the bodyguard system can cause extreme allergic reactions in some gamers!

IN CLASS EXERCISE 7.7: WIN/LOSE PART 3

Discussion: Time trials
Question:
    Are we able to think of any other examples of the "Bodyguard" win/lose condition?

Exercise 7.7 Part 3 Example Answer

The Last Guardian (Japan Studio, 2016)

FIGURE 7.32   Illustration by Jack Hollick.

The Last Guardian is an interesting example, as although perhaps not "flipping" the bodyguard mechanic, it's a fascinating variation. You play through the game as a boy co-operating with a giant cat/bird creature "Trico" – the interesting element in this case being that the mechanic "ping-pongs" between you protecting Trico and Trico protecting you. And in the process, across the playtime of the game, other than a few minor obedience issues as per any pet, I'd challenge you not to form an emotional bond with "Treacle" (as I felt our shared bond allowed me to call them by the end of the game).

Win Lose Example 4: Attack/Defend

Lecture reference: slides 46–47

FIGURE 7.33 Card Design by Andrew Thornton. Illustration by Shutterstock/deymos.

A good example of Attack/Defend (as illustrated on the GameCard Figure 7.33) is "Tower Defence." In a typical tower defence game, players win by the strategic placement of (usually static) defences to prevent waves of (Attacking) enemies from reaching a specific objective, and they lose if too many enemies successfully breach (or destroy) these defences.

IN CLASS EXERCISE 7.7: WIN/LOSE PART 4

Lecture reference: slide 24
Discussion: Attack/Defend
Question:
 Are we able to think of any other examples of the "Attack/Defend" win/lose condition?

Exercise 7.7 Part 4 Example Answer

Orcs Must Die! (Robot Entertainment, 2011)

FIGURE 7.34   Images by Shutterstock/Vuang.

In *Orcs Must die!* the win/Lose conditions remain the same, but instead of the common top-down view, you play in the third person, placing traps and fighting directly as a character, using weapons and magic to stop waves of Orcs. This hybrid (although not quite "flipped") approach theoretically makes the game more dynamic and hands-on compared to your typical tower defence games.

Win–Lose Final Notes: Achieving Stipulated Conditions

To wrap up and re-iterate – basically if you're guiding the player to achieve stipulated conditions and you've created those rules and conditions as a designer, then part of your job is to make sure those conditions are clear. If they aren't, and the player ends up losing because they don't know what the rules and the win/lose conditions are, the player will drop your game like a hot potato. Something to bear in mind!

Let's move on to the second part of the lecture:

SECTION 7.6: SOCIAL GAMING

Lecture reference: slide 50

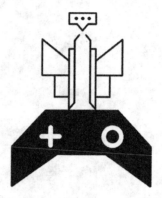

FIGURE 7.35   The Social component. Illustration by Andrew Thornton.

Overview

This section covers various types of social gaming systems, which are distinct from multiplayer design, a specialised subject taught in its own separate, self-contained module.

Let's initially look at some examples of the variations and adaptability of social game types. As an example starting point, consider "social deduction" games and how a great piece of design such as this can effectively spawn a cottage industry.

FIGURE 7.36   In the style of *Among Us*. Illustration by Shutterstock/maybielater.

Social Gaming Example: Deduction

Lecture reference: slide 50

Among Us (InnerSloth LLC., 2018) is an example of an enormously[23] popular game that uses the social deduction imposter or "traitor" mechanic, where you hide among a group of players and try to eliminate them without being discovered. This mechanic was popularised by the card game *The Werewolves of Millers Hollow*, first published in 2001 (Pallières & Marly) where players take on the roles of villagers and werewolves. The goal is to identify and eliminate the werewolves before they eliminate the villagers. This game was itself an adaptation of arguably the original social deduction game *Mafia*. Designed in 1986 (Davidoff, 1986). The social deduction concept has since become widely popular, inspiring numerous variations and adaptations, including the VR title *Werewolves Within*, the TV show *The Traitors*, (2022) and arguably influencing the design of the *Battlestar Galactica* board game (Petersen & Konieczka, 2008), reflecting the 2004 Reboot of the TV series, where nefarious crew members hide the fact that they are Cylons while bumping off other members of the crew. It's a great "badass" mechanic, and at this point, the students might be asking, "Why haven't you mentioned your infected bite game mechanic yet?" (but I'll leave that explanation to Box 7.7).

Box 7.7   Once Bitten

I've told the students for many years that someone should create a game system based on the common scenes in zombie films and TV series where someone who has been bitten tries to conceal it.[24] Wouldn't it be great to play a game that included a mechanic where you attempt to conceal a bite from your colleagues? But then I actually started to think about how you would design this into a first- or third-person game. How do you conceal a bite from a player perspective? How do other players see or suspect a bite, i.e., what feedback are the "turning" and "non-turning" players receiving? Is the turning player getting stronger (i.e., feeling no pain in dead limbs) or weaker (bits dropping off?) How long does it take, and what exactly happens when you turn? Because I imagine it is more fun being a zombie and eating humans than it is being a human trying to hide[25] in which case you might end up with a game where everyone tries to get bitten and become a zombie rather than pursue any other objective they might have had in the game. At that point, realising that developing these systems fully might be a considerable effort better served by helping the students develop their own ideas I stopped mentioning these "bite" mechanics. And here's the problem with game ideas: (and hopefully the point of this boxout) – almost everyone has game ideas, and usually thinks they are the best thing since sliced bread. Many students will be super-protective of their ideas, convinced they are sitting on the next big thing – and, certainly, as we've seen from examples, in some cases, they are. But, even with the best idea in the world, as soon as you start to drill down into the mechanics, you begin to understand how even the simplest idea can branch out into a vast array of intertwining systems, all of which need designing. And that will invariably be time-consuming and difficult. And that's before you've even started the *really* difficult part of actual development, sitting down at your computer, and facing the blank screen that needs filling with – well, *game*. The bottom line is, (following my *really in italics* theme) making games will always be *really* difficult, but if you get it right, believe me, it's *really, really* worth it. Thanks for sticking with this boxout!

SECTION 7.7: SOCIAL GAMES

Synchronous or Asynchronous?

Lecture reference: slide 51

Let's have a look at some further examples of the diversity of social games, this time beginning to categorise them by moving them into two distinct brackets – Social **Synchronous**, or Social **Asynchronous**.

Social asynchronous

Let's start with Asynchronous, as this is a little less ubiquitous than its partner Synchronous.

Social Asynchronous are games that do not require the players to be online or participate simultaneously. They allow players to respond to the other players' actions or turns at their convenience. An example would be the game *Draw Something with friends* (OMGPop, 2012), where one player must draw an image based around a word, and then this is sent to another player to guess what it is. There is no time limit here, so asynchronous games such as this allow for quick, non-scheduled play, widening their appeal across demographics. This system also fosters re-engagement what Will Luton, prominent social game designer, calls a "return trigger," in his book *Free-to-play: Making money from games you give away* (2013). We'll look at this and other re-engagement design techniques in later lectures.

Although originally 1 v 1, this game (and many other variations of it) now offer unlimited multiplayer. For a further example of asynchronous games that allow for more than 1v1, see the digital version of the classic board game *Ticket to Ride* (Days of Wonder, 2012), A good example of asynchronous gameplay without a limit to amount of players or time constraints. You'll note many of these games are smartphone or PC (i.e., tea-break in the office) focused, designed around taking turns in the short, convenient play sessions, as opposed to the commitment of sitting down at a specific time to join an online session.

Social asynchronous Example 1

Doodle Jump (Lima Sky, 2009)

Lecture reference: slide 52

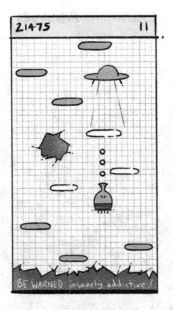

FIGURE 7.37   Illustration by Andrew Thornton.

If we look at a game like *Doodle Jump* (Lima Sky, 2009), it's you versus another player versus the game. It brings in your friends from your friends list and their scores that you're trying to beat, so it's ALL of you versus the game, and you're all trying to beat each other within that system asynchronously. This is also known as "parallel symmetric gameplay," which we'll look at in a moment.

IN CLASS EXERCISE 7.8:   SOCIAL PART 1

Lecture reference: slide 53
Discussion: Social Asynchronous
Question:
    Are we able to think of any other examples of "Social: Asynchronous" games?

Exercise 7.8 Part 1 Example Answer

Diplomacy (Calhamer, 1959)

FIGURE 7.38   Illustration by Shutterstock/M-Production.

Diplomacy, "A game of international intrigue, trust and treachery" is a strategic board game created by Allan B. Calhamer in 1959, and as it's blurb hints at, is primarily a competitive game with elements of collaboration. Interestingly, *Diplomacy* became one of the first "play by mail" (PBM) postal games in the 1960s. PBM (totally unfathomable to a modern game design class) involved sending your next move, and in the case of diplomacy, orders and diplomatic messages through the post, necessitating (for non-neighbours) a lengthy gap between turns. This game is also interesting (although it has since been translated to digital) as it is our first example of a non-digital asynchronous game – something particularly prevalent in asynchronous games, which we'll look at shortly.

Now let's look at the flip side of Asynchronous:

Social Synchronous

Lecture reference: slide 54

Social synchronous are multiplayer games where players interact with each other in real-time. This requires simultaneous participation, either between solo players or teams, and focuses on quick thinking, as the games can change rapidly around player actions. These games require a specific time commitment to play and are often designed around particular playstyles or techniques that are learned over time, fostering many loyal and passionate (to the point of voracious) communities that are not afraid to voice their opinions on any adjustments or updates. And before MP designers get too smug (although

I doubt MP shooter designers ever do) it should be noted that huge communities built up over long periods of time will not hesitate to drop these games overnight if they disagree with certain policies or design changes, as there is always another massive MP title around the corner ready to take the title away. Social synchronous games are where the big numbers happen in both social co-operative and competitive games, and where the big money comes from by utilising the "GaaS" model (see Box 7.1). This pursuit of the big money is why so many MP shooters launch on a regular basis, despite the small chances of success in such a flooded market. An example follows:

Synchronous Example

Fortnite: Battle Royale mode (Epic Games, 2017)

FIGURE 7.39   Illustration by Shutterstock/Dolzhanskyi Yaroslav.

Fortnite is a "battle royale" game where a hundred players compete to be the last person standing in a shrinking playing field, inspired by the genre popularised by games like *PlayerUnknown's Battlegrounds* (PUBG Corporation, 2017), itself inspired by the film *Battle Royale* (directed by Kinji Fukasaku from the novel by Koushun Takami) featuring a group of students forced to fight to the death on a deserted island, with only one winner. Ring any bells? Brendan Greene, the PUBG creator (known as PlayerUnknown), has cited this 2000 Japanese film as a significant influence on the game's concept. *Fortnite* continues to maximise its dominance with clever updates, including building/construction mechanics, vehicles, updated maps, and frequent in-game events with brand collaborations (e.g., *Marvel, DC, Star Wars*) and popular cultural crossovers such as in game events featuring *Marshmello* and *Travis Scott*.

> ### IN CLASS EXERCISE 7.8:   SOCIAL PART 2
>
> *Lecture reference: slide 55*
> *Discussion: Social Synchronous*
> *Question:*
>   Are we able to think of any other examples of "Synchronous" games?

Exercise 7.8 Part 2 Example Answer

Just Dance (Ubisoft, 2009)

FIGURE 7.40   Illustration by Shutterstock/luma_art.

An example of a (mostly, depending on how badly you are doing) non-violent example of a **synchronous** game is *Just Dance*. The players are tasked with synchronising their movements with the on-screen music and prompts, dancing together in real-time while attempting to perform dance routines together that mimic the choreography. The game scores players based on how accurately players match up the dance moves, and players can either compete or collaborate to achieve high scores.

SECTION 7.8: SYMMETRY

Lecture reference: slide 56

Now let's have a look at symmetry within games. Symmetrical gameplay in multiplayer games refers to a design where all players have access to the same resources, abilities, and objectives. This theoretically ensures a balanced playing field where success is determined by player skill and strategy rather than inherent advantages or differences in gameplay mechanics (EvolvingDeveloper.com, 2016). In symmetrical games, every player should start with the same conditions and compete under identical rules. This creates fair competition, making it easier to balance the game and providing a clear and straightforward competitive environment. Examples include traditional board games like Chess and Draughts, and video games like *Rocket League* (Psyonix, 2015) and *Counter-Strike* (Valve Corporation, 2000), where all players have the same capabilities and the outcome relies purely on their actions and decisions (see *here*[26] for more on Symmetry in games). In the meantime, let's look at some different types of symmetry in games.

Type 1: Parallel Symmetric Games

Lecture reference: slide 57

FIGURE 7.41   Illustration by Andrew Thornton.

This is what Game Designer and author Raph Koster calls "Parallel symmetric" in his excellent presentation on social game mechanics (Koster, 2011 – see *here*[27]). One player versus the system or game, versus an opponent versus the system or game. A simple example is an arcade cabinet. You are effectively trying to get a higher score than others who have played the game before you. Then, someone else will come along and also try to get a high score on the system, hence you are competing with the cabinet, and then, asynchronously, the other player. It should be noted that parallel symmetric works with both synchronous and asynchronous play.

IN CLASS EXERCISE 7.10: SYMMETRY

Lecture reference: slides 58–59
Discussion: Symmetry
Question:
    Are we able to think of any (non-digital) game examples of "Parallel symmetric" in the real world?

Exercise 7.10 Example Answer

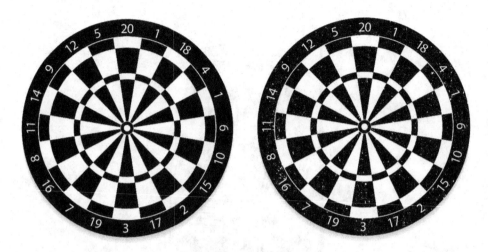

FIGURE 7.42   Illustration by Shutterstock/StudioGraphic.

Parallel symmetric gameplay in the real world includes games like Golf – you have a set of rules, and you try to use those rules to achieve the best scores within that system. The rules of golf involve skill, judgement, and strategy, but there is a clear set of rules – if you go into the rough and are unable to get your ball out, you have drops, and you have sand pits which present a greater challenge. So, there is a huge set of strategies and variables. Again, with darts, you have a very clear system utilising skill. You are trying to hit the doubles, triples, and bullseye. There are various rule systems implemented around the actual physical board, such as 301, hitting a specific target or number, etc. While it's you against the dartboard, it's also you against other person and teams. What we mean by parallel symmetric is that it's you versus the system versus a player competitor who is also versus the system.

SECTION 7.9: CO-OPERATIVE OR COMPETITIVE?

Lecture reference: slide 60

As we are starting to see from the examples, synchronous and asynchronous and symmetric can be refined down to even more specific categories – co-operative or competitive. Let's use an exercise to look at examples across all these categories and start to see how they fit together.

Example 7.11a: Leaderboards

FIGURE 7.43   Game component types. Illustration by Shutterstock/Sabbir Hossain 26.

Lecture reference: slide 62

Question: competitive or co-operative?

Example 7.11a Answer: Competitive

An easy one to start with. Leaderboards are obviously competitive – you are competing
asynchronously with all the people who have previously played the game.

Example 7.11b: Persona

FIGURE 7.44   Illustration by Stuart Atkinson.

Lecture reference: slide 63

Question: competitive or co-operative?

Example 7.11b Answer: Co-Operative and Competitive

In this instance, I'd say both. It's competitive in a cooperative fashion, so it's a little bit of both – trying to wear the best gear is not about effectively competing with other players, but can be used as a "Peacocking" mechanic if someone is seeking social status and recognition. as a tool for peer review, so it's very much a case of "Gear." You want to show your friends that you are at a higher level, or in some cases, it's about personalisation to show ownership of your character or which "clan" (see, Example 7.11c) you belong to. This kind of ownership creates more empathy towards the player character and also makes you feel as if you're expressing your own personality visually to other players, which can be important for creating and helping players form social connections based on mutual interests. From a competitive perspective, as we see in games like *League of Legends*, players often identify with their chosen champions and invest time in mastering them. This identification can increase a player's commitment to the game, driven by a desire to be seen as the best.[28]

Example 7.11c: Assisting

FIGURE 7.45   Illustration by Andrew Thornton (that also gives away the answer).

Lecture reference: slides 64–65

Question: competitive or co-operative?

Example 7.11c Answer: Co-Operative

Assisting[29] other players is co-operative. It's also, as discussed in the previous section, a "return trigger." In *Journey*, for instance, the characters are specifically designed to help each other. I've frequently found players who will guide me towards ways out of particular arenas. In some cases, you need to work your way out together, which fosters cooperation and companionship. If you haven't played it, you might wonder why people don't troll each other as frequently as they do in other multiplayer games. That's because the design doesn't support opportunities for that. First, you can't speak, but you *can* send a little musical note out of your character to communicate and effectively tell the other player where you are. Second, Jenova Chen, the designer, removed the arms from the characters after playtesting, because, somewhat depressingly, he found in early prototypes that if players had arms, they would attempt to hit each other (see article *here*[30]).

Journey is a life-affirming game. Even if you find out at the end, where it reveals the gamertag of your fellow player, that you've been playing with someone named *PuppyStab178*, it's almost impossible not to help others and foster a sense of belonging in this game. Everyone who's played *Journey* has their own story. And here's mine: After playing through an extensive section with a random player, I popped off, leaving my character (and player companion) unattended. When I returned 15 minutes later, I found *PuppyStab178* just sitting silently next to my dormant character in the game world, waiting for return and pick up where we left off. I gingerly grabbed the controller and we continued, with the nagging feeling of guilt and odd melancholy of somehow wanting to make amends to *PuppyStab178* haunting me to the tear streaked climax of the game, where we flew exuberantly (and armlessly) into the sunset together.

Example 7.11d: Gifting

GIFTING

Gift another player and they gift you back
in a re-occuring positive feedback loop.

FIGURE 7.46   Card Designs by Andrew Thornton, Illustration by Jack Hollick.

Lecture reference: slide 66

Question: competitive or co-operative?

Example 7.11d Answer: Co-Operative

Gifting is good if both you and a friend are playing the same game because it is a strong motivator for re-engagement – you and your friend are effectively helping each other with the same game. However, it's not so good if it's used as a technique to try and draw people into a game they haven't already installed. For example, you've got *Zombie Joyride* installed on Android, and you receive a notification to send out a chunk of shotgun shells for *Zombie Joyride* as a gift to friends, this seems nice, and you do it, but really all you are doing is participating in a social game version of a pyramid scheme – a surreptitious bit of design with a view to making your friends and acquaintances install *Zombie Joyride*. Beware!

Example 7.11e: Clans

FIGURE 7.47   Illustration by Andrew Thornton.

Lecture reference: slide 67

Question: competitive or co-operative?

Example 7.11e Answer: Co-Operative and Competitive

Again, I'd say this is both. Koster describes this in his GDC presentation on Social mechanics as "Association of similar nodes into a multi-cluster sub-network with its own social identity." (Koster, 2011). It is very much a case of building systems in games where you give the players opportunities to form groups and clans with like-minded people. For example, you might have a guild called "the Trekkies," where all members are *Star Trek* fans. As humans, it's really nice to be in groups, as we evolved from clans and tribal group systems, so we tend to enjoy grouping together, which is a positive aspect. Try to build that into your games, but you should also bear in mind that one of the most common words associated with clans is "rival," such as popping into your clan in Destiny to slaughter one another. Perhaps designing your clan systems more towards the cooperative end of the spectrum will guide us towards a better society. It's got to be worth a try, right?

Example 7.11f: User-Generated Content

FIGURE 7.48   Illustration by Jack Hollick in the style of Roblox "Adopt me."

Lecture reference: slide 68

Question: competitive or co-operative?

Example 7.11f Answer: Co-Operative

User-generated content is all about creativity. Whether it be creativity outside of the game or within the game, creativity is a huge driver for player motivation. As we know, creativity motivates players to play, buy, and use your game. Less cynically, creation within a game is a fantastic and intrinsic motivator because you are creating something personal that, in many cases, other people can also see. You're bringing something new into the world. Is it competitive? I imagine if you looked at all the *Roblox* and *Fortnite Creative* UGC fighting for prominence in the market, you could argue the point that it is. But let's not argue – let's call it co-operative and end this lecture series on a positive note!

CONCLUSION

In exploring win/lose conditions, we examined how games establish rulesets that determine success and failure. From the straightforward victory and defeat mechanics in classic games to the more complex and emergent gameplay evident in titles such as *Hitman* and *The Legend of Zelda: Breath of the Wild*. This section also delved into specific win/lose scenarios, such as time trials and attack/defend modes, illustrating the variety of Win and Lose conditions available to the player, as well as describing how mechanics such as QTE's can also play a formative role in designing these outcomes. The second part of the lecture focused on Social game systems, and emphasised the role of synchronous and asynchronous interactions in multiplayer settings, and by analysing examples and discussing the importance of social symmetry, we highlighted how particular systems are designed to foster co-operation, competition, or in some cases, both. At their core, social systems in games are designed to enhance player interaction, and we looked at how these systems must be understood and deployed carefully to maintain fairness and balance in social and multiplayer environments.

LECTURE SEVEN "WIN/LOSE & SOCIAL"
RESOURCE MATERIALS:

Lecture Seven in PowerPoint Format:
Lecture Seven Working Class:
   Edit and upload to a shared drive of your choice!
(These included instructor resources can all be downloaded from the **Instructor Hub**. For further information, please see the chapter "How to Use This Book.")

NOTES

1 Travis Scott's "Astronomical" concert in Fortnite attracted 27.7 million unique participants (Staff & Oloman, 2021a) *How fortnite and minecraft virtual concerts kept music alive while we weren't allowed outside, gamesradar.* Available at: https://www.gamesradar.com/how-fortnite-and-minecraft-virtual-concerts-kept-music-alive-while-we-werent-allowed-outside/
2 See Chapter 2, "Teaching," Box 2.8, "Blocks."
3 Chapter 2, "Teaching," Box 2.7 "Physics based controllers."
4 Cited as the "first board game": First board game (no date) Guinness World Records. Available at: https://www.guinnessworldrecords.com/world-records/117713-first-board-game.
5 As we've discussed in previous chapters, some games are designed as sandboxes without set win/lose conditions, but still contain objectives, challenges and rewards.
6 Harmsel, J. ter (2015) Referee age limit abolished soon in football by FIFA, Dutch Referee Blog. Available at: https://www.dutchreferee.com/referee-age-limit-abolished-soon-fifa/ (Accessed: 21 May 2024).
7 Although a Neanderthal might be more concerned about the strange bewitched light coming from out of the weird box in the corner of the cave, as opposed to concerning themselves with the rules of the game.
8 Space Invaders Hardware. Available at: http://computerarcheology.com/Arcade/Space Invaders/Hardware.html
9 arXiv, E.T. from the (2020)
10 See forums such as: Is it a 'game' if there is no win-condition?: BGG (2023) BoardGameGeek. Available at: https://boardgamegeek.com/thread/3174745/is-it-a-game-if-there-is-no-win-condition
11 See: https://minecraft.wiki/w/Ender_Dragon
12 **Jake Rice**, also known by his online alias **Jakethearchitect**.
13 See: https://westeroscraft.com/
14 Section 3.4: Maximising Motivation/Design Toolbox 2: Intrinsic and Extrinsic motivators.
15 Sounds dreamy. Not so. This was Aberdeen beach in the 1980's, and most times of the year required emergency survival equipment to get even within paddling distance of the (North) sea.
16 See "Space Invaders," (1978), "Pac-Man," (1980) and "Donkey Kong" (1981), where in all cases, player failure was marked by losing all your lives.
17 See "Aberdeen beach" note.
18 https://www.giantbomb.com/quick-time-event/3015-6/
19 Some games don't really have a "lose" condition. Think *The Sims.*
20 For a good example of emergent gameplay, see the original *Deux Ex*, where players discovered a creative way to use sticky mines to climb out of the map. By strategically placing Light Anti-Tank Weapons (LAMs) on walls and surfaces, players could create makeshift platforms to ascend to otherwise unreachable areas.
21 https://www.reddit.com/r/darksouls/comments/7hesnd/worlds_first_0_damage_run_no_blocking/
22 https://apps.apple.com/us/app/desert-bus/id470288016; https://play.google.com/store/apps/details?id=com.tueidj.DesertBus&hl=en
23 *Among us steam charts - live player count* (no date) *SteamPlayerCount.com.* Available at: https://steamplayercount.com/app/945360
24 The downside here is the fact that I, as the lecturer, told them this was a good idea obviously meant they automatically ignored it.

25 Although *Dead by Daylight* is a great example of the superpowered assailant and weak/hiding MP players working together in a game.
26 Adams (2023).
27 *Social Mechanics*. Available at: https://www.raphkoster.com/wp-content/uploads/2011/02/Koster_Social_Social-mechanics_GDC2011.pdf.
28 Yee (2006) and Przybylski, Rigby, and Ryan (2010).
29 The original meaning of the word, not the "overwatch" type of assist.
30 https://www.shacknews.com/article/75483/interview-jenova-chen-looks-back-at-journey

REFERENCES

Adams, E. (2023). *Designer's Notebook: A symmetry lesson.* Available at: https://www.gamedeveloper.com/design/designer-s-notebook-a-symmetry-lesson.

Among us steam charts - live player count, *SteamPlayerCount.com.* Available at: https://steamplayercount.com/app/945360.

Arkane Studios. (2012). *Dishonored.* Rockville, MD: Bethesda Softworks.

Arkane Studios. (2017). Prey. Rockville, MD: Bethesda Softworks.

Arkane Studios. (2021). Deathloop. Rockville, MD: Bethesda Softworks.

Atari. (1972). *Pong.* Sunnyvale, CA: Atari.

Atari Games. (1985). *Gauntlet.* Sunnyvale, CA: Atari Games.

arXiv, E.T. from the. (2020). 'Magic: The gathering' is officially the world's most complex game, *MIT Technology Review.* Available at: https://www.technologyreview.com/2019/05/07/135482/magic-the-gathering-is-officially-the-worlds-most-complex-game/.

Beenox. (2019). *Crash Team Racing Nitro-Fueled.* Santa Monica, CA: Activision.

Bethesda Game Studios. (2011). *The Elder Scrolls V: Skyrim.* Rockville, MD: Bethesda Softworks.

Blizzard Entertainment. (2004). *World of Warcraft.* Irvine, CA: Blizzard Entertainment.

Blizzard Entertainment, 2014. *Hearthstone.* Irvine, CA: Blizzard Entertainment.

Calhamer, A. (1959). *Diplomacy.* Baltimore, MD: Avalon Hill.

Capcom. (2005). *Resident Evil 4.* Osaka, Japan: Capcom.

Davidoff, D. (1986). *Mafia.* [Party game] Moscow, USSR.

Days of Wonder. (2012). *Ticket to Ride.* [Video game]. Paris, France: Days of Wonder.

Don Bluth Studios. (1983). *Dragon's Lair.* Arlington, TX: Cinematronics.

EvolvingDeveloper.com. (2016). *Multiplayer Game Balance - Part 1.* Available at: https://evolvingdeveloper.com/multiplayer-game-balance-part-1/.

Endnight Games. (2018). *The Forest.* Vancouver, Canada: Endnight Games.

Epic Games. (2017). *Fortnite.* Cary, NC: Epic Games.

Epic Games. (2017). *Fortnite: Battle Royale.* Cary, NC: Epic Games.

Fukasaku, K. (2000). *Battle Royale.* [Film]. Tokyo, Japan: Toei Company.

Garfield, R. (1993). *Magic: The Gathering.* Renton, WA: Wizards of the Coast.

Game Freak. (1996–2023). *Pokémon Series.* [Video game]. Tokyo, Japan: Nintendo, The Pokémon Company.

GameWisdom. (2021). *The Never-ending balance of Asymmetrical Game Design.* Available at: https://game-wisdom.com/critical/the-never-ending-balance-of-asymmetrical-game-design.

Ghost Town Games. (2016). *Overcooked.* Wakefield, UK: Team17.

Graft, K. (2023). *GDC 2011: Koster's big list of social mechanics for Social Games.* Available at: https://www.gamedeveloper.com/game-platforms/gdc-2011-koster-s-big-list-of-social-mechanics-for-social-games

Harmonix, Neversoft, and FreeStyleGames. (2005–2015). *Guitar Hero Series*. Cambridge, MA: Harmonix; Woodland Hills, CA: Neversoft; Leamington Spa, UK: FreeStyleGames. Published by RedOctane and Activision.

Hazelight Studios. (2021). *It Takes Two*. Redwood City, CA: Electronic Arts.

Hinterland Studio. (2014). *The Long Dark*. Vancouver, Canada: Hinterland Studio.

InnerSloth LLC. (2018). *Among Us*. Washington, DC: InnerSloth LLC.

Ion Storm. (2000). *Deus Ex*. San Francisco, CA: Eidos Interactive.

Japan Studio. (2016). *The Last Guardian*. Tokyo, Japan: Sony Interactive Entertainment.

Konami. (1987). *Contra*. Tokyo, Japan: Konami.

Lima Sky. (2009). *Doodle Jump*. New York: Lima Sky.

Luton, W. (2013). *Free-to-Play: Making Money From Games You Give Away*. San Francisco, CA: New Riders.

MCA and Philips. (1978). *LaserDisc*. [Home video format]. MCA and Philips.

MicroProse. (1994–2001). *Firaxis Games, 2012-present. X-COM Series*. Hunt Valley, MD: MicroProse; Sparks, MD: Firaxis Games.

Mojang Studios. (2011). *Minecraft*. Stockholm, Sweden: Mojang Studios.

Nadeo. (2003–present). *TrackMania series*. Paris, France: Nadeo.

Next Friday Interactive. (2014). *Nothing to Hide*. Wellington, New Zealand: Next Friday Interactive.

Nintendo. (1992). *Super Mario Kart*. Kyoto, Japan: Nintendo.

Nintendo. (1996). *Nintendo 64*. Kyoto, Japan: Nintendo.

Nintendo. (1996). *Mario Kart 64*. Kyoto, Japan: Nintendo.

Nintendo. (2006). *Wii Sports*. Kyoto, Japan: Nintendo. Distributed in the United Kingdom by Nintendo UK.

Nintendo. (2017). *The Legend of Zelda: Breath of the Wild*. Kyoto, Japan: Nintendo.

OMGPop. (2012). *Draw Something with Friends*. San Francisco, CA: Zynga.

Parkin, S. (2013). *Desert bus: The very worst video game ever created*, The New Yorker. Available at: https://www.newyorker.com/tech/annals-of-technology/desert-bus-the-very-worst-video-game-ever-created.

Pallières, P. des & Marly, H. (2001). *The Werewolves of Millers Hollow*. Paris, France: Lui-même.

Penn & Teller. (1995). *Desert Bus*. Leamington Spa, UK: Absolute Entertainment.

Playground Games. (2016–2021). *Forza Horizon 3–5*. Leamington Spa, UK: Playground Games.

Przybylski, A.K., Rigby, C.S., & Ryan, R.M. (2010). A motivational model of video game engagement. Review of General Psychology, 14(2), pp.154–166.

PUBG Corporation. (2017). *PlayerUnknown's Battlegrounds*. Seoul, South Korea: PUBG Corporation.

Psyonix. (2015). *Rocket League*. San Diego, CA: Psyonix.

Quantic Dream. (2010). *Heavy Rain*. Paris, France: Quantic Dream.

Quantic Dream. (2018). *Detroit: Become Human*. Paris, France: Quantic Dream.

Rare. (1991). *Battletoads*. Leamington Spa, UK: Rare.

Rebellion Developments. (2009). Rogue Warrior. Oxford, UK: Bethesda Softworks.

Robot Entertainment. (2011). *Orcs Must Die!*. Plano, TX: Robot Entertainment.

RubberBandGames. (2020). *Wobbly Life*. Plano, TX: RubberBandGames.

Scott, M., Burgess, J. and Gaynor, S., 2012. *Level design workshop - GDC China 2012*, SlideShare. Available at: https://www.slideshare.net/slideshow/level-design-workshop-gdc-china-2012/15306714.

Sega. (1995). *Desert Bus*. Tempe, AZ: Imagineering Inc.

Social Mechanics. Available at: https://www.raphkoster.com/wp-content/uploads/2011/02/Koster_Social_Social-mechanics_GDC2011.pdf.

Stainless Games. (2011). *Magic: The Gathering – Duels of the Planeswalkers 2012*. Newport, Isle of Wight: Stainless Games. Published by Wizards of the Coast.

Staff, E. and Oloman, J. (2021a). Travis Scott's "Astronomical" concert in Fortnite attracted 27.7 million unique participants. *How fortnite and minecraft virtual concerts kept music alive while we weren't allowed outside*, gamesradar. Available at: https://www.gamesradar.com/how-fortnite-and-minecraft-virtual-concerts-kept-music-alive-while-we-werent-allowed-outside/.

Studio MDHR. (2017). *Cuphead*. Oakville, Canada: Studio MDHR.

Taito. (1978). *Space Invaders*. Tokyo, Japan: Taito.

Technōs Japan. (1989). *Double Dragon II: The Revenge*. Tokyo, Japan: Technōs Japan.

The Traitors. (2022). [TV show] BBC One, London.

Traveller's Tales. (2005–present). *LEGO Series*. Knutsford, UK: Traveller's Tales.

Toys for Bob. (2020). *Crash Bandicoot 4: It's About Time*. Santa Monica, CA: Activision.

Valve Corporation. (2000). *Counter-Strike*. Bellevue, WA: Valve Corporation.

Valve Corporation. (2012). *Counter-Strike: Global Offensive (CS)*. Bellevue, WA: Valve Corporation.

Watts, S. (2012). *Interview: Jenova Chen looks back at journey*. Shacknews. Available at: https://www.shacknews.com/article/75483/interview-jenova-chen-looks-back-at-journey.

Yee, N. (2006). *The Psychology of Massively Multi-User Online Role-Playing Games: Motivations, Emotional Investment, Relationships and Problematic Usage*. In: Avatars at Work and Play (pp. 187–207). Dordrecht: Springer.

Index

Printed in the United States
by Baker & Taylor Publisher Services